ÉIGSE: A JOURN.
FOILSEACHÁI

DOUGLAS HYDE: IRISH IDEOLOGY AND INTERNATIONAL IMPACT

Eagarthóirí / *Editors*
LIAM MAC MATHÚNA
MÁIRE NIC AN BHAIRD

OLLSCOIL NA hÉIREANN A D'FHOILSIGH
PUBLISHED BY THE NATIONAL UNIVERSITY OF IRELAND

ÉIGSE: A JOURNAL OF IRISH STUDIES
FOILSEACHÁIN / *PUBLICATIONS*
Sraith ócáideach breise
Occasional supplementary series

3

© 2023 An Foilsitheoir, Eagarthóir na Sraithe agus na Scríbhneoirí /
Publisher, Series Editor and Contributors

ISSN 0013 2608
ISBN 978-0-9015109-5-2

Eagarthóir na Sraithe / *Series Editor*: Liam Mac Mathúna

BAILE ÁTHA CLIATH
DUBLIN
2023

CRM Design + Print Ltd., Baile Átha Cliath 12,
a leag amach agus a chuir i gcló
Layout and printing by CRM Design + Print Ltd., Dublin 12

DOUGLAS HYDE: IRISH IDEOLOGY AND INTERNATIONAL IMPACT

Drawing on the latest research on diaries, personal correspondence, memoir reflections and newspaper reports in library and State archives, this collection of essays by leading scholars on Douglas Hyde and the Irish language revival traces developments in the formulation and explication of Irish revival ideology. It also interrogates pivotal aspects of the revival movement's impact and influence as well as its interaction with the Irish diaspora and Celtic scholars in North America and Continental Europe.

Many of the essays are based on papers delivered at ACIS 2018, the Annual Meeting of the American Conference for Irish Studies, held at University College Cork, 18–22 June 2018.

ÚDAIR / *AUTHORS*

FEENA TÓIBÍN   University College Cork
REGINA UÍ CHOLLATÁIN   University College Dublin
LIAM MAC MATHÚNA   University College Dublin
AOIFE WHELAN   University College Dublin
FIONA LYONS   University College Dublin
MÁIRE NIC AN BHAIRD   Maynooth University
BRIAN MURPHY   Technological University Dublin

CLÁR AN ÁBHAIR / *CONTENTS*

ON DE-ANGLICISING THE IRISH NATION /
AR MI-SHACSANUGHADH AN CHINIDH ÉIREANNAIGH

Background

The foundation of the Gaelic League in 1893 brought changes to the political environment in Ireland. Douglas Hyde (1860–1949) gave a lecture entitled 'The necessity for de-anglicising Ireland' in 1892, which is regarded as leading to the formation of the new organisation. The object of this paper is to provide an analysis of Hyde's personal accounts of the period prior to his writing of this speech. Close reading of his diaries reveals much about his motivations, and some of the contradictions in his own lifestyle at the time of writing. Douglas Hyde was a language activist, academic and the first President of Ireland. He was one of the most prominent figures of the language revival and cultural nationalism which came to the fore at the end of the nineteenth century in Ireland. Thirteen diaries of his, written between 1874 and 1912, survive as MSS G 1036–1048, part of the collection of the National Library of Ireland. He began writing these at the age of fourteen and they are mainly written in Irish, but also at times in English, French, German and other languages.

Along with Eoin Mac Néill Hyde founded the Gaelic League in 1893 and was its President for over twenty years. The founding of this organisation brought changes to the political environment in Ireland. Douglas Hyde's lecture 'The necessity for de-anglicising Ireland' is often interpreted as heralding the formation of the League.[1] It was on 25 November 1892 that Hyde delivered this speech, addressing the Irish National Literary Society in Dublin. He is now celebrated for his words on that occasion, and for his drive to renew Irish identity, language and culture. His address looked to rally people to reclaim their Irishness and to cast aside Englishisms which had become entrenched at that time. He lamented: 'What the battleaxe of the Dane, the sword of the Norman, the wile of the Saxon were unable to perform, we have accomplished ourselves'.[2] Naturally, his primary focus was on the Irish language which the League continues to promote to this day: 'We must arouse some spark of patriotic inspiration among the peasantry who still use the language, and put an end to the shameful state of feeling ... which makes

---

[1] Hyde, 'The necessity for de-anglicising Ireland', in Charles Gavan Duffy, George Sigerson and Douglas Hyde, *The revival of Irish literature* (London 1894) 117–61.
[2] ibid. 128.

young men and women blush and hang their heads when overheard speaking their own language'.[3]

Hyde is sometimes remembered as the man who left the Gaelic League as the organisation became more politicised and militarised and '... produced other results he had not envisaged, and which, when he had fully grasped their tendency, led him to resign the presidency in the vastly different and doom-laden atmosphere of 1915 ... the league it is scarcely too much to say, was the nursery for the revolutionary generation of 1916'.[4]

However, that is not his full story. Certainly, at that time in 1915, he did not wish to pursue violent means, but his diaries do point to different feelings during the earlier period of his life. His fellow former President of Ireland, Mary Robinson described him aptly:

> What struck me about Douglas Hyde was that he had an unusual capacity to be at ease – to be comfortable – with very different sections and strands of the Irish society of his time. Coming from a Church of Ireland background, he was at home in the cottages of the local Irish-speaking Catholics in Co. Roscommon and all around Ireland. He was a convivial, fun-loving, social companion to his fellow College students. He was part of the Anglo-Irish set who met in country houses, wore cricket flannels and discussed the latest writings of Yeats, Lady Gregory and others of that set. He was a central and highly respected figure in the Gaelic language movement.[5]

Hyde was born in 1860, to Bessie and Arthur Hyde. He had two older brothers, Oldfield and Arthur and a younger sister Annette. The family lived in Frenchpark, Co. Roscommon. As the son of a Protestant minister it was unusual for him to take an interest in Irish, a language which was not spoken by his family. He did not receive any formal schooling beyond a ten-day stint in Dublin, ending in his contracting measles. Biographer Diarmid Coffey wrote:

> We probably have to thank the attack of measles for much that is admirable in Hyde, because it sent him back to Roscommon

---

[3] ibid. 136–7.
[4] F. S. L. Lyons, 'The aftermath of Parnell, 1891–1903', in W. E. Vaughan (ed.), *Ireland under the Union, II, 1870–1921, A new history of Ireland*, Vol. vi (Oxford 1996) 104–5.
[5] Mary Robinson, 'Douglas Hyde (1860–1949): the Trinity connection', *Hermathena*, QUATERCENTENARY PAPERS (1992) 17–26 (at 26).

and prevented his becoming as Anglicised as most Dublin schoolboys.... We cannot allow a measle germ to claim any important share in the formation of the Gaelic League, though to many of its enemies the rapid spread of the League throughout Ireland must have appeared like the spread of an infectious disease.[6]

Due to this illness his academic career continued at home, where he was instructed by his aunt Cecily in French and German, also occasionally by his father, but primarily progressed through his own self-led studies.

He was exposed to Irish through his relationships with local people outside of his family circle. Frenchpark in Roscommon, where he lived, was experiencing a rapid decline in spoken Irish during his childhood. Among those born from 1851–61 (Hyde's age group in other words), only 15% were Irish speakers, while the number was only 4% for 1861–71.[7] In modern terms it could probably be described as a breac-Ghaeltacht where older people had Irish but perhaps no longer spoke it as their primary language. Despite this, Hyde learned his Irish from local people, many of whom had largely discarded Irish, but who were able to share stories and songs with him when pressed by this inquisitive teenager. He mentioned that the content of his diaries contained 'many Irish songs I taught (learned) from the country people'.[8] Interestingly, one of the points he mentioned in the speech covered here is: 'do what they may the race of to-day cannot wholly divest itself from the mantle of its own past'.[9]

As he spent a lot of time in the company of local Irish Catholics, it is no surprise that at this period in his life he showed an affiliation with their nationalist views. One man in particular, John Lavin, a local Fenian, had a great influence on him. They often drank and played cards together, talking late into the night and sharing stories. Hyde wrote in November 1879, shortly after the arrest of Davitt, James Daly and James Bryce Killen in Gurteen, Co. Sligo on a charge of using seditious

---

[6] Diarmid O Cobhthaigh, *Douglas Hyde: An Craoibhín Aoibhinn* (Dublin, London 1917) 8.

[7] Garret Fitzgerald, 'Estimates for baronies of minimum level of Irish-speaking amongst successive decennial cohorts: 1771–1781 to 1861–1871', *Proceedings of the Royal Irish Academy: Section C – Archaeology, Celtic Studies, History, Linguistics, Literature*, Vol. 84, C, No. 3 (1984) 117–55 (at 136).

[8] NLI MS G 1060, p. 2. Ann mo leabhar eile mar an gcéadna, cuir me sios morán den abhrán Gaoidheilge a mhúin mé o na ndaoine tíre. 'Similarly, in my other book, I have written down many Irish songs I taught (learned) from the country people.' All translations by this author.

[9] Hyde, 'The necessity for de-anglicising Ireland', 124.

language:[10] 'Seagán O Láimhín came up in the afternoon and we were playing cards and drinking until it was after 12 o'clock and between us we drank more than a wine bottle of spirits. I got a lot of news from him about the Fenians etc.'.[11]

He gave the following amusing report of another night's socialising with Lavin and a second neighbour in March 1882: 'Seághan O Láimhín and Mícheál O Seanlaigh came up in the afternoon with poitín.... We drank many toasts to the health of O'Donovan Rossa, Stephens, the Fianna etc. etc.... I had a bad night, and a dreadful unquenchable thirst the following day. I got a lot of information from them about the Fenians etc.'.[12]

Later in his life he would go on to meet the 1867 leaders O'Donovan Rossa and John O'Leary and display respect for both. He wrote a poem expressing his admiration for O'Donovan Rossa in April 1880 'Olaim deagh-shláinte Ua Dhonabháin Rossa'.[13] Here Hyde praised the physical force philosophy espoused by O'Donovan Rossa. He later met this native Irish speaker in America in June 1891, having spent the academic year lecturing in Fredericton, New Brunswick. John O'Leary returned to Ireland in 1885. Hyde wrote in March 1892: 'Reading in the library until 10. To John O'Leary then and I spent the night talking to him. Home by 2.'[14]

Hyde began writing poetry as a pastime during his teens, and these poems show some of the same nationalist leanings. More than a hundred of his poems were published between 1879 and 1884,[15] under his pen name 'An Craoibhín Aoibhinn'.[16] He recorded their publication in his diary, e.g. 'My fifth poem which I wrote myself was published in the Irishman i.e. "Mo beannacht leat a Thír mo Ghrádh" [greetings to you o country I love]':[17]

[10] See Fergus Campbell and Tony Varley (eds), *Land questions in modern Ireland* (Oxford 2016).

[11] NLI MS G 1038, p. 132, 26 November 1879. Thainíc Seagán O Láimhín suas san tratnóna 7 bhiamar ag imirt cardaid 7 ag ól go raibh se nios mo na 12 o cloig 7 eadrainn d'ólamar nios mo na Fion-buidéul de bitáile. Fuair me cuid mhaith nuaidheacht uadh a taobh na bFéinne 7c.

[12] NLI MS G 1039, p. 143, 10 March 1882. Tháinic Seághan O Láimhin agus Mícheál O Seanlaigh suas san tratnóna agus poitín leis … D'olamar iomdha sláinte d'O Donabhán Rossa, Stephens, An Fhíanacht 7c.7c. ... B'olc an oidhce a bhi agam, & tart áidhbéul ασβὲστος orm an la'r na mhárach. Fuair me cuid maith eólas uatha air na bFínínidhe 7c.

[13] NLI MS G 1058, p. 45. 'I drink to the health of O'Donovan Rossa.'

[14] NLI MS G 1042, p. 89, 18 March 1892. Ag léigheadh san leabharlann go dti 10. Go Seán O Laoghaire ann sin & caith me an oidhche ag caint leis. Abhaile faoi an 2.

[15] An edition of these poems is in preparation.

[16] Derived from the chorus of a popular love-song.

[17] NLI MS G 1038, p. 155, 6 March 1880. clóbhualadh an cúigeadh dán annsan Eirionach do sgriobh me féin .i. 'Mo beannacht leat a Thír mo Ghrádh' 7c.

By God's power I will remember you
Thousands of miles from your shores
The hills and valleys I know
Their beauty and their bloom
Whatever my situation, til the day I die
I will always remember you
And if I cannot return again
Goodbye, goodbye, adieu.[18]

He neatly wrote out all of his efforts in his special poetry book, e.g.

Song of the destruction of Ireland, January 1878

1

Early on a beautiful morning
I was full of thoughts
As I roamed alone
Worried, thinking of Ireland ruined,
Lost and destroyed
And of the sadness of the Irish.

2

I noticed every bird
Full of fun and joy
Singing their thoughtful song in the air
Telling of the sadness
The bad luck and the harm
That has been done to Ireland.

3

Every calm calf and sheep
Thinking of the damage
That has been done to the country
The same in the mind of the cow
Who was lowing
And the hare who was jumping
In the yellow bog.

---

[18] NLI MS G 1058, p. 8.

4

In the clear water
The fish were leaping
In the bright heat of the sun
And the red and white butterflies
In the air were full
Of gladness and joy.

5

But I was saddened
Thinking of the leaders
Who are forever lost to Ireland
And of the hazy days
Full of splendour, prosperity and life
That shall not return.[19]

He continued with the following lament:

The lament of an exiled man, August

1

Greetings to you
O lovely county, county of Mayo
I am leaving, leaving, leaving,
Away from you forever and ever.

2

Greetings to you
Loyal Ireland, Ireland so green and alive
I am exiled, exiled, exiled
From loyal Ireland forever and ever.

3

There are many years, many years
Long, tired, sad
I will be walking, walking,
Through life
Without joy, without comfort.

---

[19] NLI MS G 1057, pp 5–6. See NLI MS G 1060, pp 76–7 for an alternative version.

4

There are many friends, many friends
And quiet girls tending to cows
Who are thinking of me, lamenting me
Sadly and under a cloud.

5

Island of the Saxons, island of the Saxons,
Country of the greatest and worst acts
That you will be ruined and destroyed
Forever and ever.[20]

He wrote this telling footnote at the end of the poetry notebook: 'What was in my heart, I wrote of it; my own thoughts, be they good or bad, my love for my country, for women, for drink, I wrote it. And my hatred for England in my poor song'.[21]

He noted in his diary: 'I was very pleased when I read of the actions of the Irish in Parliament, there is progress being made there now'.[22] He referred here to the Land Act of 1881[23] which sought to provide security for tenants by giving them legal rights based on Fair Rent, Fixity of Tenure and Freedom of Sale. This Act allowed the fixing of judicial rents for fifteen years by Land Courts and was hoped to be a solution to the land question as it removed the landlords' right to fix the rent payable for land they owned. It is clear from such comments that in his earlier years Hyde undoubtedly displayed nationalist and anti-English sentiment. Despite these somewhat violent attitudes, his primary focus remained on the Irish language and culture and its promotion. In the words of Brian Ó Cuív, 'it is unlikely that he seriously entertained any thought of a sacrifice in blood'.[24]

---

[20] NLI MS G 1057, pp 15–16.

[21] ibid. 186. An méid bhi ann mo chroidhe, do sgríobhas é; Mo smuainte féin, ma's maith iad no olc, Mo ghrádh do'm thír, do mnáibh, a's d'ól, sgriobh mé. As m'fhuath Sacsana, am' abhrán bocht.

[22] NLI MS G 1039, p. 39, 5 February 1881. Bhi dúil mór agam nuair leugh me gniomhthartha na nEirionach sa' bParlamint, tá dul air aghaidh anois.

[23] See Richard R. Cherry, assisted by John Wakely, *The Irish land law and land purchase acts, 1881, 1885, and 1887: with a complete collection of the rules and forms issued under each act in the Land Commission, High Court of Justice, and county courts respectively: and an appendix of incorporated statutes, edited, with full notes of the various cases decided under each section and rule: and an index* (Dublin 1888).

[24] Brian Ó Cuív, 'The Gaelic cultural movements and the new nationalism', in Kevin B. Nowlan (ed.), *The making of 1916: studies in the history of the Rising* (Dublin 1969) 8.

In addition, his nationalist sympathies need to be placed in the context of his pursuit of pastimes not associated with such sentiments. He took quickly to many country pursuits traditionally associated with the Anglo-Irish gentry. He first mentioned playing tennis, not noted as a native Irish game,[25] in his third diary in 1880 and quickly became keen on the sport, playing at first at local big houses and later laying out his own court at home: 'I was very busy today doing my best to smooth out the ground in the garden and to make a bank around it to make a tennis playing area from it'.[26] This contrasts with his calls to the Irish man in 'The necessity for de-anglicising Ireland' – 'to set his face against this constant running to England for our books, literature, music, games, fashions and ideas.... [to] become ... one of the most original, artistic, literary, and charming peoples of Europe'.[27]

He spent many hours in the company of local landlords fowling for pheasant, ducks and other birds. He played cricket[28] from an early age and also enjoyed boating. He presents many contradictions throughout his public and private life, as Dominic Daly remarks: 'The contrast between Hyde the crusader for all things Gaelic and Hyde the Anglo-Irish country gentleman was to continue all through his life ... in private life his preference was for the aristocratic and urbane'.[29]

Hyde enrolled in Trinity College Dublin in 1880, at the age of 21 and there encountered students mainly of a single class and with a prevailing un-Irish spirit. Coffey notes:

> ... at the university Hyde was brought into direct contact with much of the un-Irish side of Irish life. During his first three years in college he did not meet a single person who knew Irish ... the Trinity man ... was generally drawn from a class that in its own country regarded itself as apart from the rest of the land.[30]

However, while a student of the university he remained based primarily in Roscommon as he availed of a 'steam-packet'[31] arrangement which

---

[25] See Tom Higgins, *The history of Irish tennis*. 3 vols (Sligo 2006).
[26] NLI G 1039, 45, 19 March 1881. Bhi me an gnothach anuigh agus mé a deunadh mo dhiothcill cum an talamh san ngárrdhaidh do shleamhnughadh 7 banc do thógál na timcioll, cum áit-imirthe tennis do deunadh as.
[27] Hyde, 'The necessity for de-anglicising Ireland'· 161.
[28] See Michael O'Dwyer, *The history of cricket in County Kilkenny: the forgotten game* (Kilkenny 2006) regarding the popularity of cricket in that county during the nineteenth century.
[29] Dominic Daly, *The young Douglas Hyde* (Dublin 1974) 146.
[30] Diarmid Coffey, *Douglas Hyde President of Ireland* (Dublin and Cork 1938) 18–19.
[31] A choice between attending lectures or sitting an exam per term in lieu of same.

meant he could study alone and attend exams when necessary. During this early period at Trinity he was awarded a scholarship in Irish. Living in Dublin later in his degree course he also had the opportunity to socialise with many other Irish scholars and so-called 'enthusiasts' of the language who were based in the capital. Breandán Ó Conaire writes of

> ... a stimulating alliance between, on the one hand, his informed reading, study and personal contact with the native Irish literary and folk traditions and his participation in the affairs of the Society for the Preservation of the Irish Language and the Gaelic Union and, on the other hand, the regular round of soirée, debate and discussion in which he took an active part especially from 1884 onwards at the Young Ireland Society, the Contemporary Club, the Mosaic Club, the Pan-Celtic Society, the Historical and Theological Societies, Trinity College Dublin, as well as the more informal get-togethers in student rooms and at the homes of his friends in the capital.[32]

In 1886, a precursor to 'The necessity for de-anglicising Ireland' appeared in the *Dublin University Review*. This was 'A plea for the Irish language',[33] described by Aidan Doyle as 'a Romantic nationalist argument for Irish',[34] which laid out his feelings about Irish and its place in Irish society. His sentiments had changed from his radical statements in his younger years to a more measured assessment:

> The language of the western Gael is the language best suited to his surroundings. It corresponds best to his topography, his nomenclature and his organs of speech, and the use of it guarantees the remembrance of his own weird and beautiful traditions.... Every hill, every *lios* ['fairy fort'], every crag and gnarled tree and lonely valley has its own strange and graceful legend attached to it, the product of the Hibernian Celt in its truest and purest type, not to be improved upon by change, and of infinite worth in moulding the race type, of immeasurable value in forming its character.[35]

[32] Breandán Ó Conaire (ed.), *Language, lore and lyrics* (Dublin 1986) 35–6.
[33] Douglas Hyde, 'A plea for the Irish language', *The Dublin University Review*, Vol. II, No. 8 (August 1886) 666–76.
[34] Aidan Doyle, *A history of the Irish language: from Norman invasion to independence* (Oxford 2015) 173.
[35] Hyde, 'A plea for the Irish language', 670–1.

All this time his diary entries are written mostly in Irish, even after graduation from Trinity College, when he spent the academic year 1890–1 as a lecturer of Modern Languages in Fredericton, New Brunswick, Canada. While there he associated mainly with British army officers and spent quite a bit of time playing tennis and drinking in their mess. Despite the fact that this was his first academic job, it appears he spent little time on his academic work. Again, there is a noteworthy contrast between his usual diary entries written in Ireland, outlining his hours of reading and studying, and those written during his time in Fredericton.

He wrote in January 1891: 'Spent the last three months mar dubhras shuas go fíor pléusúrdha ["as I said above, very pleasurably"] The best things were the shooting the skating and the parties'.[36] These are pastimes which he had always enjoyed while living in Ireland, and which he continued with enthusiasm when he got to Fredericton.

One thing which differed from home was the ban on the sale of alcoholic drink in New Brunswick at that time. He did manage to access drink though, as he became friendly with the officers stationed there: 'The officers made me a member of their mess an aon áit amháin ann a dtig liom deoch uisge beatha fhághail ["the only place where I can get a drink of whiskey"] for the Scott Act prohibiting the sale of drink is vigorously enforced here'.[37]

During the period he spent in Fredericton he does not mention Irish once. However, after he continued on to the United States at the end of his academic year there, he was again embroiled in a whirl of activities with language activists there such as O'Neill Russell and O'Donovan Rossa. This chameleon-like character is typical of Hyde throughout his dealings with people of all classes, religions and persuasions. Perhaps the time he spent in such an Anglo-centric environment as New Brunswick during 1890–1 led to his greater activism on his return to Ireland.

Hyde was a supporter of Parnell and wrote a poem praising him in 1880:

1

Parnell crossed the waves to America
And they shouted a hundred thousand welcomes
Their shouts continued so long and so loud
That I must drink to his health.

---

[36] NLI MS G 1043, p. 12, no specific day mentioned.
[37] ibid. He refers here to the Canada Temperance Act which legislated for prohibition.

2
But he will come again back over the ocean
That agitation will be stilled within a season
Although the stirrings are fierce, Parnell is blameless
And we must drink to his health.[38]

Hyde also mentioned Parnell's death on 8 October 1891 in his diary upon his return home from his time in Canada 'Charles Stewart Parnell died yesterday. God help him. The best man who has come of Irish stock in the past fifty years, or thirty years at least'.[39] Having said that, not long prior to his speech in August 1892, he recounted his latest escapades as usual, sounding like quite the country gentleman, enjoying the final fling of a Big House summer: 'I went to Clonalis to a big party O'Connor Don held. Fifty people there. I played a lot of tennis until 6 in the afternoon'.[40] Notice the contrast from day to day later that same year in September:

5th Gathering up the haystacks, a meitheal of 12 or more there.
6th We put in the remainder of the hay.
7th I went to a party at Clonalis, from 3.30 to 6.20. A lot of tennis. Playing with a Mrs Little. The lords there. Spoke to O'Connor Don etc. Two good drinks. Home by 7.30.[41]

In the days immediately before his address to the National Literary Society, he wrote on 14 November 1892 that he 'stayed in the house writing about the de-anglicisation of Ireland'.[42]

Likewise, on the 21st he spent part of his day writing at home in Frenchpark. He returned to Dublin on the 24th. On 25 November he wrote:

I worked all day in the Academy writing my lecture. I gave the lecture, in Leinster Hall on Molesworth Street. Over 100 people

---

[38] NLI MS G 1058, p. 46.
[39] NLI G 1043, p. 58, 9 October 1891. FUAIR CATHAL STIUBHART PÁIRNÉULL bás andhé. Go bhfóiridh Dia air. An fear is fearr tháinig de phór na h-Eireann le leith cheud bliadhain, no le tríochad bliadhain air an laghad.
[40] ibid. 106. Cuaidh me go Cluain Mhálais go páirti mór tug O Conchubhar Donn. Leitchéad duine ann. D'imir mise a lán tennis go dti a 6 'san trathnóna.
[41] ibid. 111. **5** Ag deunamh na cocaidh féir do chrapadh. 12 no tuilleadh de mheithioll ann. **6** Cuireamar an chuid eile de'n fheur asteach. **7** Cuaidh mé go pairti ag Cluain Mhálais, o 3-30 go 6-20. Cuid maith tennis. Ag imirt le Mrs Little éigin. Na Tíghearnáyaigh ann. Caint le O Conchubhair Donn &c. Dá dhigh maithe. Abhaile faoi 7-30.
[42] ibid. 118. D'fhanas 'san tigh ag sgríobhadh ar mi-shacsanughadh Éireann.

there; a shilling a ticket. 'On the de-anglicising of the Irish Race'.
Miss Purser[43] and the Gwynnes Henry French Mrs Rowley etc.
and Mrs L'Estrange there listening to me. It lasted around an hour
and 20 minutes. It was good I believe. I was highly praised. To the
Hibernian then with Sheehan and punch there. To Sigerson[44] then
and I stayed with him until 1.30 and I drank 2 more glasses. Home
by 2.[45]

Although he mentioned that he received praise that night, it appears that
his speech had no great impact in his own mind at the time, speaking
though he was as the President of the National Literary Society. Seán Ó
Lúing describes the wider reaction:

> He encountered the scepticism the very next evening at the
> Contemporary Club, most of the members of which had attended
> his lecture. The chairman of the Club's meeting on the occasion
> was W. F. Bailey, accounted one of the most brilliant men of the
> day, a friend of the Government, widely read in the law, an
> acknowledged authority on Irish affairs. When the subject of
> Hyde's lecture came up for discussion he dismissed it with
> contempt: 'Let us turn to something of importance and reality.' He
> had no difficulty in getting the company to agree.[46]

Boyce, however, describes Hyde as 'a born propagandist' whose 'skills
were displayed from the start, with his emphasis on the urgency of the
need to halt the decay of the language and to prevent the final and
irrevocable loss of Ireland's cultural tradition'.[47] Certainly in his diary
at the time Hyde does not dwell on the lecture. This is his account of the
following day:

---

[43] See John N. O'Grady, 'Purser, Sarah Henrietta', in James McGuire, James Quinn (eds),
Dictionary of Irish biography (Cambridge 2009).

[44] See J. B. Lyons, 'Sigerson, George', ibid.

[45] NLI G 1043, p. 119. Ag obair ar feadh an laé 'san Ardsgoil ag sgriobhadh mo leictiúir.
Rinne me an leictiúir do thabhairt uaim, san Alla Laighean i Sr. Molesworth. Os cionn
100 duine ann. Sgillin ar an ticéad. 'Ar mi-shacsanughadh an Chinidh Éireannaigh'. Miss
Purser 7 na Gwynnes Hannraoi Frionnsa Mrs Rowley 7c 7 Mrs LEstrange ann ag éisteacht
liom. Mhair sé timcioll 1-20. Budh mhaith é, creidim. Bhí mé molta go mór. Go dti an
Hibernian leis an tSíothchánach, 7 puinnse ann. Go dti Sigerson ann sin 7 d'fhanas leis
go dti a 1-30 7 d'ólas 2 ghlainne eile. Abhaile faoi 2.

[46] Seán Ó Lúing, 'Douglas Hyde and the Gaelic League', *Studies: An Irish Quarterly
Review* 62, No. 246 (Summer 1973) 123–38 (at 128).

[47] D. George Boyce, *Nationalism in Ireland* (London, New York 1995) 237.

I bumped into Fräulein Kurtz and we went to the Botanical Gardens together at Ballsbridge. Strolling and a long chat with her there. To the Corlesses then for a lunch which lasted a few hours and had a bottle of champagne and a lot of sweet-talking until 4–45 when she went home.[48]

It seems he may have been somewhat distracted by his courting of Lucy Cometina Kurtz, the young Englishwoman he went on to marry the following year. The following month, December, he did again refer to the topic: 'we went together to the Contemporary Club. Arguing about the deanglicisation of Ireland there'.[49] Meanwhile, W. P. Ryan hailed the lecture as 'a startling revelation of the extent to which we had aped foreign fashions, of a nature the least suited to our character and requirements. It was a diagnosis of one of our worst diseases, one which would make either literary or national revolutions impossible'.[50]

There can be no doubt that Hyde's words did feed into a national revolution, and heralded the advent of a new cultural nationalism in Ireland. His personal diaries and poetry are valuable sources which offer much information about An Craoibhín Aoibhinn prior to this period of his life. They show the interest he had in both national and international current affairs. They show how sympathetic he was to the nationalist movement as a young man and how these matters influenced him. It is also clear that despite his huge interest in the cause of the Irish language that he was always a man apart, perhaps caught between two different worlds. In parallel with his national and nationalist interests which he exhibited publicly, his personal hobbies and interests continued to reflect his Anglo-Irish upbringing.

Feena Tóibín

---

[48] ibid. 120, 26 November 1892. Casadh Fräulein Kurtz orm as riocht 7 chuaidh mé léithe go dti na Garrdhaidh plannda ag Droicead Bháll. Spaisdeóracht 7 caint fhada léithe ann sin. Go Tigh Chorless ann sin 7 luinnse do mhair cúpla uair 7 buidéal seampéin 7 mórán cainte 7 suirighe go dti a 4-45. Nuair chuaidh sí abhaile.

[49] ibid. 121, 5 December 1892. chuadhmar le chéile chum an club comh-aimsearach. Ag árgúint ar mhi-Sacsanughadh na h-Éireann ann sin.

[50] W. P. Ryan, *The Irish literary revival: its history, pioneers and possibilities* (London 1894) 4.

A NEW GAELIC LEAGUE IDEA? THE GLOBAL CONTEXT

In his speeches in New York and Dublin in 1891–2, Douglas Hyde outlined a plan for what would eventually form the basis for the 'Gaelic League Idea'. The preservation and nurturing of not only a generation of writers but a generation of thinkers is central to the examination of the 'new Gaelic League Idea'. This continues to bring new insights into our thinking and understanding of culture, heritage and language in what is now a global and often virtual context, due to advances in technology. Although the Gaelic League is officially recorded as being founded on Monday 31 July 1893 in No. 9 Lower Sackville Street in Dublin, in a meeting called by the young scholar, Eoin MacNeill, the seeds for this movement had been sown for quite some time. Accounts indicate that there were ten people present for the founding of this organisation along with one reporter for the newspaper, the *United Irishman*. The significance of this meeting was not fully understood at the time, however, as the ambiguities in record keeping indicate that there are conflicting reports on who was present and even on which date it was held.

Much work preceded this meeting and while one of the main aims of the language revival was to create an Irish reading public, this reading public's ideas and the leaders of the movement which would make this happen, were influenced by the writings of many thinkers and philosophers prior to that, who first raised the concept of a Gaelic League Idea without framing it directly in these terms. Indeed, the creation of a reading public alongside a body of accomplished native and new Irish speakers may not have happened were it not for the writers that preceded them in literary, manuscript or journalistic forums. The birth of this revival mindset is remarkable on many levels, especially as it arose from what can only be described as a depressed and depleted linguistic milieu, resulting from a series of social and political factors over a prolonged period of time:

> the Irish language was progressively excluded from the worlds of commerce, politics, official religion, the professions and printed word as a result of complex socio-economic and political circumstances, and although Gaelic literature survived in oral and manuscript form, the overwhelming majority of Gaelic speakers remained illiterate.[1]

[1] Mary E. Daly in Mary Daly and David Dickson (eds), *The origins of popular literacy in Ireland: language change and educational development 1700–1900* (Dublin 1990) 153.

Tom Garvin states also that between 1847–1947:

> Linguistically, the country was … transformed; the language of
> the masses changed from Irish to English, and literacy in English
> replaced the non-literate use of Irish. To change language entailed
> changing cultural worlds, and millions migrated mentally from
> the medieval Gaelic world to the modern world of the English
> language.[2]

By tracing the roots and content of this journalistic writing forum
therefore, it is clear that it provided a channel for discourse and
development of a new school of thought and even a new ideology on
identity, language and culture which was deeply embedded in the
environs from which they emerged. These formal journalistic writing
practices can be traced back two hundred years beginning with the
founding of *Bolg an tSolair* in 1795. Furthermore, Irish language writing
practices as a medium of communication and administration allowed
that the language would have a role to play in the subsequent foundation
of the Irish state. The new school of thought embracing Irish and English
writing in many genres was formed in the embryonic stages of the
foundation of the Irish state as a result of the creation of a co-terminus
dual-language forum. Irish was reinstated as a *literary* language thus
allowing for a reversal of the 'changing [of] cultural worlds … of the
English Language', as referred to by Garvin, to a new modern cultural
context of the Irish language.

Ireland was not alone in this revival mindset and it would appear
that revival movements in Europe – Hungary, Poland, and Iceland in
particular – mirror the thought which developed, whereby literature and
writing forums were valued and viewed in new contexts.[3] The criteria
used for assessment of language revival is mainly oral language, but
the aims of the revival movement and the prolific amount of written
material available to support the movement in many different forums
still need an in-depth analysis in assessing the revival concept. These
writings include but are not limited to diary, journalistic and literary
sources. The Irish language became 'fixed' in the psyche of the new state

---

[2] Tom Garvin, *Nationalist revolutionaries in Ireland 1858–1928* (Oxford 1987) 2.

[3] Tomasz Kamusella, *The politics of language and nationalism in modern Central Europe* (New York 2009), Gunnar Karlsson, *The history of Iceland* (Minneapolis 2000), Anna-Ritta Lindgren, Klaus Lindgren and Mirja Saari. 'From Swedish to Finnish in the 19th century: a historical case of emancipatory language shift', *International Journal of the Sociology of Language* (2011) 17–34; Miklós Molnár, *A concise history of Hungary* (Cambridge 2014 [11 edn]).

and the reverse was also true, that the state became 'fixed' in the Irish language. This progressed to the modern-day fluidity of language, where technological change creates a network in which language is more loosely linked rather than 'fixed' in a particular culture or mindset alone, with many traversable linguistic borders.

The reliance and interdependence on Europe and the US in particular was always deemed an important aspect of the revival process. This was evident in the writings at the time and throughout the twentieth century almost until the onset of the World Wide Web in 1989. The practical implementation of the revival meant that the revitalisation of language relied predominately on the education system and formal avenues of administration. Viewing it in this way and within the framework of native speakers alone disregards the basic philosophy behind the language movement and Gaelic League, as evidenced in writings of journals of the nineteenth century in particular (*Fíor Eirionnach, Ancient Ireland, Bolg an tSolair, The Ecclesiastical Record, Dublin University Review, Irisleabhar na Gaedhilge / The Gaelic Journal*). These forums were used by future Irish leaders as platforms for thought on the progression of the nation and the language. The Irish language revival movement fostered many developments in the twentieth century which ensured a place for it in the identity of the Irish people, ranging from the ability to say a greeting in Irish to writing a book. This is a momentous achievement by any standards for a language that was considered 'dead' for three hundred years. Why then is there such doubt as to the value of the language in current Irish society? Why then is the revival not acknowledged as Seán Ó Tuama states:

> Finally one must remember that in the act of revival itself we are engaged in a new and absolutely audacious human and intellectual venture, the very planning of which and the very execution of which, will of itself help to give our culture a new dimension of experience and a unique quality of its own. In fact we are undertaking a cultural task the like of which was probably never before attempted by democratic means. It is more than likely indeed that the Gaelic League idea was one of the most exciting long-term ideas ever broached anywhere. But nobody in recent times has really presented it to the Irish people in these terms.[4]

---

[4] Seán Ó Tuama, 'The Gaelic League idea in the future', in Seán Ó Tuama (ed.), *The Gaelic League idea* (Cork and Dublin 1972) 98–109 (at 109).

It is beyond the scope of this essay to address the full success or lack of success of the revival. However, specific aspects which dictated the route and the direction that this movement would take, not least the transatlantic influence which preceded the foundation of the Gaelic League by almost fifty years, are a measure of the success of giving 'our culture a new dimension of experience and a unique quality of its own', as stated by Ó Tuama.

This essay will firstly review Hyde's diary musings starting in 1878, moving onwards to his New York visit on his way back from the year he spent in the University of New Brunswick in Canada. This trip laid the foundation for the school of thought which crossed the Atlantic in 1891–2 through print journalistic forums to form the basis for the Gaelic League. A brief overview of Irish language usage in the English press in Ireland versus pre-revival and revival journals, tracing the links in material from Ireland to the States, will further develop the importance of these links.

Examining the notion of *thall* ('there') and *abhus* ('here') which disregarded the linguistic borders in the immigrant press demonstrates a diminishing of these obstacles for the Irish immigrant, which in turn allowed Irish language communities on both sides of the Atlantic to create a revival network of sorts. This would form the basis for many strategic and robust links to develop a reading and writing public which has continued to the present day, and is also evident in many other international Irish diaspora communities.

Diary musings

Douglas Hyde, a minister's son, born in 1860 in Castlerea, Co. Roscommon and a founder of the Gaelic League, was one of the first to acknowledge the richness of the language idiom. He demonstrated in his collection and analysis of *Abhráin grádh Chúige Connacht or Love songs of Connacht* (1893) that this peasant speech had in fact preserved the poetic roots of the Irish language, elevating it to a different level of usage and understanding. If the 'poetry' still existed in the spoken language and it could be transcribed to manuscript and print sources through careful methods of recording and preservation, the role of the Irish language in the understanding of Irish identity was still relevant. This would be the cornerstone in the new literary culture of the revival movement. Hyde was chosen as the first Gaelic League President on 4 August 1893 and remained in that role until the Dundalk Ard-Fheis of 1915. Indeed, it is claimed that an account of his life until 1915 is synonymous with telling the history of the Gaelic League: 'Ba ionann, cuid mhaith, cuntas ar a shaol anuas go 1915 agus stair Chonradh na Gaeilge a insint.' ('An account of his life up to 1915 is synonymous with the history of the Gaelic League')[5]

Many of Hyde's earlier diary entries seem to indicate that New York was more favourable for the promotion of Irish than Dublin. It is no surprise therefore that the seeds of the revival were equally nurtured on both sides of the Atlantic and it is quite possible that Hyde's speech to the Gaelic Society of New York on June 16 1891, published in the *Irish American*, June 27 1891, laid the foundation for the philosophy which the Gaelic League would embrace in 1893:

> Now, I want to see the language kept alive for several reasons: first of all, because it is not good for the Irish, or any other race, to throw sentiment to the dogs; secondly I want to see the language kept alive as a great national heritage; thirdly as one of the best bonds to knit together the Irish race, and fourthly, because a bilingual race are infinitely superior to a race that speaks only one language. Here in America, as far as I can see, the one link that binds the Irish together is their Catholicity. In time past that has proved an almost sufficient link, because Irishman and Catholic were synonymous. But that will not be so in the future. The influx of German and Italian and other European Catholics will put an end to that; and if the Irish race is to hold together at all, it will have to cultivate other ties. It will have to again adopt in a foreign land the music, songs, traditions, and games of the race, and all Irishmen should at least know the Irish letters and something of the past history and glories of their land. Do you believe that Americans will think the worse of you for this, or that such a training will unfit you for a place in this vast and glorious Republic? I tell you no – a thousand times no! Respect yourselves and America will respect you. America will greedily assimilate, wants to assimilate, all that is best of the characteristics of the various races that inhabit her soil. How can she respect us if we throw sentiment to the dogs and hang our head and give up what every other nation – even little Switzerland, even tiny Denmark, holds most dear … We in Ireland owe a great deal to the Gaels of America; for if it were not for the help that we get from them, the Irish language movement would not have assumed the position it now occupies. We are both thankful and grateful to you for it.… It is sarcasm that has tended to root out the Irish language; but

---

[5] https://www.ainm.ie/, s.v. de hÍde, Dubhghlas.

when we know that you in America are admiring our efforts to revive it, that does more than anything else to keep the Irish language alive [6]

He gave this lecture on his return from a visiting professorship in the University of New Brunswick and it was further developed in the Irish journals of the day in Ireland, with full implementation plans published by Eoin MacNeill in *The Ecclesiastical Record* in December 1891 and *Irisleabhar na Gaedhilge / The Gaelic Journal*, March 1893.[7] Hyde's lecture 'The necessity for de-anglicising Ireland' delivered to the National Literary Society, Dublin 25 November 1892, is noted as the cornerstone on which the philosophy for the Gaelic League was founded. The need to remediate the demise of the strong Irish literary tradition and to assimilate cultural understanding is to the fore:

When we speak of the 'Necessity for De-Anglicising the Irish Nation' we mean it, not as a protest against imitating what is *best* in the English people, for that would be absurd, but rather to show the folly of neglecting what is Irish, and hastening to adopt, pell-mell, and indiscriminately, everything that is English, simply because it *is* English.

This is a question which most Irishmen will naturally look at from a National point of view, but it is one which ought also to claim the sympathies of every intelligent Unionist, and which, as I know, does claim the sympathy of many.

If we take a bird's eye view of our island today, and compare it with what it used to be, we must be struck by the extraordinary fact that the nation which was once, as every one admits, one of the most classically learned and cultured nations in Europe, is now one of the least so; how one of the most reading and literary peoples has become one of the *least* studious and most *un*-literary, and how the present art products of one of the quickest, most sensitive, and most artistic races on earth are now only distinguished for their hideousness.[8]

---

[6] 'Dr. Douglas Hyde', editorial, *Irish American*, June 27, 1891.

[7] 'Why and how the Irish language is to be preserved', *Irish Ecclesiastical Record*, Decenber 1891 and 'Toghairm agus gleus oibre chum gluasachta na Gaedhilge do chur ar aghaidh i nÉirinn' / 'A plea and a plan for the extension of the movement to preserve and spread the Gaelic language in Ireland', *Irisleabhar na Gaedhilge / The Gaelic Journal*, March 1893.

[8] Breandán Ó Conaire (ed.), *Douglas Hyde: language, lore and lyrics* (Blackrock, County Dublin 1986) 153.

Hyde's diary entries attest further to his vision of breaking down cultural borders and also indicate a strong connection between Ireland and the Irish-Americans in the United States. A review of the speeches within the framework of Hyde's diary entries provides new perspective on the development of the thought process which moulded the foundation of the movement rooted in both sides of the Atlantic. The many references which create this chain of knowledge are insightful and the diary entries and public writings trace the seeds of the revival movement in the United States. For example, it can be understood from the following diary entries and journalistic writings in 1878 – before Hyde went to America – that he had more faith in the progress of the movement in the US than in Ireland. One can even detect an air of frustration with the lack of progress in Ireland:

14 Mi Lughnais 1878

Pa went out shooting on the far bogs & shot three hares. He saw some grouse which were as strong as they would be in Sept another year. …

Russell sent me a paper from America yesterday with Gaelic script and a lot of news on how the Irish language is progressing in that country. It really lifted my heart. When I returned from France, I heard that Russell's people won their case and that Irish will be taught in the schools henceforth based on the plan of rewarding the masters who teach their students well in Irish. It was a great victory and Father Nolan told me that many people believed the language was saved by that. I got a list of books and MSS which are to be sold at Daly's auction. I said that it was a pity that I was not in Dublin when they were being sold and when the Master heard that he kindly said that he would give me six pounds to buy those books and the MSS and to go up to Dublin. I took him up on his offer with joy and I will be going up this Saturday, God willing.[9]

---

[9] '14 Mi Lughnais 1878 [date of year in Greek letters] … Do chuir Rusell [= Thomas O'Neill Russell] páipéur chugam andé o h America le clobualadh Gaedeilge ann 7 morán nuaideacht a dtaoib an caoi a bhfuil an teanga Gaedeilge teact ar agaidh san tír sin. D'árdaigh se mo croidhe go mór. Nuair tháinic me arais o Franc do cuala me go rugadar Russell a mhuinntir buaidh ann a g-cúis, 7 go bhfuil an teanga Gaedhelge le beith múinte annsna sgolaibh feasta air an bplan na n-duaiseadh do na máighisdribh do mhúin sgoláiridhe go maith n-Gaedheilge. Budh mór an buaidh e, 7 d'innis Athair Nolán dam go raibh cuid mór daoine do creid go raibh an teanga sabhálta trén rud sin. Fuair me liosta

The diary entries are supplemented by published material by Hyde in the *Irish Echo* in the late 1880s and in the *Celtic Monthly* as early as June 1880. Some of the poems in the *Celtic Monthly* had been republished from other sources and were the subject of an interesting debate on the revival of the language. The usage of the poetic form as the mode for debate at this early point is also interesting, allowing that Hyde would have been in the early stages of learning Irish. These present another angle on the transatlantic seeds of the revival which will be assessed in a forthcoming essay.[10] These collective publications point to the formation of an established ideology which preceded Hyde's Canadian – New York visit by approximately ten years and his later acclaimed fund-raising visit to the US as the President of the Gaelic League in 1905–6 by at least twenty-five years. The progression of thought recorded in various written and print forums can be classified as a commentary on the revival long before the founding of the Gaelic League in Ireland. In 1886 Hyde's ideology is taking shape as he voices his frustration at the lack of progress in reviving the Irish language in Ireland. There are three noteworthy points in the article entitled 'A plea for the Irish language': the need for an innovative approach to the revival which is not dependent on universities or scholarly elements alone; the distinct comparison between nurturing the Irish language and saving Irish nationality in the new world; and the emphasis Hyde puts on the importance of publishing Irish in the public platform of the newspapers. The title of the essay in a scholarly journal states the case which is gradually laying the foundation for the 'plea' to the native Irish public at home and abroad:

> I believe there is a very strong and real feeling against leaving our national language 'to the Universities'; artificial restraints have prevented it from growing here, but in America at least it is very powerful. A great part of the integrity of Irish nationality in the new world is due to the cultivation of Ireland's old language, which, proh pudor! has found a more congenial soil in the squares of New York than in the streets of Dublin.

leabhar 7 MSS atá le beith diolta ag an g-cant O Dálaigh. Dubhairt misi gurab truaigh e gan misi do beith 'nna lathair i mBaile atha Cliath nuair biadar da n-dioludh 7 nuair cualaidh an Máistir sin dubhairt se go cineálta go m-bearfadh sé sé púnta dam cum na leabhar sin 7 MSS do ceanach agus do dul suas go Bla cliath. Do thug me a ofráil go luathgáireach 7 ta me DV do dul suas Dia Sáthurn' (National Library of Ireland (NLI) MS G 1038, p. 10). All translations are by the author.

   [10] 'LITIR O'N G-CRAOBÍN AOIBÍNN,' *Irish Echo*, December 1887, September 1889; A series of poems sung or composed by 'An Craoibhín', *Celtic Monthly*, June 1880, December 1880, January 1881.

So strong is the feeling in America in favour of an attempt to preserve what many people there feel to be the purest and most seductive thing that Irish nationality can present them with, that even the *New York Herald*, the leading newspaper in America, opened its columns the other day to a portion of a speech spoken in Irish by some prominent patriot in New York, which it not only printed in Irish as delivered, but also in the native type. Have we lived to see it? Are they less materialistic over there beyond the seas than we are at home? Does the *New York Herald* actually do for us what the *United Ireland* obstinately refuses to do?[11]

Hyde's subsequent diary entries between March 1890 and January 1893 build on this conjecture. These can be taken as a subtext for the actions and writings of the revival in the United States before and around that time, in newspapers in New York, Chicago, and Boston especially – *The Irish American, The Irish World, The Boston Pilot, The Boston Daily Globe, The Philo-Celtic, Donahoe's Magazine, An Gaodhal, The Irish Echo, The Chicago Citizen* for example.[12] The most interesting part of these diary entries however is Hyde's mindset after leaving New Brunswick on his way to Boston and New York and then returning to Ireland, immediately prior to the founding of the Gaelic League. While these are insightful on the links between the Irish and the Irish-Americans, they also trace the relationship between the Boston, Chicago and New York Gaels, giving the background to the creation of Irish communities and networks, and to the development of the growth of awareness on the Irish language in the United States. O'Neill Russell kept in contact with Hyde when he was in the University of New Brunswick, Canada as a visiting professor.[13] Despite the fact that this is not clear from his Canadian diary entries, it is quite possible that Hyde was planning the details of this trip while he was there.[14]

In this first entry, the arrival of Hyde's own book preceding his arrival in Harvard demonstrates the demand for substantial works in Irish with high quality content. Irish culture needed to be reinstated in the language of the people and a new modern analysis of and perspective on the Irish

---

[11] 'A plea for the Irish language', *The Dublin University Review*, August 1886.

[12] See Fiona Lyons, '"Thall agus abhus" – Irish language revival, media and the transatlantic influence 1857–1897' (unpublished PhD thesis, submission January 2022, UCD School of Irish, Celtic Studies and Folklore).

[13] Janet Egleson Dunleavy and Gareth W. Dunleavy, *Douglas Hyde: a maker of modern Ireland* (California 1991) 162.

[14] Douglas Hyde Sealy. 'Douglas Hyde in New Brunswick 1890–1891', in Robert J. O'Driscoll and Lorna Reynolds, *The untold story: the Irish in Canada* (Toronto 1988) 237–8.

language oral tradition was proving insightful. Hyde's book, *Beside the fire* (1890), had just been published at this point and he was writing with vigour, unleashing new pioneering understandings on the role of folklore and the oral poetic tradition and their importance in the print forums of the era in the context of revival and understanding identity. Two points of particular interest here are, the visit to Harvard, considering the leading role which Harvard has in Celtic Studies in the United States and all over the world; secondly, Hyde's communication with the founders and editors of United States newspapers which can also be traced from these diary musings, his meeting with Forde from the *Irish World* in this instance, recognising that Irish Americans were trying to get newspaper pundits to print Irish to enhance their communication network. This was not merely an impromptu introduction as he clearly emphasises that he had a long conversation with Forde 'do bhi caint fhada eile agam leisean':

MI MHEADON AN t-SAMHRUIDH mdccclxli [June 1891]

3) Left Fredericton at 7–45 air maidin. Got to Boston air naoi ndolar at 9–30 at night, passing through Maine. Put up at the Crawford House, a comfortable hotel in Court St on the European plan, dollar air mo sheomra gac oidhche, vo[l]ilà tout. Deoch no dó nuair tháinig mé.

5) Went to Harvard Cambridge by electric car, just outside Boston. Hunted up Ganong & his wife & Raymond. Was shown all over that mass of luxury Harvard College. Went home & had supper with them & afterwards went to a Mr Newell a great folklorist who showed me my last book, not knowing the author. Abhaile tar éis laé caithte go maith ag an 10 san tráthnóna ['Home at10 in the evening after a day well spent'] .

10) Went to the Everett House Union Square, near the centre of N York. Met a man from Ohio & went out in a steamer with him to see the Statue of Liberty, presented to America by France & so large that 12 men could stand round the torch held in the right hand. Went to Central Park on the elevated railway & chonncamar na 10,000 i n-uachtar ag tiomáint ann a g-carráistibh ['we saw tens of thousands above driving in their carriages']. When I got back I found an Ruiseulac 7 Padhruig rómham 7 rugadar leó me go Cumann na Gaedheilge 7 bhí mé leó go dti a 12 7 d'ólamar beagán.

Bi luthgháire an mhór air an Ruiseulach mise d'fheicsint 'Russell and Pádraig there & they took me to Cumann na Gaedheilge & I was with them until 12 & we drank a little. Russell was really delighted to see me.'].

11) Russell breakfasted with me & I spent most of the day with him in Cumann na Gaedheilge & hunted in vain for O Donabhán Rossa 7 fear eile ['& another man']. Spent the evening with Padraig very pleasantly ag ól 's ag caint. Abhaile ag an 12.

12) Hunted up Bliss Carman & Gregg & asked them to breakfast with me. Went over Brooklyn[n] Bridge, looked at rifles & stores. Turned into Cumann na Gaedheilge later on. Tae leis an Ruiseullach 7 mórán cainte leisean 7 leis na daoinibh eile go dtáinig an oidhche ['Tea with Russell & a lot of talk with him & with the other people until night fell.'].

13) I went to O'Donovan Rossa in the morning and I had a long conversation with him & drinks & he took me to Patrick Forde in his office & I had another long talk with him. I came to Harlem then to see a baseball game but I didn't stay too long there. The temperature was 90 in the shade. Onward to Cumann na Gaedheilge then & a drink with Breathnach, & dinner with Russell & and we went together to Irish music by the Mac Giolla Mhuire band in Madison Hall, the largest hall I was ever in. Very good music. Home at 11[15]

It is clear from these entries that Douglas Hyde was not unknown among noteworthy figures in the Irish community in the United States and that the Irish connection was an established two-way network by this time. The entries show the context of his bilingual address to the New York Gaelic Society on 16 June, which was very well received. This speech was subsequently published in *The Irish American* on 27 June 1891.

---

[15] '13) Chuaidh go h-O Donabhán Rossa air maidin 7 bhí caint fhada agam 7 deochanna leis 7 do rug seisean mise go Padraig Forde ann a oifig 7 do bhi caint fhada eile agam leisean. Tháinig me go H-aarlem ann sin le cluiche, na baseball d'fheicsint acht níor fhanas ro fhada ann. Bí an glaine 90 san sgáile. Go Cumann na Gaedheilge ann sin 7 deoch leis an mBreathnach, 7 dinnéur leis an Ruiseullach 7 cuadhmar lé chéile go ceól Eireannach san Madison Hall le banda Mhic Giolla Mhuire, an halla bu mho d'á raibh me ariamh ann. Ceól an mhaith. Abhaile ag an 11' (NLI MS G 1043, pp 35–8).

MI MHEODHON SAMHRUIDH [June, 1891]

15) A very hot day 113 in the sun and 95 in the shade. I bought a Colt firearm & bullets &c for $20 & a ticket to Niagara and back for $16. I wrote a talk on the state of Irish &c. In the evening I went to Cumann na Gaedheilge. They had a Feis for me. 15 or 20 people there. Talking Irish. They had a nice supper. Wine with ice and punch. We drank a lot. There were six talks in Irish and as many, or more, in English, and all of them praising me. We stayed talking and drinking until 3 in the morning. I wasn't drunk but I had enough to drink. Six of them came back to the hotel with me at 4 am.

16) Russell came to me and brought me with him to Mlle Carusi without eating any food. I talked to her and she clasped my hand gently and lovingly and gave me a rose. I lay on my bed at midday. The weather-glass (barometer) 100 in the shade. Then a storm. Cumann na Gaedheilge had a big meeting in the evening. I gave a talk in English and in Irish. Coleman in the chair. One person kissed my hand and every one of them shook my hand. Home at 12. Drinks.

21) … And I came back and I went with Pádraig and Russell to the School of Irish in the Bowery. There were 30 people there. All had Irish. I gave a talk and I believe it was a very good talk. Many were speaking there. After that we went with O'Donovan Rossa out to Tailtinn and we were welcomed, and a good dinner, and a nice young woman before me and a lot of punch and cigars talk until 10 in the night. Home to Cumann na Gaedheilge with Russell and some doctor, . . .

23) I went out to Donovan Rossa. Talked & a drink with him & he brought [me] up to the top of the Herald building where I could see the whole city.[16]

---

[16] '15) Lá áidhbheul-theith glaine 113 san ngréin 7 95 san sgáile. Cheannuigh mé gunna piléir le Colt 7 peilleiridhe 7c air $20 7 ticéad go Niagara 7 air ais air $16. Sgríobh me labhairt ar stáid na Gaedheilge 7c. Cuaidh me san trathnóna go Cumann na Gaedhelge. Tugadar Féis air mo shon-sa. 15 no 20 duine ann. Ag labhairt Gaedheilge. Suipeur deas aca. Fíon le leac oidhre tríd 7 puinnse. D'ólamar go leór. Bhí sé labhairt ann san ngaedheilg 7 an oiread no níos mo i mbeurla 7 iad uile dom' mholadh-sa. D'fhanamar ag caint 'sag ól go di a 3 air maidin. Ni raibh mise air meisge acht do bhí mo sháith ólta agam. Tháinig seisear aca a bhaile do'n teach ósta liom. ag an 4. a.m.

By the date of the following final piece, 1894, although the revival movement and indeed the Gaelic League were up and running, the US influence on Hyde is still very strong. Allowing that the first diary entry referring to the correspondence with O'Neill Russell dates back to 1878, this continuous thread of musings over a sixteen-year period accrues added importance and validity to the thought process which eventually was to be the cornerstone of the Irish language revival movement. When added to the many societies on both sides of the Atlantic which created a new plan of action to implement the ideals which were coming to the fore, the evidence for the ideology of the revival as one rooted in international concepts is substantial. While the foundation of the Gaelic League was the culmination of years of organisation and discussion, the Gaelic League Idea as referred to by Ó Tuama was a much greater marker of this period. The writing practices and processes and subsequent journalistic print forums played a key role in this 'human and intellectual venture, the very planning of which and the very execution of which, will of itself help to give our culture a new dimension of experience and a unique quality of its own', as referred to earlier by Ó Tuama. The print forums acted as instruments of translation and transmission of this ancient 'language', albeit with a new message, combining visibility in the usage of the Irish language itself and conveying the message to Irish language communities on both sides of the Atlantic. As this ideology and these methods of transmission developed, this expanded to other international contexts which go beyond the scope of the present essay. Although it may be on a lesser scale, this is also evident in journalistic forums in Canada, Australia, Argentina, New Zealand and even Asia.

This final example in 1894 refers to the use of Irish and English at the same event with a rapturous reception to both addresses. While Hyde

16) Tháinig an Ruiseullach faoi mo dhéin 7 rug sé leis mé go Mlle Carusi gan aon bhiadh d'ithe. Labhras léithe 7 d'fháisg sí mo lámh go carthanach 7 go gradhamhuil 7 thug rós dam. Luidh me air mo leabuidh i meadhon laé. Glaine aimsire 100 san sgáile. Stoirm ann sin. Cruinniughadh mór ag Cumann na Gaedheilge san trathnóna. Rinne mise labhairt i mbeurla 7 i nGáedheilge. Colman san g-cáthaoir. Bhí duine ann do phóg mo lámh, 7 chraith gach aon aca lámha liom. Abhaile ag an 12. Deochanna.

21) . . . Tháinig mé air ais 7 chuaidh mé le Pádraíg 7 an Ruiseullach go Sgoil na Gaedhilge 'san mBowery. Bhí 30 duine ann. Gaedheilg aca uile. Rinne mise labhairt 7 labhairt an mhaith creidim. Bhí mórán ag labhairt ann. Tar éis sin cuadhmar le h O Donabhán Rossa amach go Tailtinn, 7 bhí fáilte rómhann, 7 dinnéar maith, 7 cailín óg deas rómham, 7 a lán puinnse 7 sigarridhe agus caint go dti a 10 san oidhche. Abhaile go Cumann na Gaedheilge le Ruiseullach 7 dochtúir éigin, . . .

23) Chuaidh mé amach go Donabhán Rossa. Caint 7 deoch leis, 7 thug sé suas go bárr tógbhála an Herald o a bhfaca me an cháthair uile.' (NLI MS G 1043, 39–42).

clearly had used the dual-language approach in his diary entries long before this, by this time the dual-language situation was already becoming a progressive aspect on the public platform of the revival. Again, Hyde uses his reception in New York as a source of comparison to the welcome he has received in Cork maintaining the international framework as a benchmark for revival:

Samhain MDCCCLXLIV [November 1894]

30. Ó Murchadh took me to the Cork Young Men's Society, where the Gaelic League was gathered. They presented me with an address, framed in oak, written on parchment and a poem by Stúndún similarly framed. I spoke for a long while in English and in Irish and they understood me well. I then gave a lecture there on Gaelic Literature over the last three hundred years. There was warm applause and huge enthusiasm and I only ever received as warm a welcome as I received there previously in New York, perhaps. Ó Glaosáin, an tAthair Ó Laoghaire, Ó Suiliobháin, An Pléimionnach Óg (an Síoladóir) and many others were there. Home by 12 with Ó Murchadh. [17]

This tracing gives an insight into the effect that the nurturing of the transatlantic network had on the progression of the revival. The occasional use of both English and Irish in the diary writings demonstrates Hyde's comfort in using both languages and that it was a natural practice for him as part of the writing process. Although these are diary entries, this dual language usage is insightful with regard to the language situation as part of the intellectual context and approach of the revival. Another valuable aspect of these diary entries is the recognition of modern print forums alongside the use of Greek letters. For Irish to flourish it would be dependent on productive use of these public forums, which Eoin MacNeill understood when he was discussing the founding of the first Irish language newspaper in 1897, emphasising

---

[17] '30 . . . Rug O Murchadh leis me go Cumann na bhFear Og Chorcaigh, 'n áit a raibh Leug na Gáedheilge cruinnighthe ann. Thairg siad dham dileagra no *address*, fréimeálta i ndair, sgríobhtha ar phár. 7 dán do rinne an Stúndúnach fréimeálta mar an gcéadna. Rinne mé cómhrádh fada i mbeurla 7 i nGaedheilg 7 thuigeadar mé go maith. Tug mé leictiúr uaim ann sin air Litridheacht Gaedheilge na trí céad bliadhain cuaidh tharrainn. Bhí teas-bhualadh lámh 7 *enthusiasmus* mór 7 ni bhfuair mé ariamh acht i Nuadh-Eabhroch, b'éidir, a leitheid d'fháilte teith a's fuair mé ann sin. Bí O Glaosáin, an tAthair O Laoghaire, O Suiliobháin, An Pléimionnach Óg (an Síoladóir) 7 mórán eile ann. Abhaile faoi12 le O Murchadh' (NLI MS G 1044, no page numbers).

that the focus had now changed from 'protesting' against the authorities
to 'testing the Irish reading public'.[18] Although Máirtín Ó Cadhain
stresses the community voice in the context of achieving revival aims
on these public forums, it seems by now that it was more important to
present Irish in the print forum than the voice of the community if the
revival were to move on to a broader societal level.[19]

Irish press sources in Ireland
A brief overview of Irish language usage in the English press in Ireland
versus pre-revival and revival journals, tracing the links in material from
Ireland to the States, gives further understanding of the rationale underlying Hyde's emphasis on international links.

   Titles on columns in newspapers indicate that the concept of identity
for the Irish emigrant was not specific to one domain. The headings used
for columns on international affairs in *Irisleabhar na Gaedhilge / The
Gaelic Journal* (1882–1909) and *An Claidheamh Soluis agus Fáinne
an Lae* (1899–1932), the two main Irish language revival periodicals
spanning a period of more than fifty years, indicate a distinction between
national and international reportage in the titles – being 'there' or 'here'
('*thall*' or '*abhus*'), in the 'western world' or the 'eastern world'
('*domhan thiar*' or '*domhan thoir*'), 'at home' or 'away' ('*i mbaile*' or
'*i gcéin*'). Clearly, however, columnists did not view the material related
to the international community as completely separate from that of the
native one. These titles reflect the conflict which was evident in the
immigrant psyche through the perception of living in a foreign land,
forging a need to create a network with the home community while
coming to terms, not only with a new geographical world, but for native
Irish language speakers, with a new language world. Again, this attests
to the utilisation of the journalistic web developing on the writing
processes which laid the foundation for the thinking behind the revival.
These processes were the links between those who viewed the Irish
language as a preservation project, and those who saw it as a real possibility for reinstating an element of identity which would supplement
rather than burden further the understanding of nationality, adding to the
modernisation of the Irish people of the twentieth century in a global
context. As a result of 'the Irish language [being] progressively excluded
from the worlds of commerce, politics, official religion, the professions
and printed word as a result of complex socio-economic and political

---

[18] 'Fáinne an Lae', *Irisleabhar na Gaedhilge / The Gaelic Journal*, Samhain 1897, 1.
[19] Máirtín Ó Cadhain, 'Conradh na Gaeilge agus an litríocht', in Seán Ó Tuama (ed.),
The Gaelic League idea (Cork and Dublin 1972) 52–62 (at 52).

circumstances' as referred to by Daly and Dickson at the beginning of this essay, timing really was of the essence. This 'timing' is a key factor in journalistic discourse and at this watershed in early twentieth-century Ireland, addressing the linguistic border was almost as important as addressing the political and geographical borders in order to traverse boundaries encompassing identity and heritage. This would help to initiate the reversal of what Garvin refers to as the mental migration 'from the medieval Gaelic world to the modern world of the English language' which entailed 'changing cultural worlds', as mentioned earlier.

The borders in the context of a language world can best be understood within the challenges that immigrants had to overcome settling into a strange country in which a language, which was not part of their language world, was being spoken:

> No border is as effective as a language border ... What really is a language world? An environment or cultural ecology in which someone lives; it is an environment which plays a role in one's personality, in their identity. A person spends their life in that environment. He finds his relationships and his thoughts there. He remembers all that he has learned from the time of his youth – from parents, from teachers, from friends, from books that he has read – all in *one* language ... Be that as it is, the average person is unaware that he is living in a language world. In order to understand that he muse emigrate to a place in which another language is to the fore.[20]

The role of journals and newspapers in the creation of a network of sorts of Irish speakers assisted the migration process in establishing links which helped to diminish the importance of the role of political and geographical borders in that way for emigrants, while coming to terms with a new hybrid identity. Links to the native language formed part of the identity chain. Using this perspective and rationale for news reporting, 'Irish' news should probably have come under the 'foreign'

---

[20] 'Níl aon teorainn chomh héifeachtach le teorainn teanga ... Cad is domhan teanga ann le fírinne? Timpeallacht nó éiceolaíocht chultúrtha ina maireann duine, timpeallacht a bhfuil páirt aici ina phearsantacht, ina fhéiniúlacht atá ann. Caitheann an duine a shaol sa timpeallacht sin. Faigheann sé a chaidreamh agus a chuid smaointe ann. Is cuimhin leis na rudaí go léir atá foghlamtha aige ón am go raibh sé óg – ó thuismitheoirí, ó mhúinteoirí, ó chairde, ó na leabhair atá léite aige – agus an rud uile in aon teanga amháin ... Bíodh gurb ea, ní bhíonn a fhios ag an ghnáthdhuine go bhfuil sé ag maireachtáil i ndomhan teanga. Chun an méid sin a thuiscint caithfidh sé dul san imirce go dtí áit ina bhfuil domhan teanga eile i réim.' Tarlach Mac Con Midhe, 'Domhain teanga', *Comhar*, Aibreán 2010, 18–21 (at 19).

material ('there') in the United States. However, a study of material in and about Irish language in the American newspapers shows that it too had a cultural and community focus, which was perceived as local as opposed to foreign news, strengthening the relationship between the home and immigrant community, instead of focusing solely on creating new connections with the adopted country. This journalistic web reveals new perspectives on the global revival process, bringing fresh interpretations to the concept of citizenship and identity. In order to preserve the old and new identity in the new language world this meant that, mentally, both the Irish emigrant and the Irish revivalist needed to be '*thall*' [there] and '*abhus*' [here] at the same time.

The use of periodicals and newspapers from the pre-revival journal *Bolg an tSolair* in 1795 to the revival journals of the late nineteenth and early twentieth centuries, secured a place for the subsequent presence of the Irish language as part of the communication revolution of the early twentieth century.[21] If the focus was to change from that of language preservation to the 'living language' of the people, the creation of public discourse and communication networks in the public sphere of the media was essential. The content of newspapers and periodicals shows that the revivalist mindset was viewed in a global framework as opposed to one which was solely rooted in narrow nationalist principles.[22] So, what was the viewpoint of the Gael and what insights are provided on Irish society and on public discourse as delivered in the idiom of the Irish language of this period? Was it shaping a new language or a new ideology on public discourse in the Irish language and on the evolving new society? The debates on language issues are very prominent in the native press with detailed accounts of related activities providing insights to a sub-culture of an Irish language rooted community which was not necessarily native-speaking. Many reports attest to the Gaelic league functioning at many levels of society while providing extra practical supports to local people under the guise of the Irish language movement.[23] The fundamental focus on communication in the immigrant

---

[21] Asa Briggs and Peter Burke, *A social history of the media: from Gutenberg to the internet* [Third Edition] (Cambridge 2014) 89, 98; Regina Uí Chollatáin, '*An Claidheamh Soluis agus Fáinne an Lae:* "the turning of the tide"', in Felix Larkin and Mark O'Brien (eds), *Periodicals and journalism in twentieth-century Ireland* (Dublin 2014) 31–46; Regina Uí Chollatáin, 'Trasnú teorainneacha agus náisiúin in iriseoireacht na Gaeilge sa naoú haois déag', in Fionntán de Brún and Séamus Mac Mathúna (eds), *Teanga agus litríocht na Gaeilge i gCúige Uladh sa naoú haois déag* (Béal Feirste 2012) 107–33.
[22] Uí Chollatáin, '*An Claidheamh Soluis agus Fáinne an Lae*'.
[23] Paton, Monica, 'The dynamics of the clerical-lay relationship in the Roscommon Gaelic League', *Éire-Ireland*, vol. 48, Issue 3&4 (Fall/Winter 2013) 129–54.

press also serves as a subtext to the revival discourse, allowing for a broader interpretation of the concept of language revival.[24]

Despite a minority readership and output, Irish language in the media forum in the revival period was used for most areas of public discourse, be it related to news 'at home' or 'away'. The Irish language column in the *Irish Independent* being '*abhus*' [here], echoed these sentiments and was clear about its foreign policy from the start, for example:

> *Sinn Féin* ['Ourselves']
> There will be an account of current affairs and events in this section of the paper. From day to day, according to the *Gaeilgeoir*'s ['Irish speaker's'] view of life. Precedence will not only be given to Irish affairs – we shouldn't get rid of that – our own affairs will be given first, middle and last place; but because of that and as a result of that, world affairs will not be completely eliminated from our view, as they come to pass in other countries. Anything that the human person is interested in, the Irish person is interested in.[25]

The first Irish language revival periodical and newspapers were preceded by Gaelic columns in regional newspapers, many of which continued throughout the twentieth century. In the context of the journalistic web between North America and Ireland, undoubtedly the most productive and one of the earliest of these columns was that which was edited by John Glynn in the *Tuam News and Western Advertiser* in the 1870s.[26] More recent research indicates that these columns in the revival period functioned at a broader level than reports of Gaelic League activities and the endorsement of the Irish-Ireland philosophy. The *Irish Independent* and the *Weekly Freeman* for example, engaged with current

---

[24] Unpublished research on this by the author, by Fiona Lyons, by Máirín Nic Eoin on *An Gaodhal*, by Deirdre Ní Chonghaile on the sean-nós song tradition in Philadelphia is also bringing new perspectives to the role of these Irish-American journals where the function of Irish language journalism is viewed in a different context. See ACIS/CAIS UCD June 2014. Panel: Digitizing *dúchas*: reappraising the global history of the Irish language. See also Newspaper and Periodical History Forum of Ireland Conference, UCC, November 2014: 'Home thoughts from abroad: history, the press and diaspora'. Panel: 'Transnational journalism and digitization: Irish Language sources'. Monica Paton's ongoing unpublished research on the Gaelic League *tímirí* [helpers], focusing on the Irish regional press also reviews the role of Irish language in rural communities in Ireland during and subsequent to the revival period.

[25] 'Sinn Féin', *Irish Independent* 2/1/1905.

[26] Philip O'Leary, *The prose literature of the Gaelic Revival 1881–1921: ideology and innovation* (Pennsylvania 1994) 7.

and topical issues of the day including national and international material, often demonstrating a conflicting and hybrid identity.[27] Marie Louise Legg's (1999) study of the provincial press in the context of newspapers and nationalism provides a valuable insight to the role of this forum in the development of identity in a regional and rural milieu. These sources are useful in the study of what may be termed as the emergence of a sub-culture in rural Ireland in the revival period which was nurtured by Gaelic League activities, and language revival was central in these gatherings and projects. Ongoing research indicates that this sub-culture, through the work of the Gaelic League *timirí* ['helpers'] in conjunction with the County Councils of the time, sustained many rural communities in a broader sense, something which entailed much more than language maintenance alone, and was not dissimilar to the way the Irish societies and journalistic sources functioned for immigrant diaspora communities in the United States and beyond. This revival approach which was rooted in nurturing community values transcending language maintenance alone, allows for a deeper appreciation of the need for the Irish immigrant to maintain links with the language as a communication tool in building a sense of belonging to the community abroad also. Language was the tool for communication but in the context of revival it was also an emblem of community and identity. The social aspect of this sub-culture therefore went beyond language maintenance and revival alone, which subsequently assigned an economic value to the language, inadvertently assisting the post-revival movement in the mid-twentieth century. Again, highlighting how the revival ensured that language was progressively included in societal structures as opposed to the previous era when Irish language was deliberately 'excluded from the worlds of commerce, politics, official religion, the professions and printed word as a result of complex socio-economic and political circumstances'. This led to the evolution and transformation of new understandings on the fundamental role of the Irish language as part of society and culture. This is particularly evident in reports and accounts in the press and periodicals in the comprehensive documentation of

[27] Aoife Uí Fhaoláin, '*The Irish Independent* agus ábhar Gaeilge 1905–1922: peirspictíocht stairiúil ar theanga agus ar chultúr na hÉireann i gcomhthéacs idé-eolaíocht "Irish-Ireland" agus athbheochan na Gaeilge' (unpublished PhD thesis, submission January 2015, UCD School of Irish, Celtic Studies, Irish Folklore and Linguistics, University College Dublin); Aoife Uí Fhaoláin, 'Language revival and conflicting identities in the *Irish Independent', Irish Studies Review* (2014) http://dx.doi.org/10.1080/09670882.2013. 872388 (accessed 8 December 2020); Nollaig Mac Congáil, 'Saothrú na Gaeilge ar nuachtáin náisiúnta Bhéarla na haoise seo caite: sop nó solamar?' in Réamonn Ó Muireadhaidh (ed.), *Féilscríbhinn Anraí Mhic Giolla Chomhaill: tráchtais léannta in onóir don Athair Anraí Mac Giolla Chomhaill* (Baile Átha Cliath 2011) 112–91.

membership, class attendance, community impact and links with home and abroad through the activities of the Gaelic League by its teachers and *timirí*, a fact which has really only merited a footnote in revival history and analysis to date.

The international influence aided this 'inclusion' immensely, expanding the scale of the role of language revival within a socio-economic framework, while simultaneously promoting literary and cultural values and acknowledging the 'language world' of many immigrants. For example, the first Irish language periodical *Irisleabhar na Gaedhilge / The Gaelic Journal* (1882–1909), although sporting a primarily scholarly focus, reports on events in the United States as Irish language news. Many reports and lists of newspapers with Irish content, and accounts of events demonstrate a clear interdependence between media platforms on both sides of the Atlantic.[28] The account of Father O'Growney's welcome to New York in 1895 is one example of this which also bears resemblance to Hyde's visit to the States a few years earlier. Noteworthy also here is the reference to the three societies, the Irish Language Society of Providence, the New York Philo-Celtic Society, and the New York Gaelic Society and the dual-language approach which Hyde refers to in his diary entry in 1894 using his New York welcome as a comparison on his visit to Cork. The use of Irish at these gatherings and the fact that O'Growney's message focuses on the influence of the Irish abroad on those at home instead of the other way around mirrors Hyde's approach:

> Father O'Growney has received a real Irish welcome in America. The first to grasp his hand at the landing-place was Rev. Martin L. Murphy who came from Springfield, Ohio, a journey of nearly 1,000 miles to meet him. Mr M.J. Henehan, on behalf of the flourishing Irish Language Society of Providence, R.I.; Hon. Denis Burns and Captain Thomas D. Norris, from the New York Philo-Celtic Society, and Messrs. Henry Magee and Patrick Reynolds, of the New York Gaelic Society, attended to welcome the visitor, and escorted him to the Metropolitan Hotel. On the Saturday following, the Gaelic Society gave a reception to Father O'Growney at the Broadway Central Hotel. Chief Justice Daly presided, and later in the evening, the chair was taken by Mr. E.T. McCrystal, President of the Society. An address in Irish, printed

---

[28] Regina Uí Chollatáin, 'Deisceabail agus soiscéalta: ceannródaithe athbheochana agus fóram na hiriseoireachta', in Tracey Ní Mhaonaigh (ed.), *Léachtaí Cholm Cille* 44 *Oidhreacht Uí Ghramhnaigh* (2014) 22–45.

below was presented to the guest, who replied in Irish. Other Gaelic speeches and Gaelic songs and recitations followed. On Sunday evening, Father O'Growney was the guest of the Philo-Celtic society. The Hon. Denis Burns presided and speeches in Irish and a concert of Irish music and songs occupied the evening. In writing home, Father O'Growney has expressed great delight at the spirit and earnestness manifested by the friends of the Gaelic League in America. He says that those working in the same cause at home should take increased courage from the attitude of their American fellow-workers, who are watching eagerly the progress of the movement in the old land.[29]

Clearly the space created for transmission of the language via these Irish societies in North America was also important in the network it provided for the global Irish community. The last page of *Irisleabhar na Gaedhilge / The Gaelic Journal* in the 1890s generally gave a list of newspapers with Irish language content under the heading 'The Gaelic Papers'. This list did not separate Irish papers in Ireland from those abroad in the United States or the United Kingdom, for example. Again, the economic impact of this is evident with references to supporting the Irish language press in Ireland with cheques, with the aim not only of producing the print journal but of increasing circulation, thereby increasing cultural awareness of the role of the language in 'changing cultural worlds' as Garvin stated, but in the reverse with the Irish language taking a central role in the new understanding of Irish culture:

> … to be applied towards defraying the cost of publication of the GAELIC JOURNAL, with a view to reducing it to a lower retail price, thus contributing to increase its circulation. The gentlemen named are members of Cumann na Gaedhilge, New York, and their generosity deserves gratitude and approbation of all readers of the Journal and friends of this movement.[30]

The column 'News of the Movement' did not differentiate between the native and emigrant community in its reports with all reports being published, be they '*thall*', ('there') in the United States or '*abhus*', ('here') in Ireland (*Irisleabhar na Gaedhilge / The Gaelic Journal*, April 1897). Generally, the subscription list for the Oireachtas fund, the Irish language literary and cultural festival, also has as many subscribers from

---

[29] *Irisleabhar na Gaedhilge / The Gaelic Journal*, 1 January 1895, 159.
[30] *Irisleabhar na Gaedhilge / The Gaelic Journal*, November 1896.

the United Kingdom and the United States as Ireland (*Irisleabhar na Gaedhilge / The Gaelic Journal*, May 1900), while regular reportage of Irish language usage at meetings is recorded. Some examples include an account of the establishment of the London branch of the Gaelic League on 5 October 1896, entitled 'The Irish language movement in London' (*Irisleabhar na Gaedhilge / The Gaelic Journal*, November 1896), 'An able and well-informed article, entitled, "How the Celtic Revival Arose", by Mr. M.A. O'Byrne, of New York, to the *Catholic World* for March', along with the announcement of new branches in Pawtucket, Rhode Island and Detroit, Michigan (*Irisleabhar na Gaedhilge / The Gaelic Journal*, April 1896, 190). One of the better examples of the coverage of the angle of the movement in the United States in *Irisleabhar na Gaedhilge / The Gaelic Journal* relates to the first Oireachtas:

> Mr Patrick O'Byrne, of the Gaelic Society, New York, was present at a meeting of the Central Branch, Gaelic League, Dublin, on the 24th September, and was accorded an Irish welcome. In returning thanks, Mr. O'Byrne dealt with the present position of the movement in America, and continuing, said: Your Oireachtas was, I think, taken up better by the Press in America than anything that has happened on this side of the Atlantic for some time past. The novelty appealed to them. The very idea of the Irish people having a literary competition in their own language in Dublin was so extraordinary that they eagerly took notice of it. They in America … were happy that such a very large measure of success had attended the efforts of the Gaelic League in establishing an institution having for its objects the literary cultivation of the tongue of our fathers. He considered that there were two great reasons which should induce every Irishman to join the movement for the preservation of the Irish language – first, it offered a common platform to those of different shades of political and religious thought; and secondly that it formed a strong bond of union between the Celtic peoples of Ireland, Scotland and Wales. He concluded by again thanking the meeting for the hearty welcome accorded him, and said that he might take it upon himself to say on behalf of the Gaelic Society of New York that anything they could do to assist them they would do.[31]

[31] *Irisleabhar na Gaedhilge / The Gaelic Journal*, October 1897, 95.

The endorsement in the main Irish language revival journal of this unified approach, transcending geographical borders, was important at the time. The reportage and discourse in these journals, and drawing also on Hyde's diaries as written sources of memory, is significant in the attempt to determine the multifaceted nature of the identity of immigrant communities and the understanding of the citizenship which they envisaged for themselves within their new country. Margaret Beetham has long argued that such periodicals are also part of a complex social process:

> Each article, each periodical number was and is part of a complex process in which writers, editors, publishers and readers engaged in trying to understand themselves and their society: that is, they struggled to make their world meaningful.[32]

This is just a small sample of the material which demonstrates the interdependence of both communities on either side of the Atlantic. Timothy McMahon argues that gatherings like the Oireachtas allowed the local native community to connect with something that was greater than them, allowing them membership of a greater movement.[33] The combination of gatherings like the Oireachtas, the work of the Philo-Celtic societies and the journalistic forum were central therefore to the communication network and to the sense of community which was being formed in creating the Gaelic League Idea. The reportage mirrors the ideology on the overall context of the revival – discussing the rhythm and pulse of current world affairs while simultaneously preserving traditional values and the literary and cultural heritage.

An overview of some of the content of *An Claidheamh Soluis* as the first Irish language national newspaper demonstrates a diversity of subject matter also. The writers could not discuss or provide reports on these subjects without having some concept of internationalisation and of the importance of broadening this Gaelic mindset at home and abroad. Furthermore, this was not based on speculation and musing alone and was viewed as important at the time it was written, as discussed in *An Claidheamh Soluis* in 1903:

---

[32] Margaret Beetham, 'Towards a theory of the periodical as a publishing genre', in Laurel Blake, Aled Jones and Lionel Madden (eds), *Investigating Victorian journalism* (New York 1990) 19–32 (at 20).

[33] Timothy G. McMahon, (ed.), *Éire-Ireland*, vol. 48, Issue 3&4, Fall/Winter 2013 (Boston 2013); Timothy G. McMahon, *Grand opportunity: the Gaelic revival and Irish society, 1893–1910* (New York 2008) 186.

Of course *An Claidheamh Soluis*, like all weekly newspapers, to a certain extent depends for its facts on the daily press; but unlike the majority of papers published in Ireland, it does not take either its facts or its views wholesale from English sources. For its facts it draws quite as largely on the continental press, and for its views it depends on itself. In point of fact, three quarters of our news matter is really original comment rather than a *resumé* of facts and the comment is always that of Gaels with the Gaelic viewpoint.[34]

The international content in *An Claidheamh Soluis* reflects this with a variety of topics and countries under review. Some of the material related to language movements and official structures would subsequently be instrumental in the formation of the ideology and identity of the nation in question.[35] In order to influence public opinion however, reportage was consistently acknowledged as the key element in the diffusion of this revivalist ideology. As mentioned already, due to the instant impact of live journalism the timing of this reportage was central to the implementation of the revivalist ideology and structures at this juncture:

Let us continue reporting to our own paper. We should take trouble to send reports too to the Dublin as well as to the local newspapers. It is not easy to win against the officialism of this country and we dare not lose, and we have said often enough before, to succeed there must be at our backs an intense and widespread public opinion. The metropolitan press is the great channel of communication and should be used as far as possible by the League.[36]

The immigrant press
An examination of the various forums of language usage helps in reviewing the boundaries of the new life of the immigrant in a new language world. If a language world is an

environment or cultural ecology ... which plays a role in one's personality, in their identity ... finds his relationships and his thoughts there. He remembers all that he has learned from the time of his youth – from parents, from teachers, from friends, from books that he has read – all in *one* language[37]

---

[34] 'Gleo na gcath', *An Claidheamh Soluis*, 6/6/1903.
[35] Uí Chollatáin, *An Claidheamh Soluis agus Fáinne an Lae 1899–1932*. Aguisín a deich.
[36] 'The rising tide', *An Claidheamh Soluis*, 5/8/1899.
[37] Mac Con Midhe, 'Domhain teanga', 19. See footnote 20 for original Irish text.

what cultural baggage did emigrants carry or discard to deal with this new 'language world' within the new geographical landscape? For example, despite the fact that newspaper and manuscript evidence indicates that the Irish language was in use in the context of reportage on events in the United States as early as the period of the American Revolution in North America,[38] when an act regarding language signage was passed in 1848 to help immigrants to settle in, Irish was not one of the languages listed, despite the fact that approximately 151,003 Irish emigrants entered the city of New York in 1848.[39] There is a clear indication here that either the 'cultural baggage' that was discarded was the Irish language or the level of literacy in Irish meant that signage would not assist the migration process. This adds further substance to the theory of the necessity for production of reading material in print journals to promote the language revival in the States in order to capture the intergenerational transfer which could be lost without written language records.

Current research on newspaper material is inconsistent, as it is mainly understood that the Irish language column was not evident prior to the *Irish American* column in 1857. Some sources indicate the first newspaper to have had Irish language content was the *Shamrock* or *Hibernian Chronicle* (New York 1810–24), with Irish language also in *The Globe and Herald* (Philadelphia 1824), *Emerald* (Boston 1836 for 3 months), *Irish Shield and Monthly Milesian* (New York 1829), *Truth Teller* (New York 1825–55). Dorothy Ní Uigín refers to *The Citizen* (New York 1853), *The Irish Citizen* (New York 1867) and the *Boston Pilot* (1836), as some of the attempts that were made to keep the Irish language in the discourse of the immigrant community.[40] Ní Uigín states that the use of the Irish language itself is not referred to specifically except that there was much discussion on the Irish language in the first

---

[38] Tomás Ó h-Íde, 'Emancipation through exile: Irish speakers in the Americas', in Michael Newton (ed.), *Celts in the Americas* (Cape Breton 2013) 56–75 (at 61).

[39] Ken Nilsen, 'The Irish language in New York 1850–1900', in Ronald H. Bayor and Timothy J. Meagher (eds), *The New York Irish* (Baltimore and London 1996) 252–74 (at 256).

[40] Dorothy Ní Uigín, 'An iriseoireacht Ghaeilge i Meiriceá agus in Éirinn ag tús na hathbheochana: an cúlra Meiriceánach', *Léachtaí Cholm Cille XXVIII. Iriseoireacht na Gaeilge* (1998) 25–47; Dorothy Ní Uigín, 'Tréimhseacháin agus colúin de chuid, agus a bunaíodh faoi thionchar Chonradh na Gaeilge. Sa chéad fhiche bliain den fhichiú haois', Cuid a haon, *Feasta* (Bealtaine 2009) 40–3; Cuid a dó: 'Tréimhseacháin logánta a raibh baint indíreach ag Conradh na Gaeilge leo', *Feasta* (Meitheamh 2009) 9–13; Cuid a trí: 'Irisí craoibhe an Chonartha i Londain agus i Meiriceá agus colúnaíocht Ghaeilge in Éirinn', *Feasta* (Iúil 2009) 19–23; Cuid a ceathair: 'Tréimhseacháin nuabhunaithe Gaeilge', *Feasta* (Lúnasa 2009) 19–23; Cuid a cúig: 'Tréimhseacháin Ollscoile, liteartha, léannta agus acadúla', *Feasta* (Meán Fómhair 2009) 21–4.

few editions of the *Irish Citizen*.[41] It is probably safe to assume therefore that Irish language content itself is sparse prior to the columns such as those in the *Irish American* (New York 1849–1914), *The Irish News* (San Francisco 1860s), *The Irish People* (San Francisco 1860s), *Celtic World* (Minneapolis 1880s), *Irish Standard* (Minneapolis 1880s), *American Celt* (St Louis), *The Irish Times* (St Paul) and *The Monitor* (San Francisco 1878–1920). The use of the Irish language in North American based newspapers increased between 1848 and *c.*1870 with some Irish language content in the *Oneida Morning Herald*, the *Mohawk Courier*, *The New York Herald*, *The New York Sun*, and *The Corrector*. There are quite a few references also to the use of Irish in the Fenian newspapers in America:

> They printed newspapers, the *Phoenix* and the *Irish People* in New York for example, and the *United Irishman* in San Francisco, which spoke out directly for the Fenians. In an examination of these and other newspapers which were connected to the Fenian movement, the *Irish-American*, the *Irish Nation*, the *Gaelic American*, the *Irish World* in New York, and the *Citizen* in Chicago, for example, one can see that the editors had great respect for the language. Clearly, they believed that the Irish language was an important aspect of cultural nationalism.[42]

The fact that Irish language content came to the fore in this forum primarily in the latter half of the nineteenth century helps in interpreting the evolution of the understanding of the new identity of the Irish immigrants, viewing Irish language and cultural revival as constructive links between their new life and the community with which they wanted to maintain links in Ireland. This also demonstrates that they did not want this language to be suppressed in the process of being subsumed into a new cultural entity. At the very least this raises questions as to why the immigrant community would employ this 'dead' literary language in public forums in their adopted country. This question goes

---

[41] Ní Uigín, Cuid a trí, 30

[42] 'D'fhoilsíodar nuachtáin, mar shampla an *Phoenix* agus an *Irish People*, i Nua Eabhrac, agus an *United Irishman* i San Francisco, a labhair go díreach ar son na bhFíníní. Nuair a scrúdaítear iad agus na nuachtáin eile a raibh baint ag Fíníní leo mar shampla an *Irish-American*, an *Irish Nation*, an *Gaelic American*, an *Irish World* i Nua Eabhrac agus an *Citizen* i Chicaco feictear go raibh ard-mheas ag na heagarthóirí ar an dteanga. Is léir gur chreid siad gur ghné thábhachtach de náisiúnachas cultúrtha na hÉireann ab ea an Ghaeilge.' Fionnuala Uí Fhlannagáin, *Finíní Mheiriceá agus an Ghaeilge* (Baile Átha Cliath 2008) xii-xiii.

beyond the understanding of language maintenance alone but adds to the concept of the Gaelic League Idea in an international context. Unlike the native press in Ireland, in the United States the lack of orthographical consistency seems to be more of a basic literacy issue than that of linguistic or political debate. If the Irish emigrant had to abandon the language and culture to integrate fully into the new community and engage in the new 'psyche' of the new country, the language seemed to take on a new role in their new identity and lives, as recognised by Hyde. This further reinforces the importance of close examination of these literary sources and writing practices as linguistic and societal commentary, and as instruments in furthering present perspectives on citizenship, as opposed to historical evaluation alone as referred to earlier by Beetham and further current research.[43]

Irish American (1849–1915)

Nilsen states that the weekly *Irish American* 'has been largely over-looked by those who have written on this subject', allowing that some of the content uses spelling in 'that particular orthography that is neither proper English nor Irish'.[44] This is key to understanding the function of the journalistic platform which did not overemphasise language accuracy and may account for the lack of attention to these sources to date. Indeed, the font and spelling issues were the source of much controversy which, in reality, cloaked more in-depth questions of culture, nation and identity among the right-wing element of the revival movement.[45] For example, on 18 July 1857 the *Irish American* announced that they had acquired the Gaelic font and that Irish language poetry and prose would then be printed. The following week (25/7/1857), the Irish 'column' was printed for the first time. Although the *Irish American* had printed Irish prior to this, the concept of the Gaelic column differentiates from Irish language content alone as it served a different role in both literary and communicative terms. After the death of the renowned poet, Pádraig Cúndún in 1857, his poems were published in the *Irish American* in 1858, but there were approximately 450 Irish language columns in the newspaper by 1881. This is helpful in the understanding of the transatlantic context of the revival, especially when Douglas Hyde connected the beginning of the revival with the

---

[43] Michael Cronin, *Translating Ireland: translation, languages, cultures* (Cork 1996) 116.

[44] Ken Nilsen, 'The Irish language in New York 1850–1900', in Ronald H. Bayor and Timothy J. Meagher (eds), *The New York Irish* (Baltimore and London 1996) 252–74 (at 259).

[45] Brian Ó Conchubhair, 'The Gaelic font controversy: the Gaelic League's (post-colonial) crux', *Irish University Review* 33.1 (2003) 46–63.

founding of *Irisleabhar na Gaedhilge / The Gaelic Journal* in 1882, twenty-five years after this. The concept of using the public sphere of the media for language revival took root in the United States much earlier than in Ireland, which also vaguely mirrors the ancient Irish written tradition of the *file* ['poet'], yet another example of a deliberate direction in viewing change in the cultural worlds.

The column in the *Irish American* was irregular between 1861 and 1863, and placed emphasis on 'Easy lessons in Irish' by Father Ulick J. Bourke focusing on the Irish learner, or at least the illiterate native Irish speaker. The focus was changing from preservation of cultural sources to revival of a communicative language for usage in the public domain and in public discourse. The column was published again in 1869 and 1877 and it was used for the teaching of Irish, which resulted in a published book. Readers contributed to the column 'Written Irish' in 1877 which was used as a means to study the Irish language with a view to increasing its usage in a communicative way:

> From a number of communications in the Irish language, which we have received since resuming our Gaelic publications, we select the following as specimens of what can be done with the Irish as a medium of written correspondence. The letters will serve also as a study of ordinary colloquial language for those who are desirous to learn.[46]

As a result of Irish classes and of the column itself, a new forum was gradually being established for the new Irish speakers and writers to practise the craft of writing. The forum in the United States therefore recognised the two publics, the established native Irish speaker and the enthusiastic learner. Patrick O'Beirn, a native Irish speaker from Donegal was one of those who learned to write Irish in New York, reflecting another aspect of the literary progression of Irish emigrants and the need to make the spoken language a literary print language to ensure its survival as a voice of this new community. It is worth noting that O'Beirn is hailed as one of the most famous Irish language poets of that period of revival in the United States.[47]

According to Máirtín Ó Cadhain, the modern language and the problems related to reviving a language in the native country did not seem to be an issue for *An Gaodhal,* the Brooklyn-based periodical founded by Galway emigrant Michael Logan in 1881. The main function

---

[46] 'Written Irish', *Irish American*, 29/9/1877.
[47] Also known as Patrick O'Byrne, he is already mentioned above: see footnote 31.

of the Irish language presence in this milieu was to provide a voice for the immigrant, reinstating their ownership of the language. By doing this it acknowledged its role in the hybrid identity of the Irish immigrant in the United States. Interestingly, Ó Cadhain attributes this 'voice' in the immigrant press to the Gaelic League:

> Some of this Irish in the new writing is clumsy enough. But none of it is as bare and rough as the *patois* which poor Michael Logan received in the 19th century. As a form of writing, it is similarly lacking and quite awkward also. Despite that, it is *modern* literature about *modern* affairs in a *modern* style. Above all else it belongs to us, the only voice of our own that we as Gaels have – thanks to the Gaelic League. [Emphasis added][48]

It is worth noting that Hyde's material referred to earlier in the *Celtic Monthly* in the early 1880s added to the visibility of the usage of Irish language in the public sphere of the media for debate and communication also. Therefore, while *An Gaodhal* and the *Gaelic Journal / Irisleabhar na Gaedhilge* were certainly forerunners in the development of the Irish language revival periodical, the writings in more cultural English-language publications by Hyde in particular are worth including in the historiography of the Irish language media. Hyde's reference to the *Gaelic Journal* as being the start of the Irish language revival is also open to analysis as he was clearly aware of Irish language journalistic writing which preceded the *Gaelic Journal* in the US. The immigrant Welsh newspaper *Y Drych* (*The Mirror*), which was in print around the same era in New York is yet another example of the role of the public sphere of the media in defining identity for the immigrant:

> First published in New York City in 1851, the newspaper relocated to Utica in 1860, where it continued to be published for over a century. *Y Drych* was so pivotal to Welsh American life for such a long period of time that the definitive study of the paper's history is not just a 'biography of a newspaper' (A. Jones and B. Jones

---

[48] 'Cuid den Ghaeilge seo sa nua-scríbhneoireacht tá sí ciotach go maith. Ach níl cuid ar bith di chomh maol mantach leis an *bpatois* a fuair Mícheál Ó Lócháin bocht ón 19ú céad. Mar scríbhneoireacht tá sí uireasach útamálach go maith freisin. Ainneoin sin is litríocht nua-aimsire faoi chúrsaí nua-aimsire i bhfriotal nua-aimsire í. Thar gach ní eile is linn féin í, an t-aon ghlór dár gcuid féin atá againn mar Ghaeil – a bhuíochas sin ar Chonradh na Gaeilge.' Ó Cadhain, 'Conradh na Gaeilge agus an litríocht', 62.

2001a: xi)[49], but also an exploration of how the disparate Welsh American communities evolved, saw themselves and communicated with one another. In addition to reflecting the culture of the Welsh in America, the newspaper sought to shape it: its pages reveal 'a series of concerted attempts by its editors and main correspondents to define a Welsh identity, an ideology, if you like, for the Welsh in America' (A. Jones and B. Jones 2001b: 44).[50]

In 'shaping' the culture as opposed to 'reflecting' it in the Irish language immigrant press in the US, we understand more fully the transatlantic concept of revival. An overview of what was shaping this culture is helpful in identifying the links between the Gaelic League Idea on both sides of the Atlantic.

Although Irish language usage declined in the *Irish American* in the mid-nineteenth century this was probably a result of the founding of *The Phoenix* in 1859. Irish language pieces published in *The Phoenix* provided the emblem of identity, but there was no Irish language column. During the 1860s there were Irish language articles in *The American Celt* (St Louis), *The Citizen* (Chicago) and *The Irish Echo* (Boston Philo-Celtic Societies journal). John O'Mahony's *Irish People* had a Gaelic column in 1869 and there were many similarities between the content of the column in the *Irish People* which lasted until 1871 and that of the *Irish American*.

One of the more interesting examples from the point of view of public discourse in Irish language journalism in the New World is *The Monitor* which was founded in San Francisco (1878–1920), and of which Father Peter Yorke was editor for a period, and Mary Butler the Irish correspondent. This paper seems to have crossed all boundaries as an instrument in the global revival process. Butler was a contributor to *An Claidheamh Soluis* and she had a column on Irish language affairs in *The Irish Daily Independent* from 1899 onwards, although this was mostly written in English. She was also the Irish correspondent for *The Pittsburgh Post* and *The Philadelphia Leader*.[51] Yorke's role in *The*

---

[49] The work cited is Aled Jones and Bill Jones, *Welsh Reflections: Y Drych and America, 1851–2001* (Llandysul 2001) ix.

[50] Gethin Matthews, 'Miners, Methodists and minstrels: the Welsh in the Americas and their legacy', in Michael Newton (ed.), *Celts in the Americas* (Sydney, Nova Scotia 2013) 94–116 (at 108). The closing work cited is Aled Jones and Bill Jones, 'Y Drych and American Welsh Identities, 1851–1951, *North American Journal of Welsh Studies* 1:1 (2001) 42–58 .

[51] Ní Uigín, Cuid a trí, 35.

Monitor is described as energetic, fearless and sometimes overzealous:

> In 1894 the post of editor of the expanding archdiocesan
> newspaper, *The Monitor*, was added to his growing list of
> responsibilities. Yorke was just thirty years of age, bright, hard-
> working, and respected.
>
> The turning point in Yorke's career coincided with his
> appointment as editor of *The Monitor*. Riordan had advanced him
> to that post in order to combat organized anti-catholicism, then
> rampant in many parts of America and also apparent in San
> Francisco. Only after Fr Yorke's total success did Riordan come
> to realize the magnitude of what he had done. Yorke's editorials
> and public lectures had educated, laughed, and gouged the bogus
> patriotism of the anti-catholic American Protective Association
> out of San Francisco. ... Yorke refused ever again to heed his
> archbishop's normal institutional concerns for prudence and
> caution in public matters. Obsessed by the need to right every
> fancied slight to Irish and Catholics, Yorke became a permanent
> embarrassment and irritant to the hierarchy and a sheer delight to
> the admiring Irish-American working class.
>
> Irish leaders in America with causes to champion and opinions
> to air logically turned to the establishment of newspapers....
> Almost all American cities with an Irish population possessed their
> own ethnic press. Yorke, replaced as editor of the official *Monitor*,
> would not be silenced; instead he established his own highly
> successful Irish-American weekly, *The Leader*, in 1902. Removing
> himself in this way from the immediate supervision of his religious
> superiors, Yorke was free to wallow in public controversy and to
> torment those with whom he took exception over the issues of the
> day.[52]

At this time, the press took on a new importance for Irish leaders in
America with almost all Irish city populations having their own ethnic
press. The use of the Irish language as part of this voice renders it a
relevant aspect of the Irish identity for the Irish emigrant, enhancing the
new identity in their adopted country. By this time, the international
reportage regarding language revival in the States and the milieu in
which it was fostered was becoming as important as what was happening
in Ireland. Yorke was a controversial character in this domain who would

---

[52] James P. Walsh and Timothy Foley, 'Father Peter C. Yorke: Irish-American leader',
Studia Hibernica 14 (1974) 90–103 (at 91–2).

not be silenced by the restraints of his ministry or otherwise. If challenging the authorities was a factor of immigrant communities, he was up for the challenge and this forum afforded him a freedom which his ministry did not.

In 1899 also Patrick Forde's *Irish World* continued with discussion on the value of the Irish language as an ancient language in the first place, and then as a living language which would include a newspaper column. In 1879 the Irish community in Brooklyn convinced the management at *The Irish World* that they should publish Irish language pieces regularly. Considering that this took twenty years to come to fruition, Hyde's diary entries in 1891 where he documents his meeting with Forde are a further indication of this transatlantic influence on the revival movement.[53] The Gaelic column or the 'Irish Department' was not implemented until 1899 because apparently Forde really had no intention of going through with it. Allowing for Forde's success as a citizen of the United States, his hesitancy is somewhat understandable in light of the perceived challenge to authority with the use of a language which was not considered the main language of the population. Although it did not have a strong Irish column, the column 'Voice of the People' in 1873 included letters which examined 'The restoration of the Celtic language'.[54] The *Irish World* also published a significant amount of discussion on the provision of Irish language classes and on various societies which would help to revive the Irish language. The seeds were planted mainly through a noteworthy letter from Michael Logan on 25 May 1872, announcing that he would give Irish classes. Many scholars have since linked the establishment of these Philo-Celtic societies to the inspiration of the founding of the Society for the Preservation of the Irish Language in Ireland in 1876, while also linking the subsequent foundation of *Irisleabhar na Gaedhilge* / The *Gaelic Journal* in 1882 with that of *An Gaodhal* in Brooklyn in 1881.[55] This would suggest that the progression of the revival movement and language usage in this

---

[53] Proinsias Mac Aonghusa, 'An Ghaeilge i Meiriceá', in Stíofán Ó hAnnracháin (ed.), *Go Meiriceá siar: na Gaeil agus Meiriceá: cnuasach aistí* (Dublin: Clóchomhar Tta. do Chumann Merriman, 1979) 13–30 (at 21).

[54] 'The Irish language', *Irish World* 22/3/1873.

[55] William Mahon, 'Ar thóir na Gaeilge: tionscadal lámhscríbhinní an Philo-Celtic Society (Bostún) 1873–1893', in Ríona Nic Congáil, Máirín Nic Eoin, Meidhbhín Ní Úrdail, Pádraig Ó Liatháin, Regina Uí Chollatáin (eds), *Litríocht na Gaeilge ar fud an domhain* (Baile Átha Cliath 2015) 155–90; Ken Nilsen, 'The Irish language in nineteenth century New York city', in Ofelia Garcia, Joshua A. Fishman and Mouton de Gruyter (eds), *The multilingual apple: languages in New York city* (New York 1997) 52–69; Nilsen, 'The Irish language in New York 1850–1900', 272.

context was to the fore in the United States, indicating a role for the Irish language as a central element of the identity of the Irish immigrant.

By 1886 the movement had also taken root in Boston and the journal of the Philo-Celtic Society of Boston, *The Irish Echo*, was issued in January of that year. In September 1887 Irish was published in it for the first time, in the form of the alphabet and a poem 'Cáitlín mo mhuirnín', with minor language lessons to follow.[56] The Gaelic font put some readers off and in April 1889, the Irish column was printed in Roman font, again showing a focus on literacy as opposed to anything more complex. Poems and prose were published and there were quite a number of controversies also. Despite all this, the *Irish Echo* was quite successful and apparently sometimes sold 30,000 copies.[57] A double final edition for March–April 1894 is an indication of the content of the journal for the previous forty years.

Hyde, as a notable figure, and his writings clearly signified a new departure in the understanding of the Irish oral and written traditions. In the context of Hyde's diary entries, as mentioned earlier, Irish being acknowledged at other levels in the United States at this stage with the foundation of the Professorship (Chair) of Celtic in the Catholic University in Washington the following year in 1895, and the foundation of the first Irish courses in Harvard in 1896, is interesting. It was after this in 1897 when the debate on the founding of the first Irish language newspaper in Ireland started to produce results in Ireland. This was a point at which the role of the publications had moved from 'protesting' to the authorities to 'testing' the Irish public, as referred to earlier.[58]

The periodical culture and journalistic forum was one of the main instruments which played a role in the concept of bridging language preservation, with full revival ensuring a modern literary as well as a modern spoken language. Historical and linguistic research sometimes implies that the Irish abandoned their language when they arrived in the New World, but the newspapers and periodicals of the era build on current research on profiling these immigrant population in certain areas, where evidence to the contrary is available.[59] Clearly the link between language, identity, and citizenship/migration was a source of some conflict in the revival period both at home and abroad, but as the debate

---

[56] Séamus Ó Diolúin, *Mícheál Callánach Ó Séaghdha (1818–1901)* in Nic Congáil et al. (eds), *Litríocht na Gaeilge ar fud an domhain*, 215–32.

[57] Mac Aonghusa, 'An Ghaeilge i Meiriceá', 24.

[58] Eoin Mac Néill, 'Fáinne an Lae', *Irisleabhar na Gaedhilge / The Gaelic Journal*, November 1897.

[59] Nicholas M. Wolf, *An Irish-speaking island: state, religion, community, and the linguistic landscape in Ireland, 1770–1870* (Madison 2014).

on the language gained momentum the Irish language content in the papers achieved more significance in strengthening the revival movement in both domains:

> As talk about the Irish language increased, pieces like this became part of the newspapers. Letters began to recommend revival of the Irish language in the *Irish World* in America in January 1872. 'Shall it be revived ... the tongue that the immortal Liberator loved so well', said a certain Michael Noonan. On the 25th of May that year there was a letter authored by the pen name 'Gael': 'The Irish language should be cultivated in order to maintain Irish ideas and Irish nationality in their integrity.'[60]

Conclusion

An analysis of this kind demonstrates that what was involved was not merely a movement on the margins, but a movement which was rooted in global understandings and language, which envisaged that a marginalised mindset would not be a part of the living language and of the community to which it belonged. Whether the forum itself was fostered in the '*domhan thoir*' [eastern world] or in the '*domhan thiar*' [western world] in a transatlantic context, whether drawing on traditional writing practices or formulating new ways of engaging with reportage, journalistic practice and the styles associated with it were central to the global and transatlantic process of the revival. However, this transatlantic process relied heavily also on communication and writing forums and practices prior to the revival period. The role of journals and newspapers in the creation of a network of sorts of Irish speakers facilitated the migration process establishing links for emigrants while coming to terms with a new hybrid identity. Links to the native language formed part of the identity chain and the seeds for a new ideology on public discourse in the Irish language and society were sown at this time:

> For the majority of Irish speakers, Irish was the language that was most natural for them to use with family, friends, and neighbors. It is an encouraging sign that modern researchers are starting to

---

[60] 'De réir mar mhéadaigh an chaint i dtaobh na Gaeilge tionsclaíodh "giodáin" mar seo i bpáipéir. Thosaigh litreacha ag moladh an Ghaeilge a athbheochan san *Irish World* i Meiriceá in Eanáir, 1872. "Shall it be revived ... the tongue that the immortal Liberator loved so well", adúirt Michael Noonan áirithe. Ar 25ú lá de Bhealtaine an bhliain sin bhí litir ann faoin ainm chleite *Gael*: "The Irish language shall be cultivated in order to maintain Irish ideas and Irish nationality in their integrity."' Ó Cadhain, 'Conradh na Gaeilge agus an litríocht', 52–3.

hear the voices of the many Irish immigrants who arrived in this city with their language and culture intact.[61]

New perspectives on the global revival process and profiling of Irish language speakers help in understanding the concept of citizenship and identity that these emigrants adopted in their new country. Although the Irish language was not in everyday use in every Irish immigrant household, its presence as a visible aspect of the new identity which allowed the immigrant to be '*thall*' and '*abhus*' ['there' and 'here'] at the same time, merits more than a footnote in current sociolinguistic research.

By locating his initial public statements of language revival in New York and in Dublin, Hyde consolidated the foundation of the language revival movement, which was preceded by entries in his diary and discourse on the revival in journalistic forums on both sides of the Atlantic for almost fifty years prior to that. These print and diary sources indicate that the language change which enabled the 'progressive exclusion of Irish in the worlds of commerce, politics, official religion, the professions and printed word' and the 'changing of cultural worlds, [where] millions migrated mentally from the medieval Gaelic world to the modern world of the English Language' were at an earlier stage in the transatlantic context of the revival. Between 1847 and 1947 gradual inclusion of Irish in these areas mainly as a result of the new Gaelic League Idea as part of the revival process depended and continues to depend on the international network and approach which Hyde initiated and pioneered. This was subsequently engineered through the many methods outlined in this essay, not least the journalistic forums.

Regina Uí Chollatáin

---

[61] Nilsen, 'The Irish language in New York 1850–1900', 274.

DOUGLAS HYDE'S INTELLECTUAL LINKS
WITH JOHN QUINN, LADY GREGORY AND W. B. YEATS

Introduction

This paper examines some of the intellectual reach of the Gaelic League in the revival period, focusing in particular on the years 1898 to 1906. Lady Gregory's big house at Coole Park, near Gort, Co. Galway, served as the initial meeting place for her, Douglas Hyde, W. B. Yeats and the Irish-American financial lawyer John Quinn, who was based in New York. Building on the twin successes of the *Punch and Judy* show which Hyde and Norma Borthwick staged in Irish at the end of 1898 and the placing of a commemorative tombstone on the poet Anthony Raftery's grave in 1900, the early years of the twentieth century saw Coole Park serve as the locus for creative collaboration between Hyde, Gregory and Yeats. They worked together on some of Hyde's earliest plays, including *Casadh an tsúgáin* ('The twisting of the rope'), *Pleusgadh na bulgóide; or the bursting of the bubble* and *An tincéar agus an tsídheóg* ('The tinker and the fairy'), to which latter play George Moore also contributed. But it was the cultural discussions occasioned by the arrival of Jack B. Yeats and his friend John Quinn for the Killeeneen feis to be held beside Raftery's grave at the end of August 1902, which led to the intellectual cross-currents which prompted Quinn to organise highly successful coast-to-coast American tours for Yeats in 1903–4, and Hyde in 1905–6. Hyde's trip took him to the White House twice, as well as to over fifty cities and twelve universities throughout the United States. In all, he collected $64,000 for the Gaelic League, a sum said to be equivalent to between one and a half million and two million dollars today. This paper seeks to provide an overview and concise analysis of Hyde's interaction with the other three important turn-of-the-century figures, and briefly assess the impact of this intellectual milieu on the policies and activities of the Gaelic League.

One of the characteristic features of any movement or organisation is the great variation in the commitment and involvement of its members and supporters. This is true not only of the roles they undertake, but of the length and depth of their engagement in different activities. To illustrate this, we may consider the case of some leading members of the Gaelic League in the three decades from its inception in 1893 until 1922. This period includes events such as the resignation of the League's founding President, Dr Douglas Hyde, in 1915 and the establishment of the Irish Free State in 1922. We may summarise the pattern of active involvement and roles of some of the most prominent activists in the organisation as follows:

- Douglas Hyde, 1893–1915 (co-founder, President)
- Eoin MacNeill, 1893–1909 (co-founder, honorary Secretary, editor, Vice-President, President), but with stretches of inactivity after 1902 or thereabouts, and of activity after 1915
- Seosamh Laoide, 1893–1915 (honorary Treasurer, editor)
- Patrick H. Pearse, 1898–1913 (editor)
- Tomás Bán Ó Concheanainn, 1899–1911 (organiser, chief organiser)
- Pádraig Ó Dálaigh, 1901–15 (General Secretary)
- Stiofán Bairéad, 1902–21 (Treasurer)
- Fionán Mac Coluim, 1902–22 (organiser, chief organiser)

All of these rather well-known figures would be closely, many of them indeed primarily, identified with the Gaelic League organisation itself. But there were others who were also well-known, some indeed famous, but whose active and direct participation in the language movement was confined to shorter periods and/or specific activities. This is true of the three people whose relationship to Douglas Hyde is discussed in this paper, *viz.* John Quinn (1870–1924), Irish-American financial lawyer and patron of the arts, Lady Augusta Gregory (1852–1932), founder of the Abbey Theatre and a prime mover in the Irish literary revival, and W. B. Yeats (1865–1939), pioneering poet and dramatist of the Irish literary revival. Quinn, Gregory and Yeats were all close friends of Hyde's at the start of the twentieth century and their intellectual relationship with him played a significant part in the early development of the Gaelic League and its impact on public opinion. As noted already, it was John Quinn who organised Hyde's highly successful American tour of 1905–6,[1] and despite a serious falling out over the riotous reception accorded Synge's play, *The playboy of the western world*, by Clan na Gael supporters in the United States some years later, they maintained friendly contact until Quinn's death in 1924. Lady Gregory kept an open house in her residence at Coole Park, Co. Galway, where she entertained writers and artists. Hyde paid his first visit there in 1897, performing with Miss Norma Borthwick in an Irish-language *Punch and Judy* show in December 1898. Hyde returned to Coole regularly on short visits for a number of years, and it was there that Lady Gregory translated many of his plays into English, and typed them up.

---

[1] Liam Mac Mathúna, Brian Ó Conchubhair, Niall Comer, Cuan Ó Seireadáin and Máire Nic an Bhaird (eds), *Douglas Hyde: my American journey*, Foreword by President Michael D. Higgins (Dublin 2019).

W. B. Yeats

We may first consider the links between W. B. Yeats and Douglas Hyde, as they go back farthest. Born in 1865, Yeats was five years Hyde's junior. The two got to know each other in the 1880s. Yeats is first mentioned in Hyde's diary entry for 2 June 1885.[2] Yeats recalls in his *Autobiographies* how he first met Hyde as an undergraduate at Trinity, and conveys a picture of a young man, who had become as one with his Frenchpark neighbours:

> I have a memory of meeting in college rooms for the first time a very dark young man, who filled me with surprise, partly because he had pushed a snuffbox towards me, and partly because there was something about his vague serious eyes, as in his high cheek-bones, that suggested a different civilization, a different race. I had set him down as a peasant, and wondered what brought him to a college, and to a Protestant college, but somebody explained that he belonged to some branch of the Hydes of Castle Hyde, and that he had a Protestant Rector for father. He had much frequented the company of old countrymen, and had so acquired the Irish language and his taste for snuff, and for moderate quantities of a detestable species of illegal whiskey distilled from the potato by certain of his neighbours. He had already – though intellectual Dublin knew nothing of it – considerable popularity as a Gaelic poet, mowers and reapers singing his songs from Donegal to Kerry.[3]

In his entry for 23 January 1887, Hyde tells how he and Yeats walked the four miles to the writer Katharine Tynan's house at Clondalkin on a Sunday afternoon.[4] In fact, Hyde was soon helping his younger friend,

---

[2] See National Library of Ireland (NLI) MS G 1040, image 89; cf. Dominic Daly, *The young Douglas Hyde* (Dublin 1974) 57. Hyde maintained a diary in Irish from 1874, when he was just fourteen, until 1912. This is in thirteen volumes, which are held in the National Library of Ireland as NLI MSS G 1036–48. They have been digitised and may be consulted online. For discussion of entries in the early diaries, see Máire Nic an Bhaird and Liam Mac Mathúna, 'Douglas Hyde (1860–1949): the adolescent behind the diarist', in Rebecca Anne Barr, Sarah-Anne Buckley and Muireann O'Cinneide (eds), *Literacy, language and reading in nineteenth-century Ireland* (Liverpool 2019) 28–50, and Máire Nic an Bhaird and Liam Mac Mathúna, 'Early diary insights into Roscommon's impact on Douglas Hyde, Ireland's first President', in Richie Farrell, Kieron O'Conor and Matthew Potter (eds), *Roscommon: history and society* (Dublin 2018) 515–37.

[3] William Butler Yeats, ed. Douglas N. Archibald and William H. O'Donnell, *The collected works of W. B. Yeats. Vol. III. Autobiographies* (New York 1999) 180–1.

[4] NLI MS G 1041, image 89; cf. Daly, *The young Douglas Hyde*, 87.

who was very interested in Ireland's native traditions and culture, but lacked competence in the Irish language. For instance, Hyde provided three stories in translation from the Irish for Yeats's *Fairy and folk tales of the Irish peasantry*, published by Walter Scott in 1888. Yeats acknowledges that one of these was the best tale in his collection.[5] He then observes that he believed he 'had something to do with the London publication of his [viz. Hyde's] *Beside the fire* [1890]' which he goes on to describe as 'a book written in the beautiful English of Connacht, which is Gaelic in idiom and Tudor in vocabulary, and, indeed, the first book to use it in the expression of emotion and romance, for Carleton and his school had turned it into farce'.[6] In his Introduction to *Fairy and folk tales of the Irish peasantry* Yeats thanks Hyde for 'valuable and valued assistance in several ways', and individual notes on Irish words and phrases acknowledge them as Hyde's.[7] However, Hyde tended to be somewhat wary of his younger colleague, even when they were both members of organisations such as the National Literary Society in the 1890s. At a personal level, he found Yeats's torrent of ideas, all delivered and expressed with supreme confidence, to be rather trying at times.

In recognition of his tact and demonstrated ability to keep the peace between the elderly Sir Charles Gavan Duffy (1816–1903), whose literary views and standards had been formed in the heyday of the Young Ireland movement in the 1840s, and the fiery young Yeats, who was brimming with up-to-the-minute ideas, Hyde was appointed President of the National Literary Society in August 1892. Yeats had actually been the prime mover in the establishment of this organisation,[8] which of course was also the body to which Hyde delivered his celebrated, ground-breaking lecture entitled 'The necessity for de-anglicising Ireland' on 25 November 1892. The friendship between Hyde and Yeats was quite close at this period. Hyde's diary records that he and Yeats travelled to Cork together on 23 January 1893:

> Cuaidh mé go Corcaigh. le Yeats, leis an g-coiste 9.15. Bhí Cúnt
> Pluinnceud ⁊ O Mathghamna ann rómhainn. Chuadhmar don tig
> osta Victória ⁊ bhí dinnéar againn ⁊ dá ghlaine maith puinnse
> agam-sa. Chuadhmar do'n chruinniughadh annsin do cuireadh ar
> bonn leis an gCumann Náisiúnta Litirdhea do chur ar agaidh. Bi
> Dini O Liatháin (<u>Lane</u>) ann san gcáthaoir ⁊ rinne seisean caint i

[5] Yeats, *Autobiographies*, 181.
[6] ibid.
[7] Daly, *The young Douglas Hyde*, 129.
[8] ibid. 153–4.

dtosach ag léigheadh o sgribhinn. Labhair mise ann sin go righ-mhaith. Thainig Yeats am' dhiaigh-se ⁊ an Cúnt 'nnar ndiaigh-ne. Bhí timcioll 150 duinne ann ⁊ lucht-ionaid gach cumann litirdhea i gCorcaigh mar aon. ...[9]

'I went to Cork with Yeats on the 9.15 coach-train. Count Plunkett and O'Mahoney were there before us. We went to the Victoria Hotel where we had dinner and I had two good glasses of punch. Then we went to the meeting which had been arranged to promote the National Literary Society. Dinny Lane was in the chair and he spoke first, reading from a script. I then spoke and did so very well. Yeats spoke after me, and the Count after us. There were about 150 people present, including representatives of every literary society in Cork.'[10]

This is an interesting illustration of the wide public interest in national cultural matters at the time and is indicative of the latent reservoir of support which was available to be tapped by an organisation such as the Gaelic League, founded in Dublin just six months later. We also know that Yeats stayed at Hyde's home, Ratra House, Frenchpark, Co. Roscommon, 13 April–1 May 1895.[11]

When Yeats and Lady Gregory met Hyde at Coole Park at the start of the new century, they encouraged him to compose plays in Irish, and helped him in his endeavours by providing plot lines and cordial critical appraisal. Indeed, the full extent of the input which Yeats had into the plot of Hyde's first play, *Casadh an tsúgáin*, 'The twisting of the rope', is not widely appreciated. A number of entries in Hyde's diary throw light on the extent of the collaboration involved:

28 August 1900
Cuir Yeats ag sgriobhadh drama mé ar casadh an tsugáin ⁊ sgríobhas cuid mhór dhé ón scenario do tarraing seisean amach dam.

'Yeats set me to writing a play on "The twisting of the rope", and I wrote a good part of it from the scenario he drew out for me.'

---

[9] NLI MS G 1044, image 6. The orthography here and elsewhere is that of the original diary.

[10] Translations are by the author, unless otherwise stated. Cf. Daly, *The young Douglas Hyde*, 160.

[11] See notes to Yeats, *Autobiographies*, 466. The visit is also recorded in Hyde's diary, volume NLI MS G 1044, images 66–7.

29 August 1900
Ag criochnughad Casadh an tSúgáin. Tuirseach 7 rud beag tinn.
Thug Laedi Gregori buideál seampaén dam ag dinéar.
'Finishing "The twisting of the rope". Tired and a bit sick. Lady
Gregory gave me a bottle of champagne at dinner.'

30 August 1900
Táinig an Mairtíneach chum dinéir 7 léigh mé Casadh an tsugáin
dó andé 7 bhí sé lán-shásta.

'Martyn[12] came to dinner and I read "The twisting of the rope" to
him yesterday and he was fully satisfied with it.'

31 August 1900
Léigh mé casadh an tsugáin andé 7 andiú don bhainteargna 7 do
chló-sgríobh sí é om' bhéal i mBéarla. Lá breágh. biseach orm.
sgriobhas cuid de drama beag eile.

'I read "The twisting of the rope" to Lady Gregory yesterday and
today and she typed it in English from my dictation. A fine day. I
was better. I wrote part of another little play.'[13]

Yeats had an active, if somewhat faltering, connection with the Gaelic
League at the turn of the century, although the stresses which would
soon see the language movement and the literary revival take separate
paths are set out by Roy Foster in an account of some events in the
second half of 1901:

> Cultural enterprises continued to spark into life in Dublin, but
> WBY [W. B. Yeats], who was becoming worried at Gaelic League
> zealots causing trouble in literary organizations, preferred to stay
> at Coole. A letter he sent to D. P. Moran's new journal the *Leader*
> on 26 August effectively argued against the pure Fenian line in
> cultural matters, and provided a self-defence against the continuing
> campaign waged against his 'West-Britonism' in the columns of
> *An Claidheamh Soluis*. When he did venture to Dublin in October

---

[12] Edward Martyn of Tulira Castle, Ardrahan, Co. Galway was a playwright and leading
personality of the Irish literary revival. He had introduced Lady Gregory and Yeats to each
other at his home in 1896.
[13] NLI MS G 1045, from images 131–2; also detailed in Daly, *The young Douglas Hyde*,
135.

to preside at a Gaelic League concert in the Gresham Hotel, he
trod very carefully indeed and obviously bore in mind the rancour
aroused by Leaguers in the National Literary Society. After a
programme that included Moore's *Melodies* as well as step-
dancing, WBY spoke in English on the Irish language. 'It was no
use disguising from themselves that they had now going on in
Ireland a war of civilisation, and upon that war not only did the
issue of Irish Nationality hang, but the very greatest issues that a
man could concern himself with.' He moved on to attack English
commercialism and vulgarity, and to call for a new Irish dramatic
movement: short plays in Irish, without scenery, played all over
Ireland 'in barns'. 'They should revive the old Irish drama' (an
undefined concept).[14]

Nor is there any doubt but that Yeats had the utmost regard for Hyde's
English-language renderings of Irish folktales and songs. Writing in
1902, Yeats recalled his first reading of *Love songs of Connacht*, initially
published in book form in 1893:

> The prose parts of that book were to me, as they were to many
> others, the coming of a new power into literature. I find myself
> now, as I found myself then, grudging to propaganda, to
> scholarship, to oratory, however necessary, a genius which might
> in modern Irish or in that idiom of the English-speaking country
> people discover a new region for the mind to wander in.[15]

Thus, although Yeats thought highly of Hyde's literary abilities, he
always felt – and regretted – that the public man, *engagé* in current
affairs, had relegated these qualities to a subsidiary place, as Daly
observed:

> Ceaseless travel, speechmaking and pamphleteering made it
> impossible for him to find time, as Yeats would have him do, 'for
> the making of translations, loving and leisurely, like those in
> *Beside the Fire* and the *Love Songs of Connacht*.' Henceforth for
> Yeats, he was 'the great poet who died in his youth'.[16]

---

[14] R. F. Foster, *W. B. Yeats: A life. I: The apprentice mage 1865–1914* (Oxford and New
York 1998 [1997]) 235.
[15] W. B. Yeats, *Samhain*, 1902, reprinted in Mrs. W. B. Yeats, *Explorations: W. B. Yeats*
(New York 1962) 93.
[16] Daly, *The young Douglas Hyde*, 136.

Recalling how he and Lady Gregory gave Hyde scenarios for plays, Yeats contrasts the difficulty he had in wresting poetry from words with the ease with which Hyde seemed to compose:

> In later years Lady Gregory and I gave Hyde other scenarios and I always watched him with astonishment. … When I wrote verse, five or six lines in two or three laborious hours were a day's work, and I longed for somebody to interrupt me; but he wrote all day, whether in verse or prose, and without apparent effort. Effort was there, but in the unconscious.[17]

However, Hyde's companions saw to it that he got a break from his writing:

> Lady Gregory kept watch, to draw him from his table after so many hours; the gamekeeper had the boat and the guns ready; there were ducks upon the lake. He wrote in joy and at great speed because emotion brought the appropriate word. Nothing in that language of his was abstract, nothing worn-out; he need not, as must the writer of some language exhausted by modern civilization, reject word after word, cadence after cadence, he had escaped our perpetual, painful, purification.[18]

However, the underlying truth may well have been that Yeats was always a little in awe of, and probably somewhat envious of Hyde's easy way with people, with individuals, and perhaps more particularly, with 'the people', as a collective, when they congregated before him in crowds, or when he addressed them as a virtual or imagined community through print. A decade or so later, in 1912, Yeats confronted the question of the Abbey's unpopularity in verse, publishing 'At the Abbey Theatre' in the *Irish Review*. This poem was a direct challenge to Hyde, addressing him by his well-known pseudonym 'An Craoibhín Aoibhinn' ('The Pleasant Little Branch', here with the spelling *Aoibhin*, an orthographic by-form of the adjective) to explain why the theatre could put on nothing that pleased the Dublin audience, and implying that Hyde himself knew how to manipulate popularity.

---

[17] Yeats, *Autobiographies*, 324–5.
[18] ibid. 325.

DEAR Craoibhin Aoibhin, look into our case.
When we are high and airy, hundreds say
That if we hold that flight they'll leave the place,
While those same hundreds mock another day
Because we have made our art of common things,
So bitterly, you'd dream they longed to look
All their lives through into some drift of wings.
You've dandled them and fed them from the book
And know them to the bone; impart to us –
We'll keep the secret – a new trick to please.
Is there a bridle for this Proteus
That turns and changes like his draughty seas?
Or is there none, most popular of men,
But, when they mock us that we mock again?

As it happened, Hyde revelled in such calls to public debate and adroit
as ever, happily responded smoothly in verse, claiming that he thought
as one with the Irish people, while Yeats 'bewildered' them:

A narrower cult but broader art is mine,
Your wizard fingers strike a hundred strings
Bewildering with multitudinous things,
Whilst all our offerings are at one shrine.
Therefore we step together. Small the art
To keep one pace where men are one at heart.[19]

In fact, Yeats himself conceded as much, saying of Hyde: 'He had
the folk mind as no modern man has had it, its qualities and its defects.'[20]
   Hyde's 1905–6 American tour retraced much of the journey Yeats had
undertaken just over two years previously. On 16 December 1905 Hyde
wrote to Yeats, passing on a cheque for £77 due to him for his talks in
California. Reporting positively on his own endeavours, Hyde assured
Yeats that he was also furthering the cause of the national theatre and
that the poet himself was fondly remembered: 'I have been working very
hard since I came here, speaking at either four or five meetings every
week, generally for nearly an hour and a half. I think I have persuaded

---

[19] See Foster, *A life*, 455, for discussion of the verse dialogue. For the texts themselves
see *Irish Review* (Dec. 1912) 505 and (Jan. 1913) 561.
[20] Yeats, *Autobiographies*, 324. Seán Ó Ríordáin in his diaries quoted this intriguingly
apposite assessment of Hyde. I am grateful to Dr Pádraig Ó Liatháin, who is working on
Ó Ríordáin's diaries, for this reference.

everybody I spoke to of the necessity for our movement. Many people have inquired lovingly about you, especially at the young ladies colleges, and I am sure everyone will be glad to see you again if you come out next year. I have said all the good I could think of about the theatre.'[21] In doing this, Hyde was reciprocating the effort Yeats had put into informing his own American audiences, two years earlier, about Hyde and his work. This is a point made forcefully by Quinn himself in a letter to Yeats dated 13 July 1906, written a few weeks after Hyde's return to Ireland. Quinn was in retrospective mode at the time, reviewing the bigger picture and surveying the tours he had organised for Yeats and Hyde. He assured Yeats: 'You did more to make him [*viz*. Hyde] known here than anyone else and I finished the job that you began. You did it generously and Hyde should never forget it. … Outside of the Irish Societies he was almost unknown here a year ago except to some Irish, who weren't numerous enough to make up a corporal's guard. Today he is almost an international figure.' Quinn had achieved what he set out to do when he envisioned the tours for both Yeats and Hyde: 'You and Hyde have done more for the elevation of the Irish in this country and for the increasing respect with which Irish ideals and aspirations are regarded in this country than any other two men of your day and generation. The people were getting tired of mere politicians, whose sole stock in trade consisted of abuse of Englishmen and promises of the good things they were going to do.'[22]

Lady Augusta Gregory
Lady Gregory was introduced to Yeats by Edward Martyn at his residence, Tulira Castle, Co. Galway in 1896, at a time when she was becoming increasingly interested in the Irish literary revival. Ironically, although Yeats himself never progressed beyond the elementary stage in learning Irish, Lady Gregory's acquaintance with the young poet and her increasing familiarity with his writings were major impulses for her own, more successful, efforts to acquire the language. While she never quite mastered the skills of understanding and speaking the oral language, Lady Gregory did achieve considerable competence in the written word. She also had a growing appreciation of the richness of the folklore still to be found among the country people living about her in the west of Ireland. In addition, she was increasingly influenced by the ideas being promulgated by Dr Douglas Hyde, both by way of speeches

---

[21] NLI MS 18,253/2/5.
[22] Alan Himber, *The letters of John Quinn to William Butler Yeats* (Ann Arbor, Michigan 1983) 76–80.

reiterating the thrust of his 1892 de-anglicisation lecture, and through
the dynamic activities of the Gaelic League. Further, more personal,
motivation came from the interest in learning the language expressed by
her son Robert, about the time of his sixteenth birthday in May 1897.
Like most others of the period, Lady Gregory depended on Fr Eugene
O'Growney's *Simple lessons in Irish* to guide her in learning the
language. Although the more immediate appeal of hunting was soon to
divert Robert from language learning, his mother worked her way
through the exercises, checking the pronunciation with Mike Dooley,
one of her tenants. When she travelled to London in autumn of that year,
she made contact with Norma Borthwick of the Southwark Irish Literary
Society, a pioneering Gaelic group, and arranged for a series of lessons.[23]

It was also at Tulira, in the summer of 1897, that Gregory first met
Hyde. Her biographer, Judith Hill, tells us that 'she was immediately
attracted to his enthusiasm, his sensitivity to the nuances of the language
and the way he was haunted by the fragility of the dying oral culture'.[24]
Hyde was already on the trail of Anthony Raftery, the early nineteenth-
century itinerant poet, whose work he was to edit and publish in 1903.
Hyde's first note to Lady Gregory was dated 19 August 1897 and
expressed his regret at not being able to accept her invitation to Coole
Park, for he had always heard that 'Gort abounded in shanachies and in
correct Gaelic', and 'he was very sorry to miss this opportunity of
proving it'.[25] But he was able to visit her soon afterwards, and Lady
Gregory's diary for Sept.–Oct. 1897 includes the following entry:

> And Dr. Douglas Hyde came – full of enthusiasm & Irish – I took
> him & Sharp to the cromlech & to Kilmacduagh – & he began
> talking Irish to Fahy, near Cranagh – who to my pride came out
> with legends of Finn & Ussian galore – I was able to help Dr. Hyde

[23] Judith Hill, *Lady Gregory: an Irish life* (Cork 2011) 180. As part of the group's new
and lively desire to learn Irish, and evidently to further the young Robert's interest in the
language, Edward Martyn presented him with a copy of Bedell's Old Testament in Irish,
Leabhuir an tsean Tiomna, printed in Dublin by Grierson and Keene in 1827, dedicating
it (on the top half of a page) 'To Robert Gregory / from / Edward Martyn / Tillyra Castle.
/ 9 September 1897'. Following Robert's tragic death, piloting a plane in the Great War
early in 1918, Lady Gregory returned the book to Martyn, with this touching message
inscribed on the lower half of the same leaf: 'Returned to Edward Martyn / in memory of
Robert Gregory / killed in action Jan 23.1918. / A. Gregory'. This volume is now held in
the Edward Martyn Library, which is attached to St Teresa's Church, Clarendon Street,
Dublin.

[24] Hill, *Lady Gregory*, 181.

[25] Janet Egleson Dunleavy and Gareth W. Dunleavy, *Douglas Hyde: a maker of modern
Ireland* (Berkeley, Los Angeles, Oxford 1991) 132.

to get some MS from 'one Connor', who had left there for Galway a year ago, & who I finally traced to a butcher's shop in Clare[n]bridge – but whether they are worth anything I know not.[26] Gregory's introductory highlighting of Hyde's enthusiasm is noteworthy. This fervour with regard to the revival of the spoken language and his scholarly engagement with the collection of folklore and study of the language's literature were characteristic of the man, and hallmarks of his personality: they impacted positively on almost everyone he met throughout his long life. While Lady Gregory and Hyde helped each other generally in a variety of ways, they collaborated closely in two particular areas, namely, the creation of original drama in Irish and the promotion of Raftery's memory.

Fired by Hyde's zeal, Lady Gregory helped him to source oral renderings and manuscript copies of Raftery's poems. She took the initiative in locating Raftery's grave in Killeeneen cemetery, near Craughwell in east Galway, and in raising funds for the placing of a memorial stone on the spot. Inspired by her comparison with the Greek epic poet Homer, the inscription she chose was a simple one, consisting only of the poet's surname. A year earlier, in an article in *An Claidheamh Soluis* (16 September 1899), Tomás Ó Concheanainn, the first Gaelic League *timire* or organiser, described a conversation at Coole where Lady Gregory siad it was a pity that there was no stone to mark Raftery's grave.[27] Lady Gregory's article 'Raftery, the poet of the poor', written at Hyde's suggestion for *An Claidheamh Soluis* (14 October 1899), was an appeal for subscriptions for Raftery's stone; it also included some stories about Raftery and a verse of his, which was later printed by Hyde in *The religious songs of Connacht*. As it happened, however, Lady Gregory herself paid for most of the cost of the stone – a high stone with a single word 'Raftery' – that was unveiled and blessed at a Gaelic League feis in Killeeneen, County Galway, on 26 August 1900.[28]

Importantly, Hyde was more understanding of the ideals of Lady Gregory and the other leaders of the Irish literary revival than some of

---

[26] James Pethica (ed.), *Lady Gregory's diaries 1892–1902* (Gerrards Cross, Buckinghamshire 1996) 154. In footnote 145 the editor observes: 'In a letter of 23 October 1897 to Hyde, AG [Augusta Gregory] mentions obtaining this manuscript from "one Connolly" (NLI). It appears not to have contained significant material since Hyde fails to mention it as a source in his publications, though he cites other material AG provided.'

[27] Tomás Ua Concheanainn, 'Anonn agus anall', *An Claidheamh Soluis* (16 Seacht-mhí, 1899) 419–21.

[28] Murphy, Maureen, 'Lady Gregory and the Gaelic League'. In Ann Saddlemeyer and Colin Smythe (eds), *Lady Gregory, fifty years after* (Gerrards Cross, Buckinghamshire and Totowa, N. J. 1987) 143–62 (at 151).

his colleagues in the Gaelic League, including Eoin MacNeill and Patrick Pearse, whose ideological antagonism towards the concept of a national Irish literature in the English language was bolstered by Fr Peter Yorke's 'The turning of the tide' lecture in Dublin on 6 September 1899. Already in April 1899 Hyde had written to Lady Gregory of his annoyance that the Gaelic League's newspaper seemed to oppose the idea of anything Irish in English – for example, the Literary Theatre. Fearing that his ally at Coole might be alienated because of sniping at her theatre in *An Claidheamh Soluis*, on 7 May 1899 Hyde wrote quite a firm letter in Irish to its first editor and his long-time friend, Eoin MacNeill:

> I beseech you please to say nothing in *Claidheamh* against the Literary Theatre. Many of our friends, especially Lady Gregory are on the Executive Committee, so don't go against them. ... They are not enemies to us. They are a halfway house. They wanted, and did their best to do *Oisin* and *Padraig* in Irish, at the same time, in the theatre.

Hyde wrote that neither they, nor George Sigerson's group,[29] another 'halfway house', should be condemned.[30] The viewpoint of the anti-Literary Theatre element in the Gaelic League was expressed by P. H. Pearse in a letter to MacNeill as editior of *An Claidheamh Soluis*, 13 May 1899: 'The Irish Literary Theatre is in my opinion more dangerous, because glaringly anti-national, than Trinity College. If we once admit the Irish literature in English idea, then the language movement is a mistake. ... Let us strangle it at its birth.' However, by 1905 Pearse himself was speaking well of Lady Gregory's plays, although others still held to the ideas he had expressed previously.[31]

The first steps with regard to drama in Irish were taken during Hyde's Christmas visit to Coole in 1898. He and Miss Norma Borthwick gave a *Punch and Judy* show in Irish for local children at St Colman's Hall in Gort. This was an unqualified success and inspired Lady Gregory to urge Hyde to write an Irish play for a Dublin audience. She dated the beginning of a drama in Irish to that event:

---

[29] This was the National Literary Society.
[30] Gareth W. Dunleavy, 'The pattern of three threads: the Hyde-Gregory friendship', in Saddlemeyer and Smyth, *Lady Gregory, fifty years after*, 131–42 (at 134–5). For the letter in question, which is in Irish, see NLI MS 10,874/9/9, Douglas Hyde to Eoin MacNeill, 7 May 1899.
[31] Dunleavy, 'The patterns of three threads', n. 17 on p. 411.

I hold that the beginning of modern Irish drama was in the winter of 1898, at a school feast at Coole, when Douglas Hyde and Miss Norma Borthwick acted in Irish in a Punch and Judy Show, and the delighted children went back to tell their parents what a grand curse An Craoibhin had put on the baby and the policeman.[32]

These two projects concerning Raftery and drama in Irish formed a natural part of wider collaboration between Hyde and Lady Gregory. For instance, Lady Gregory was actively involved in the preparations for the first meeting of the Kiltartan Branch of the Gaelic League which took place at Kiltartan School on 9 January 1899, with her friend Father Fahey, Gort's Irish-speaking parish priest, in the chair. Hyde spoke in Irish, which Lady Gregory confessed she didn't understand, and in English. She felt that his remark, 'Let English go their road and let us go ours and God forbid their road should ever be ours' was too political.[33]

When Lady Gregory returned to London in spring 1900 she translated some of Hyde's poems from Irish, translations which Yeats read one evening to Mark Twain and to Mrs Clemens.[34] Hyde's reaction pleased her and she was proud of her growing ability to read Irish. He wrote to her on 5 June 1900, saying: 'I had no idea that you had translated anything like so many, or that you would have been able to translate them anything like so well'.[35] He then invited her to write the preface to his book of Raftery poems, and asked her to give Yeats a Gaelic League button, which he enclosed with the letter: 'Please give it him from me. I hope he'll wear it. It will be a talisman against the *banditti* of the League.'[36] This was almost certainly the same button which Fr O'Growney had enclosed for Yeats in a letter he sent to Hyde in 1899, in which he wrote the following note at the top of the first page: *Cnaipe do Yeats agus / do'n Athair O'Fathaigh san nGort.* ('A button for Yeats and for Fr Fahey in Gort.') The letter, in Irish, was sent from Sisters' Hospital, Los Angeles, Cal., dated *Ochtmhí* ['October'] 7/1899 and signed Eoghan O Gramhna.[37]

---

[32] Lady Gregory, with a foreword by T. R. Henn, *Poets and dreamers: studies and translations from the Irish by Lady Gregory including nine plays by Douglas Hyde* (Gerrards Cross, Bucks. 1974) 136.

[33] Murphy, 'Lady Gregory and the Gaelic League', 146.

[34] ibid. 147.

[35] Dunleavy, 'The pattern of three threads', 135.

[36] ibid. The letter is dated September 1900, no specific day being cited.

[37] The letter quoted from here was donated to the UCD School of Irish, Celtic Studies and Folklore by Mrs Mary Sealy, December 2013.

When Hyde came to Coole for the shooting just after Christmas 1900, Lady Gregory showed him her translations of some of the early Irish saga tales. However, Hyde regarded the colloquial style as inappropriate.[38] He thought that the translating was really work for a scholar and disliked her practice of combining different versions in order to form a single narrative. However, she only wanted his approval, which he gave, and was not put out by his misgivings.[39] He continued to be doubtful and vaguely discouraging: 'I do think you are plucky to tackle the great cycle ... It is more difficult than it seems at first sight,' he wrote in March. But by May he was persuaded and enthusiastic: 'I am rejoiced to hear you have progressed so far with your Tain series. You are really wonderful. I shall be ever so curious to know and see what you have done.'[40] After that he gave her manuscripts, information on other scholars' work, and helped her with some of the translations.[41]

In another effort to advance the work of general, non-political, nationalist forces in Ireland Lady Gregory edited *Ideals in Ireland*, a collection of essays by 'A. E.', D. P. Moran, George Moore, Douglas Hyde, Standish O'Grady and W. B. Yeats, which was published in 1901. Standish O'Grady's 'The great enchantment' was the only contribution not concerned at some level with the Irish language and/or the Gaelic League. Notwithstanding the fact that Lady Gregory did not contribute an essay herself, her hand is clear in her selection, in her Introduction, and in her translation of Hyde's two essays and some of Raftery's work for Yeats's 'The literary movement in Ireland'. Significantly, not only was Hyde author of two of the essays, rather than the customary one, but the high esteem in which Lady Gregory held the President of the Gaelic League found direct expression in her Prologue, where she observed: 'Douglas Hyde, our Craoibhin Aoibhin, stooped down to make an earthenware candlestick, but when he lifted his head he knew it was not a candle he had lighted, but a star he had discovered, and is now lighting up all the western sky.'[42] Lady Gregory gave the Gaelic

---

[38] Pethica, *Lady Gregory's diaries*, p. 293; cf. Hill, *Lady Gregory*, 226–7.

[39] ibid.

[40] Douglas Hyde to Lady Gregory, 13 March 1901 and 1 May 1901: see Pethica, *Lady Gregory's diaries*, 293.

[41] Lady Gregory to Wilfred Scawen Blunt, 7 April 1902: see Pethica, *Lady Gregory's diaries*, 293. Cf. Hill, *Lady Gregory*, 226–7.

[42] Lady Gregory (ed.), *Ideals in Ireland* (London 1901). Further evidence of the high regard in which she held Hyde is to be seen in the fact that he was author of one of the three literary pieces quoted by way of prelude to the book proper, the other two being Walt Whitman and Turguénieff (Turgenev). The following is the quatrain composed by 'An Craoibhin Aoibhin':

League the royalties for *Ideals in Ireland* and she also suggested to Yeats that the proceeds from the Spring 1901 issue of *Beltaine*, the occasional journal of the Irish Literary Theatre, should be given to the League as well. Yeats not only agreed, but decided that *Beltaine* should be 'A Gaelic propaganda paper this time'. *Beltaine* was in fact succeeded by *Samhain* but its profits for the October 1901 issue were donated to the League.[43]

Hyde stayed at Coole after the Gaelic League feis at Killeeneen in 1900. While there, Lady Gregory and Yeats set him to writing a play in Irish which might be produced by the Gaelic League: 'We thought at our first start it would make the whole movement more living and bring it closer to the people if the Gaelic League would put on some plays written in Irish.'[44] While Hyde, Yeats and Lady Gregory all agree that Yeats provided a scenario based on his Red Hanrahan story, 'The twisting of the rope', from *The secret rose* (1897), Hyde was of course familiar with the basic idea of the twisting of a straw rope to get rid of an unwanted suitor. He had already described it in the note to his version of *An súisín bán* ('The white coverlet') in *Love songs of Connacht* (1893). Although Hyde did not use the words of this song in his play, another of the songs, *Tadhg agus Máire* ('Teig and Mary'), may have inspired dialogues spoken by Una and Hanrahan in the play.[45]

As well as collaborating actively with Hyde on the plots of his plays, Lady Gregory translated them into English. Some of Hyde's plays were actually first published, with translation by Lady Gregory, in *Samhain*, the literary journal founded by Yeats. Among these were *Casadh an tsúgáin* in October 1901, *An naomh ar iarraidh* ('The missing saint') in October 1902 and *Teach na mbocht* ('The poorhouse') in October 1903. The last mentioned, originally scripted in collaboration with Lady Gregory, was rewritten by her as *The workhouse ward* (1909). *An tincéar agus an tsidheóg* ('The tinker and the fairy') first appeared in the *New Ireland Review*, May 1902; *Pléusgadh na bulgóide* ('The bursting of the bubble'), a good-natured, if biting, satire on Trinity College Dublin, in

---

Ní rachaidh mise go bráth ar gcúl,
Má's éigin bheith umhal duit, is mór mo leun,
Muna dtig liom siubhal, muna dtig liom siubhal,
Muna dtig liom siubhal ar mo pháirc féin.

[43] See Murphy, 'Lady Gregory and the Gaelic League', 150–1.
[44] Quoted from Lady Gregory, *Our Irish theatre* (1972) 54, in Murphy, 'Lady Gregory and the Gaelic League', 153.
[45] ibid.

the same *Review*, May 1903;[46] *An cleamhnas* ('The matchmaking')
appeared in *Irisleabhar na Gaedhilge / The Gaelic Journal*, in December
1903. All were afterwards published individually.[47] Lady Gregory also
translated *Rígh Séumas* ('King James'), and *Maistín an Bhéarla* ('The
mastiff of the English language').[48] Hyde's practice of interweaving
work and play is neatly illustrated by the following observation recorded
by Lady Gregory in *Poets and dreamers*:

> 'The Lost Saint' was written last summer. *An Craoibhin* was
> staying with us at Coole; and one morning I went for a long drive
> to the sea, leaving him with a bundle of blank paper before him.
> When I came back at evening, I was told that Dr. Hyde had
> finished his play, and was out shooting wild duck. The hymn
> however, was not quite ready, and was put into rhyme next day,
> while he was again watching for wild duck beside Inchy marsh.[49]

When the time came for Hyde to set out on his lecturing and fundraising
tour of America, 1905–6, he was honoured with a great municipal
reception consisting of speeches, toasts and well-wishes in the Gresham
Hotel, Dublin, on 6 November 1905. Yeats had agreed that Lady
Gregory should present Hyde with flowers on behalf of the Irish
National Theatre Society, of which he had once been Vice-President.
Less than three weeks later, on Saturday, 25 November, Hyde journeyed
together with John Quinn to Washington D. C., having been invited to
the White House to dine with President Theodore Roosevelt. The
President proved to be very knowledgeable about both Irish and Norse
mythology and was able to draw comparisons between them. Indeed,
Roosevelt told his visitors that he had been brought up by Irish nurses
and that Cú Chulainn and Fionn Mac Cumhaill had been familiar and
vivid figures to him before he ever saw their names in literature. In a
letter he wrote to Lady Gregory just four days later, Hyde was able to
tell her of the President's high regard for her work: '… and on Saturday
to lunch with President Roosevelt, who spoke so nicely about your work

---

[46] See Liam Mac Mathúna, 'Na róil a bhí ag an gCraoibhín Aoibhinn, an Géagán Glas
agus "G. G." i gcumadh *Pleusgadh na bulgóide; or The bursting of the bubble* (1903)', in
Éadaoin Ní Mhuircheartaigh, Róisín Ní Ghairbhí and Pádraig Ó Liatháin, *Ó Chleamairí
go ceamairí: drámaíocht agus taibhealaíona na Gaeilge faoi chaibidil* (Baile Átha Cliath
2021) 19–33.

[47] See Daly, *Young Douglas Hyde*, 216–17. Later in the 1930s, new editions, in Irish only,
were published by An Gúm in the new independent state.

[48] See Murphy, 'Lady Gregory and the Gaelic League', 154.

[49] *Poets and dreamers* (1974) 137–8.

and the Irish sagas in general. It was a delightful experience meeting him. There was nobody there except himself and his own family and Mr. Quinn and myself.'[50]

After quite a long period of regular contact and interaction, involving visits to Coole and frequent correspondence, Lady Gregory and Hyde became increasingly preoccupied with the demands of their respective, separate commitments, as Maureen Murphy notes. She goes on to observe:

> Their correspondence fell off in 1905 and was irregular after that until the 1911 Abbey tour to America when Hyde, pressured by Clan na Gael threats to cut off American financial support to the Gaelic League, cabled a short statement from Dublin, affirming that there was absolutely no connection between the Abbey and the League. Strictly speaking, he was quite correct, but Lady Gregory saw it as an act of gratuitous disloyalty.[51]

However, their old relationship was still evident in a long letter Lady Gregory received from Hyde, which was written on 14 July 1910. In this he shared his greatest triumph with his old friend, describing the scene as the University Senate, by a narrow majority, decided that Irish should form an essential part of the university curriculum – indeed, should be a requirement for matriculation. 'It is the greatest blow ever struck for the recovery of our nationality, and it is bound to profoundly affect the country.'[52]

But, of course, this predated the *Playboy* row and their serious falling out over the Abbey Theatre's tour of Synge's play in America, 1911–12. The protests and disturbances by Clan na Gael members which the play provoked were adversely affecting the fundraising tour of the States being undertaken at the same time by Shane Leslie and Fr Micheál

[50] Letter from Douglas Hyde to Lady Gregory, dated 29 November 1905, NLI MS 18,253/2/3. Indeed, we know from an earlier letter of Roosevelt's, also held in the National Library of Ireland, that his book collection included both Lady Gregory's work on the Cú Chulainn sagas and Hyde's *Literary history of Ireland*: 'My dear Mr. Gill: I thank you very much for the Cucullain Saga. I had ordered it myself, and now have canceled the order and have ordered Douglas Hyde's "A Literary History of Ireland."' (Typewritten letter from Theodore Roosevelt (signed), Oyster Bay, N. Y., on WHITE HOUSE, WASHINGTON notepaper, to Mr. T. P. Gill, 51 west Forty-eighth Street, New York, N.Y., September 22, 1903; NLI MS 48,522). Gill was a journalist, politician and secretary of the Department of Agriculture and Technical Instruction; see s.v. Gill, Thomas Patrick in www.dib.ie.
[51] Murphy, 'Lady Gregory and the Gaelic League', 155.
[52] Hyde to Gregory, 14 July 1910. See Dunleavy, 'The pattern of three threads', 140.

Ó Flannagáin (O'Flanagan) on behalf of the League. While not explicitly stating as much themselves, the Abbey group were happy for people to infer that the Gaelic League supported the play. Eventually in exasperation, John Devoy, head of Clan na Gael, and editor of *The Gaelic American* asked Hyde to issue an official denial that the League was associated with the Abbey. Hyde immediately did so, not once, but twice – the second telegram also sent at Devoy's request, as he had felt that the first one was not strong enough. Lady Gregory and John Quinn were both incensed. Hill observes: 'Quinn was furious, only too aware that the withdrawing of League support would strengthen their enemies. Augusta, however, did not doubt Hyde's personal support, speculating to Yeats that Devoy must have lied to him to make him repudiate them; in fact, he had not distanced the League enough for Devoy.'[53] Augusta wrote to Hyde, sadly and tactfully: 'Oh Craoibhin, what are these wounds with which we are wounded in the houses of our friends? ... We are fighting your battle if you did but know it, and the battle of all who want to live and breathe.'[54] Hyde wrote in response: 'I am sorry you minded my wire.' It was sent, he explained, in 'answer to two insistent cables in two consecutive days, demanding repudiation of connection with the Players, cabled by our own delegates. ... I might have said much more, but you yourself will acknowledge I could not have said less.'[55]

The matter of the cable continued to interpose itself in their correspondence. In May 1912 Hyde wrote to Lady Gregory: 'As you know, there is nobody in Ireland whose interests I would consult more than your own, if I could without harm to the Gaelic League.'[56] In an undated letter, probably written in May 1912, Lady Gregory sought to reassure Hyde: 'Yes, indeed, you would not willingly have done anything to hurt us, and I have always said you did what you believed best for the interest of the League....'[57] So, as Hill comments, 'undeniably the Gaelic League was forcing Hyde into a different set of allegiances and the episode remained an issue between them for some time'.[58] Although Murphy notes that among Gregory's papers are two letters from Hyde, written six months apart, trying to explain his position to her, it appeared to Murphy that Gregory never completely forgave

---

[53] Hill, *Lady Gregory*, 379.
[54] Dunleavy, 'The pattern of three threads', 141.
[55] ibid.
[56] ibid.
[57] ibid. 141, 412.
[58] Hill, *Lady Gregory*, 379.

him.[59] Dunleavy commented that it was 'curious, but perhaps indicative of the still cool relationship between them, that he did not inform his comrade of nearly twenty years of his departure from the League until December 1915.[60] This was in a letter, enclosing his latest book, which was addressed to Lady Gregory at Coole Park, Gort, Co. Galway. She had evidently been in New York for an extended period. The tentative nature of the letter confirms that they had indeed drifted apart and were no longer in regular contact:

> A Bhaintighearna dhílis[61]
> I am sending you another little book.[62] I would have sent it before but I knew you were away. I do not know if you are home yet, but I suppose you are. I heard the other day that Robert had been ill and in hospital. I never knew until he had gone away again or I would have called to see him. I hope he is quite well again now.
> I am no longer President of the Gaelic League. I kept them together for 22 years, but the war was too much for me! I shall tell you about it when I see you!
> With all good wishes for Christmas
> Mise do chara buídheach
>   An Craoibhín
> I hope you left John Quinn well. I suppose you saw him when in New York.[63]

However, shared personal tragedy was to bring them closer together again a few years later. In a letter of October 1916 Hyde thanked Augusta Gregory for her note on the death of his daughter Nuala. He described her death and funeral, and concluded, 'What a dreadful year this has been both public and private. Ireland seems in a hopeless muddle. So does everything. The Gaelic League included.'[64]

Perhaps prompted by her grief following the death of her son Robert when his plane crashed during the Great War in January 1918, Lady

---

[59] Murphy, 'Lady Gregory and the Gaelic League', 155. Unfortunately, the actual period in question remains unclear, as there has been a slip in the editing at this point: the text has two superscript numbers '46' (pp 155, 156) and endnote 46 on p. 415 clearly relates to the superscript on p. 156.

[60] Dunleavy, 'The pattern of three threads', 142.

[61] Lit. 'Dear faithful Lady'.

[62] This was presumably *Legends of saints and sinners* which was published in 1915.

[63] NLI MS 22,957.

[64] Dunleavy, 'The pattern of three threads', 142.

Gregory took the initiative in penning a short letter opposing the enforcement of conscription in Ireland in May of that year. She typed it up and sent it to a number of newspapers, having persuaded some of her literary friends – W. B. Yeats, James Stephens, George Russell ('AE') and Douglas Hyde (An Craoibhín) to add their support as co-signatories. The text of a clipping from *The Nation*, May 25 1918, shows a printed version:

> IRISH WRITERS AND CONSCRIPTION.
> Sir, - We, the undersigned writers, feel compelled to appeal and protest against the enforcement of Conscription in our country, believing, as we do, that such action will destroy all hope of peace in Ireland and goodwill towards England in our lifetime. – Yours, &c.,
>
> (Signed) A. Gregory.
> W. B. Yeats.
> James Stephens.
> George Russell ("Æ")
> Douglas Hyde (An Crasibhín). [*sic*]
> May 17ᵗʰ, 1918.[65]

A Dublin auction recently brought to public notice a signed autograph letter (in pencil) on the same subject which Hyde sent to Lady Gregory from his Roscommon home at Ratra, July 14, 1918, when he was still recuperating from a rather serious illness. He tells her:

> I met Yeats in Dublin, & he gave me your kind message … I came home at the end of June, but am not much better, I cannot fish or boat or bicycle, and when the grouse come I fear I won't be able to shoot! ... I enclose a poem which may amuse you. I wrote it in a white heat when Lloyd George made his conscription speech.

The poem he enclosed with the letter was the well-known *Almost any O or MAC to almost any Englishman, with almost any Englishman's answer*, and is 'a most effective polemic', as the auction house catalogue states. The copy they refer to was printed on one side of a folio sheet, inscribed in manuscript 'July 1918. *An Craoibhín do scríobh agus é tinn ar a leabaidh*' ('Written by Douglas Hyde while he was sick in bed.').

---

[65] The original letter and clipping are held in Stuart A. Rose Library, Emory University, Atlanta, TN 37678.

It carries the caption, 'On reading Christopher Benson's "Hymn for Empire Day"'.[66] Writing to Hyde shortly afterwards, on 20 July 1918, probably in response to this letter and its verse enclosure, Lady Gregory reminded him of what they had achieved: '... but you and I anyhow didn't put off the rebuilding until Home Rule! Your League encompasses the end of the earth – and our theatre is anyhow marking time till we can hand it over to a National Movement.'[67]

All in all, one has to conclude that despite its vicissitudes, the early friendship of Hyde and Gregory and their shared passion for Ireland's people and culture, as expressed in the country's two languages, lived on as heartfelt mutual respect. Writing to John Quinn in a generous effort to heal the *Playboy* rupture in a 1912 New Year's letter, Hyde had called Augusta Gregory 'a wonderful, wonderful woman, with the pluck of a Joan of Arc'. For her, despite her disappointment in him in 1911, he was the man who had 'given the imagination of Ireland a new homing place'.[68]

John Quinn

In late August 1902, two years after the inscribed tombstone was placed at Raftery's grave, another feis was held in Killeeneen. Hyde, Jack B. Yeats, W. B. Yeats and John Quinn were all staying at Coole Park at Lady Gregory's invitation so that they could attend that year's nearby feis. Quinn's visit to Coole actually formed part of his first trip to Ireland and England. He had sailed from New York on 15 July. When he was in London he bought nearly a dozen paintings from Jack B. Yeats as well as portraits of John O'Leary, Douglas Hyde and George Russell ('AE') from his father John. As his biographer, B. L. Reid, observes, Quinn 'was setting out to collect images of his heroes in the cultural and political life of Ireland'.[69] Reid conveys well a sense of the vigour, enthusiasm and cultural interests of this thirty-two-year-old Irish-American in his account of Quinn's engagements in Dublin and Galway:

> In a mere week in Dublin and Gort Quinn found time to meet, to impress and be impressed by, W. B. Yeats and his sisters Lily and Lollie, Russell, T. W. Rolleston, Douglas Hyde, George Moore, Edward Martyn, and Lady Gregory. At Killeeneen, Craughwell,

[66] Fonsie Mealy Catalogue 2017, lot 403, p. 41. From the collection of Mrs Catherine Kennedy, 'Nu', grand-daughter of Lady Gregory and daughter of Robert Gregory.

[67] Dunleavy, 'The pattern of three threads', 413 (n. 50).

[68] ibid. 142.

[69] B. L. Reid, *The man from New York: John Quinn and his friends* (New York 1968) 7–8.

on the last day of August, Quinn joined in a Gaelic Feis at the new tomb which lady Gregory had erected of the blind Connacht poet Raftery, and Jack Yeats decorated a program of the day with charming sketches of Quinn, Lady Gregory, Hyde, W. B. Yeats and himself. At Lady Gregory's great house of Coole Park Quinn heard Hyde read one of his Gaelic plays, and it must have been at this time that he added his initials to those carved in the bark of her famous signatory beech tree.[70]

Quinn stayed at Coole for just two nights, but it is clear that the intellectual vigour and fervour of his discussions with W. B. Yeats and Hyde, in particular, had a deeply inspirational effect on him, moving to action this consummate strategist and organiser. He decided to invite first Yeats and then Hyde to tour America, lecturing and raising funds. Yeats crossed the Atlantic in 1903–4, Hyde in 1905–6.

Quinn was back in Dublin in late October 1904. In order to honour Quinn's interest in the efforts to found an Irish theatre, Lady Gregory invited all the players to meet him at a reception and supper on the evening of Tuesday, 25 October. Standish O'Grady sat at the left of the hostess, with Quinn at her right, followed by Douglas Hyde.[71] On the following Friday Quinn lunched with Douglas Hyde in Harcourt Street, and Hyde made a verse for him in Irish. One of Quinn's goals on this trip to Ireland was to plan a lecture tour for Hyde and the Gaelic League in America. Reid tells us:

> Quinn was anxious to promote Hyde and his cause, admiring both as native Irish, nonclerical, nonpolitical, and intellectual. He assured Hyde of nearly certain success and promised to take care of all the practical details of the tour. But Hyde was doubtful and finally agreed to take the plunge only after Quinn had personally agreed to guarantee him against any loss. … Again at tea with Lady Gregory, Quinn met the Hydes, W. B. Yeats, and another of George Moore's sparring mates, Edward Martyn.[72]

---

[70] Reid, 8–10, with image of the feis programme in question on p. 9. Hill also notes how the occasion was commemorated by Jack B. Yeats and lives on for posterity in the memorable drawings he applied to a copy of the feis programme: 'His [viz. John Quinn's] quick interest was greeted with spontaneous affection, expressed in Jack Yeats's scrawls on the feis programme where Quinn's rather austere profile takes its place with Hyde, a comfortably seated Lady Gregory, a meditative W.B. Yeats, Jack and a frenetic feis dancer' (Hill, *Lady Gregory*, 248).

[71] Reid, *The man from New York*, 25.

[72] ibid. 28.

At George Russell's, Quinn stated that for him the most interesting thing he had discovered in Ireland was that 'all those who were denounced turned out to be very charming people'. Reid notes that 'he commented several times in his journal on the habitual and brilliant malice in the conversation of Dubliners. Indeed, Quinn recorded that '[t]he 'only three men in Dublin who have not said sharp things about others' were Russell, O'Grady and Hyde'.[73]

This is not the appropriate context for a detailed account of Quinn's magisterial management of Hyde's 1905–6 tour, which has been treated at some length by the author and others in a separate publication.[74] Quinn was a perfectionist, brilliantly capable, meticulous and effective in all he undertook. For instance, a vast amount of his correspondence lives on. In the case of his letters to Hyde two copies are regularly extant – the original one mailed to Hyde, and the copy retained by Quinn himself. Indeed, rather than penning them by hand, his practice was to dictate his letters and have them taken down and typed, thus facilitating the maintenance of records – they could run to eighteen typescript pages! The letters which Quinn sent to Hyde are in the National Library of Ireland, while his own personal copies are now in the New York Public Library, as indeed are Hyde's hand-written letters to him.

The people Quinn corresponded with were numerous and of varied background. In the United States he acted as attorney for Maud Gonne in her bitter divorce proceedings against John MacBride, and thus began an exchange of letters which lasted from 1906 to 1921. By a happy coincidence for the theme of this paper, Quinn's very first letter to Maud Gonne, dated 24 May 1906, was written when Hyde's trip was still ongoing, and contains some fascinating insights into the tour from Quinn's perspective. Quinn estimated that he had spent between one and three hours a day over a year-long period organising Hyde's great American journey. Hyde and his wife Lucy were due to spend just a few weeks more in the United States, before returning to Ireland on the Lucania. Quinn was looking forward to the completion of his major efforts and, understandably, felt very pleased with the spectacular success of the tour, tinged as his satisfaction was, however, with a note of self-pity. At any rate, he took the opportunity to take stock and the following is the summary assessment he sent to Maud Gonne:

> Hyde has had a great trip out here. He has been here seven months and has traveled over 19,000 miles and has spoken to over 75,000

---

[73] ibid. 31.
[74] See Liam Mac Mathúna, 'Introduction', in Mac Mathúna et al., *Douglas Hyde: my American journey*, xxiii–lxviii.

persons. He will take back with him $50,000 net, over and above all expenses and exclusive of the $5,000 which he returned to San Francisco. When you consider the fact that he came here without any organization and was practically unknown except to a mere handful of insignificant Gaelic Leaguers, I think the results of the tour are marvellous. Mr. Thomas Concannon, above referred to, came out here heralded as the 'chief organizer of the Gaelic League in Ireland,' but he was an utter failure. He was vain, conceited, arrogant, and bursting with vanity. I saw that the thing would be a failure with Concannon trying to arrange things (because he mussed everything he touched and got into all sorts of difficulties) and so I put my shoulder to the wheel. In fact I began to arrange for the Hyde lectures just one year ago and there has scarcely been a day pass that I have not devoted from one to three hours to the work, and I am beginning to feel it is now time to consider myself. I think I have done in the last three years as much work for Ireland as any man in America. It is not in me to do things by halves, and so far as the organizing and advertising work I have been doing for the past three years is concerned, I must drop it altogether. There are three kinds of Irishmen: The first kind give advice and nothing but advice; the second kind give money, and the third kind give themselves. I have given both myself and money, and hereafter I will try and qualify in the second class and save myself a little.

Hyde and Mrs. Hyde sail on the 'Lucania' on the 9th, and they will both, I imagine, be very glad to get back to their quiet place in Ireland.[75]

The Londravilles, who edited the correspondence between Quinn and Maud Gonne observe that Quinn seemed unable to delegate work to others and that few people could match his aptitude for management and ability to get things done, noting that 'This also allowed him to voice the perfectionist's bitter complaint that he had to do everything himself'.[76]

The interaction of the four people discussed in this paper, took place in many ways and over quite a long period, albeit mainly in the first decade of the twentieth century. For example, it had been at W. B. Yeats's request that Quinn first helped Gonne in her difficulties with John

[75] Janis and Richard Londraville (1999), *Too long a sacrifice: the letters of Maud Gonne and John Quinn* (Selinsgrove and London 1999) 36.
[76] ibid. 22.

MacBride, going on to obtain affidavits of his drunken behaviour while on tour in the US. This information served as an important part of the case she was building against her husband, as she sought legal separation from him and custody of their young son, Seán.[77] Quinn's friendship with his Irish acquaintances continued after the American tours. For instance, he told Gonne of his plans for a short visit to Ireland in 1909: 'I am going to spend a day or two at Lady Gregory's place and a day or two with Douglas Hyde, and I expect to sail from Queenstown.'[78]

The bitterness unleashed by the *Playboy* controversy, already referred to, is clear in the blunt reference to Hyde in a letter which Quinn sent to Gonne, dated 15 March 1912: 'I was very much disgusted at Hyde's attitude.'[79] As noted already, matters had come to a head because Shane Leslie and Fr Micheál Ó Flannagáin were engaged in a fundraising campaign on behalf of the Gaelic League in the United States at the same time as the Abbey Theatre Company was touring. The *Playboy* was being attacked by John Devoy's Clan na Gael organisation and the public protests were stymying the League's fundraising efforts, because it was felt that the Abbey players were implying that they were endorsed by the League, although this was not the case. In Quinn's words:

> The fact is, as I was informed at the time, that Devoy and that crowd insisted that they would not help Father O'Flanagan and Shane Leslie, who were out here collecting on behalf of the Gaelic League, unless the Gaelic League repudiated the Abbey Theatre Company. O'Flanagan, although he had previously praised the work of the Company in public speeches both here in the [city and in] Boston and in Chicago, very promptly knuckled under and asked Hyde to 'repudiate,' and Hyde timidly and weakly did so. If Hyde were a mere politician one might make the defense for him that the same rule of honorable dealing does not and cannot apply to a political leader in every case that a man would feel bound by in his private relations. But the Gaelic League has been fond of boasting that it is above politics and is governed by principle and is independent and non-partisan.[80]

On the other hand, Hyde was the unwitting trigger for a curious interaction between Gonne and Quinn, which tells us something about

---

[77] Londraville, *Too long a sacrifice*, 20–3.
[78] 4 June 1909, Quinn to Gonne, ibid. 42.
[79] ibid. 92.
[80] ibid.

the personalities of both. Writing to Quinn from Paris on 8 March 1914, Gonne enquires:

> Have you seen Willie Yeats? In Dublin at Douglas Hyde's house I saw the reproduction of a portrait drawing of you by [Augustus] John. I want one so much. Have you a copy you could send me? It is a wonderful drawing of you. It looks harder than you do generally, but I have seen you look like that occasionally. It has all that strength and determination, which makes me feel wild that you do not belong to Ireland *entirely*, for you would have led the people and made history as *Parnell* did. With the Irish people, in the Isle of Destiny that would be possible.[81]

One wonders whether this is a line of thinking which had been proffered to John MacBride and Yeats – and perhaps others – before Quinn? At any rate, practised in the ways of the world, Quinn didn't rise to the bait. He was over a page into his reply of 18 March 1914 before he responded succinctly to the urgent request for a portrait reproduction of himself:

> I shall of course be glad to send you a reproduction of the John drawing. The first reproductions were done very well; the last have come back rather dark and smoky. I will have a good one made and send it to you with pleasure.[82]

There is no hint here of Quinn answering Ireland's call, as mediated by Maud Gonne!

Later rounds of correspondence between Quinn and his friends were prompted by the aftermath of the 1916 Easter Rising in Dublin, when Quinn liaised anxiously and copiously with both Leslie and Hyde, first trying to get Casement's sentence commuted, then in an effort to get Eoin MacNeill out of jail as early as possible.[83] It may also be noted that Quinn wrote to Sir Horace Plunkett in 1918, requesting that Hyde be appointed to the National Convention, and to Lady Gregory in the 1920s in support of Hyde being appointed to the Free State Senate, of which Yeats was already a member.

Conclusion

However, these responses to the pressures created by the 1916 Easter Rising (and in Hyde's case to those which arose out of his resignation

---

[81] ibid. 124.
[82] ibid. 126.
[83] See, for instance, the letter of 14 March 1917, from Quinn to Gonne, ibid. 188.

from the Presidency of the Gaelic League in 1915) were mere postscripts. The 'real' world of the four friends and colleagues discussed here had been new and young, and everything had seemed possible to them some two decades earlier. But the four friends did in fact accomplish much together, especially in that initial period. The *fin-de-siècle* and turn-of-the-twentieth-century collaboration between Douglas Hyde, W. B. Yeats, Lady Augusta Gregory and John Quinn had resulted in vibrant cooperation between the Irish literary revival and the Irish language movement. Hyde and the Gaelic League benefited in myriad ways: for instance, drama in Irish was created and substantial funds to further the language cause were raised in Ireland, and more especially, in America. But above all else, this collaboration of leading cultural intellectuals in Ireland and Irish-America helped to ensure that the Irish language, and the ideology and ideal of a de-anglicised, Irish Ireland moved centre stage in Irish cultural life, a place where they continue to maintain a significant presence to this day, resisting all attempts to ignore or dislodge them. John Quinn, Lady Gregory and W. B. Yeats – and Douglas Hyde – all had a two-fold interest: the language, literature and culture of Ireland and the literature, culture and arts of the whole world. So too had the Gaelic League / Conradh na Gaeilge, in its heyday and at its highpoint, when the world was a seamless cultural garment, resplendent with a distinctive Irish hue.

Liam Mac Mathúna

IRISH INDEPENDENT COVERAGE OF DOUGLAS HYDE'S VISION FOR A DE-ANGLICISED IRELAND

From its foundation in 1905 the *Irish Independent* was Ireland's best-selling daily newspaper.[1] Given its impact on public opinion at the time, an analysis of the *Irish Independent*'s coverage is central to enhancing our understanding of the Irish language revival movement and the influence of its leading activists. Chief among these language activists was Dr Douglas Hyde, whose vision for a de-anglicised Ireland shaped much of the *Independent*'s discourse on the revival movement.[2] Print media provided an essential platform for the dissemination of revivalist ideals from the late nineteenth century onwards. Major issues pertaining to the Irish language revival and other related movements, including Gaelic culture, nationalist politics, Irish produce and religious conservatism, were debated in both English and Irish using this journalistic forum. By the turn of the twentieth century, a new wave of nationalist spirit was sweeping the country with a particular emphasis on native culture including the Irish language, Gaelic games, traditional music, folklore and literature. Newspapers, periodicals and journals played a pivotal role in developing this nationalist culture in line with the 'Irish-Ireland' ideology espoused by Douglas Hyde, D. P. Moran and others.[3] The objective of the 'Irish-Ireland' movement was to establish a truly Irish nation, free from the influence of British culture and customs. The Irish language was recognised as a defining trait of national identity which would provide a cornerstone for the foundation of a Gaelic nation. The present article will assess how this transformative ideology was presented to the Irish public at the time. The promotion of the 'Irish-Ireland' philosophy and the Irish language revival in the decades before the foundation of the Irish Free State will be examined, focussing on the *Irish Independent* as an illustrative example of how a dual-language journalistic platform was used to promote and develop this revivalist mindset.

---

[1] For an overview of the *Irish Independent*, see Mark O'Brien and Kevin Rafter (eds), *Independent newspapers: a history* (Dublin 2012).

[2] For biographical information on Hyde, see Risteárd Ó Glaisne, *Dúbhglas de h-Íde (1860–1949): ceannródaí cultúrtha 1860–1910* (Baile Átha Cliath 1991), Risteárd Ó Glaisne, *Dúbhglas de h-Íde (1860–1949): náisiúnach neamhspleách 1910–1949* (Baile Átha Cliath 1993), Janet Dunleavy and Gareth Dunleavy, *Douglas Hyde: a maker of modern Ireland* (Berkeley and Oxford 1991), Brian Murphy, *Forgotten patriot: Douglas Hyde and the foundation of the Irish presidency* (Cork 2016).

[3] For biographical information on D. P. Moran, see Patrick Maume, *D. P. Moran* (Dundalk 1995).

Douglas Hyde and 'Irish-Ireland'

Echoes of the 'Irish-Ireland' mentality can be traced back to Douglas Hyde's renowned lecture on 'The necessity for de-anglicising Ireland', delivered to the National Literary Society in Dublin in November 1892. In this speech, Hyde set out his view of the various obstacles preventing the Irish from prospering as a nation:

> On racial lincs, thcn, wc shall best develop, following the bent of our own natures; and, in order to do this, we must create a strong feeling against West-Britonism, for it – if we give it the least chance, or show it the smallest quarter – will overwhelm us like a flood, and we shall find ourselves toiling painfully behind the English at each step following the same fashions, only six months behind the English ones; reading the same books, only months behind them; taking up the same fads, after they have become stale *there*, following *them* in our dress, literature, music, games, and ideas, only a long time after them and a vast way behind.... We must teach ourselves to be less sensitive, we must teach ourselves not to be ashamed of ourselves, because the Gaelic people can never produce its best before the world as long as it remains tied to the apron-strings of another race and another island, waiting for *it* to move before it will venture to take any step itself.[4]

Self-reliance was emphasised throughout Hyde's speech which called on the people of Ireland to resist the increasing prevalence of British culture. Throughout his address, Hyde reinforced his primary motivation – the pressing need to rid Ireland of British influence. This correlates with Kiberd's assertion that 'postcolonial writing does not begin only when the occupier withdraws: rather it is initiated at that very moment when a native writer formulates a text committed to cultural resistance'.[5] In 1892 Hyde, like Moran after him, felt that it was time to fully re-gaelicise Ireland through 'cultural resistance'. Historical accounts of the decades that followed provide ample evidence of the public response to his cultural call to arms.

Newspaper reports on Hyde's 'de-anglicising Ireland' speech in the national dailies indicate support for the 'Irish-Ireland' ideology from the *Irish Daily Independent* and the *Freeman's Journal*, while the *Irish Times* expressed its opposition:

---

[4] Breandán Ó Conaire (ed.), *Language, lore and lyrics: essays and lectures* (Dublin 1986) 169. The text of Hyde's speech is reproduced in full in Ó Conaire, *Language, lore and lyrics*, 153–70.

[5] Declan Kiberd, *Inventing Ireland: the literature of the modern nation* (London 1995) 6.

The *Irish Daily Independent* praised 'this excellent lecture' and recommended its publication. The *Freeman's Journal* referred to the 'extremely able and interesting lecture' (26 November 1892) and the *Irish Times* was predictably hostile.[6]

This variation in reportage reflects the prevailing attitudes of these papers at the time. The *Irish Times*, founded in 1859,[7] aligned itself with pro-British factions, while the *Freeman's Journal*, established in 1763,[8] broadly supported the nationalist movement at this time, publishing revivalist material in English and Irish.[9] The *Irish Daily Independent*, founded in 1891 as a pro-Parnell paper, strongly supported the nationalist cause. The *Daily Independent* was described by the Gaelic League newspaper, *An Claidheamh Soluis*, as '[the] first daily paper to introduce the regular publication of articles in Irish'[10] and was praised for its inclusion of material in Irish:

> For some weeks past an Irish Language section has been appearing once a week in the *Irish Daily Independent*. Not only matter in English dealing with the movement in a highly appreciative spirit, but also short Irish articles are printed in this section. We congratulate the *Independent* on its enterprise which will certainly not make the paper less popular with a vast number of its readers.[11]

Máire de Buitléir also contributed a regular column to the *Daily Independent* from 1899 onwards. Though the column was usually in English, its main focus was on the Irish language movement.[12] This

---

[6] Ó Conaire, *Language, lore and lyrics*, 51.

[7] See Mark O'Brien, *The Irish Times: a history* (Dublin 2008).

[8] See Felix Larkin, '"A great daily organ": *The Freeman's Journal*, 1763–1924' *History Ireland*, Issue 3, Vol. 14, 2006. http://www.historyireland.com/20th-century-contemporary-history/a-great-dailyorgan-the-freemans-journal-1763-1924/

[9] For an analysis of Irish language material in English-medium newspapers, see Nollaig Mac Congáil, 'Saothrú na Gaeilge ar nuachtáin náisiúnta Bhéarla na haoise seo caite: sop nó solamar?', in *Féilscríbhinn Anraí Mhic Giolla Chomhaill: tráchtais léannta in onóir don Athair Anraí Mac Giolla Chomhaill*, ed. Réamonn Ó Muireadhaigh (Baile Átha Cliath 2011) 112–91.

[10] 'Notes', *An Claidheamh Soluis* , 25 November 1899, 583. For further examples, see also 'Notes', *An Claidheamh Soluis*, 17 February 1900. 'Notes', *An Claidheamh Soluis*, 31 March 1900.

[11] 'Notes', *An Claidheamh Soluis*, 21 October 1899: 10; quoted in Regina Uí Chollatáin, *An Claidheamh Soluis agus Fáinne an Lae 1899–1932* (Dublin 2004) 58.

[12] Dorothy Ní Uigín, 'An iriseoireacht Ghaeilge i Meiriceá agus in Éirinn ag tús na hathbheochana: an cúlra Meiriceánach', *Léachtaí Cholm Cille* 28 (1998) 25–47. Biographical information can be accessed at De Buitléir, Máire (1873–1920), *ainm.ie*, http://www.ainm.ie/Bio.aspx?ID=13. See also Máiréad Ní Chinnéide, *Máire de Buitléir: bean athbheochana* (Baile Átha Cliath 1993).

provides us with an early example of the dual-language approach to publicising and debating the revival that was continued in the *Irish Independent*.

When the *Daily Independent* faced financial difficulties in 1900, prominent businessman William Martin Murphy stepped in, first combining the *Daily Independent* with his *Daily Nation*, before redesigning and relaunching the paper as the *Irish Independent* in January 1905.[13] Support for the Irish language and the nationalist movement was evident in the new paper from the outset, building on the nationalist ideology expressed in its predecessor. In its first editorial on 2 January 1905, the *Irish Independent* declared its allegiance to the nationalist movement, including the Irish language revival: 'To the Irish Language and Industrial Revival Movements, as to every movement for the National and material regeneration of Ireland, we shall give our heartiest support.'[14] This declaration of support was backed by the publication of a regular Irish language column penned by Eoghan Ó Neachtain for almost ten years, from its first issue in January 1905 until the outbreak of the First World War in August 1914.[15] In addition, the *Irish Independent* published various columns, reports, letters, reviews and advertisements in Irish from 1905 onwards, as well as material in English relating to the language movement.[16] Later columnists and contributors included Aodh de Blácam, Colm Ó Murchú ('Taube') and Liam Ó Rinn.[17]

'Irish-Ireland' ideology in the Irish Independent

As Ó Neachtain's daily column in the *Irish Independent* was titled 'Irish Ireland. A Leaguer's point of view. Éire na nGaedheal', links with both the 'Irish-Ireland' ideology and the Gaelic League were manifest from its inception.[18] Its bilingual title is also noteworthy as this is reflective of the paper's dual-language approach to promoting the Irish language

[13] See Patrick Maume, 'Parnellite politics and the origins of Independent Newspapers', in O'Brien and Rafter, *Independent Newspapers*, 1–13.

[14] 'Ourselves', Editorial, *Irish Independent*, 2 January 1905, 4.

[15] For biographical information, see Eoghan Ó Neachtain (1867–1957), *ainm.ie*, http://www.ainm.ie/Bio.aspx?ID=357

[16] See Aoife Whelan '"Irish Ireland" and the *Irish Independent*, 1905–22', in O'Brien and Rafter, *Independent*, 67–80.

[17] For biographical information, see Aodh de Blacam (1891–1951), *ainm.ie*, https://www.ainm.ie/Bio.aspx?ID=12 ; Colm Ó Murchú (1889–1939), *ainm.ie*, https://www.ainm.ie/Bio.aspx?ID=216 ; Liam Ó Rinn (1886–1943), *ainm.ie*, https://www.ainm.ie/Bio.aspx?ID=106

[18] 'Irish Ireland: A Leaguer's point of view. Éire na nGaedheal', *Irish Independent*, 2 January 1905, 4.

revival and the 'Irish-Ireland' movement in the early decades of the twentieth century. Another aspect of Ó Neachtain's column that captured the spirit of the 'Irish-Ireland' concept was his inclusion of historical and martyrological information highlighting significant historical events that happened 'on this day' in the past from sources such as *Féilire na Gaedhilge* and *Féilire Oenghusa*.[19] Examples of such material include:

> Eanair 12 – 'Éamonn De Búrca do rugadh 1729. Do cailleadh Art Mac Murchadha, 1417. (Éamonn De Búrca was born 1729. Art Mac Murchadha died, 1417.)' – Féil. na G.[20]
>
> Márta 3. – 'Roibeárd Emmet do rugadh, 1778. (Robert Emmet was born, 1778.)' – Féil. na G.[21]
>
> Mí na Nodlag 28. – Marbhadh na leanbh i mBeithil, leis an Imrir, le hIruaith. Dhá fhichid dhá chéad 7 dhá mhíle mac do cuireadh chun báis, ar mháighibh suairce Bheithil imacuaird. (The killing of the infants in Bethlehem, by the Emperor, by Herod. Two thousand, two hundred and forty children were slain, on the pleasant plains of Bethlehem round about.)' – Féil. Oen.[22]

The target readers of this column were likely to already have some proficiency in Irish as the columns did not include a 'gluais' or glossary for learners, unlike other newspapers such as the *Leinster Leader* or *Weekly Freeman* that set out to teach the language through their Gaelic columns.[23] As the Irish language and Irish history were not widely taught in primary schools in the previous decades, many language enthusiasts were keen to learn more about Ireland's history and heritage. This approach correlates with Hyde's assessment of the general population's unawareness of their own history and heritage, as reported by *An Claidheamh Soluis* in 1899: 'Not only were the people ignorant of the language that their fathers and grandfathers spoke before them for

---

[19] See Earnán de Siúnta, *Féilire na Gaedhilge: An Buachaillín Buidhe do scríobh* (Dublin 1904) and Elva Johnston and Donnchadh Ó Corráin, *The martyrology of Oengus the Culdee* (Cork 2010). Distributed by CELT online at University College, Cork, http://www.ucc.ie/celt/online/G200001.html

[20] 'Irish Ireland: A Leaguer's point of view. Éire na nGaedheal', *Irish Independent,* 12 December 1906, 4.

[21] 'Irish Ireland: A Leaguer's point of view. Éire na nGaedheal', *Irish Independent*, 3 March 1906, 4.

[22] 'Irish Ireland: A Leaguer's point of view. Éire na nGaedheal', *Irish Independent*, 28 December 1906, 4.

[23] Father O'Growney's *Simple lessons in Irish* were published in the *Weekly Freeman* from 1895 to 1896. *Freeman's Journal*, 20 October 1899, 5, quoted in Mac Congáil, 'Saothrú na Gaeilge ar nuachtáin náisiúnta Bhéarla', 142

countless ages; they were ignorant of their own class history, the history of their race, of their country, of their people.'[24]

In addition to its Gaelic column and other Irish language material, the *Irish Independent* also endorsed the 'Irish-Ireland' mindset through journalistic material published in English, thereby practising a dual-language approach to the promotion of Irish. From time to time, a note was inserted immediately following Ó Neachtain's column directing readers to the 'Irish Language Notes' on another page: 'Our "Irish Language Notes" and a number of interesting news items will be found today on page 7.'[25] These notes indicate an important link between the regular Gaelic column and the reports in English on the promotion of 'Irish-Ireland' through revival events and activities. This provides a clear example of the *Irish Independent*'s dual-language approach to the promotion of the revival and all things Gaelic. An insight into the type of material contained in these 'Irish Language Notes' can be found in the following extracts from 8 February 1905. In 'The Gaelic League and the University Question', readers are told that 'The League, looking to the future, sees clearly that the only way to build up a newer and happier and more prosperous nation is to educate the youth of the country to be frankly Irish in thought and action', while in the report 'Facts and Figures for "Irish Language Week"', an appeal for funds is issued: 'Irish Ireland will soon be asked to make its annual contribution towards the upkeep of the Gaelic League for the year, 1905–6.'[26] Undercurrents of the 'Irish-Ireland' concept are evident in both excerpts from the 'Language Notes' column which functioned as a complement to the Gaelic column and was perhaps more influential in engaging non-fluent Irish language enthusiasts. This correlates with the use of English to promote Irish by Hyde and other revival activists, as discussed by Ó Cuív:

> Hyde and the other pioneers of the Gaelic revival movement made good use of the English language in order to foster an interest in the Irish language and our history and traditions, and we must remember that there is still today a vast reading public, by no means unsympathetic to Irish, which can be reached more easily through the medium of English. By ignoring these readers we would do a great disservice to Irish.[27]

[24] 'Dr. Douglas Hyde in Belfast: the educative influence of the Irish language', *An Claidheamh Soluis*, 23 December 1899.

[25] Advertisement, *Irish Independent*, 8 February 1905, 4.

[26] 'The Irish language. (Special to the "Irish Independent")', *Irish Independent*, 8 February 1905, 7.

[27] Brian Ó Cuív, 'Irish in the modern world', in Brian Ó Cuív (ed.), *A view of the Irish language* (Dublin 1969) 127.

Another example of this dual-language methodology is the *Independent*'s report on Douglas Hyde's visit to Killarney, Co. Kerry in May 1907. This report (written in English) claims that Hyde's speech raised key questions regarding the role of Irish in the creation of a truly Irish nation. The excerpt below captures the links Hyde envisioned between the Gaelic League and cultural nationalism as simultaneous forces in the struggle against West Britonism:

> [Hyde] was very impressive when he referred to the struggle for the revival of the Irish Language and Irish customs as a life-and-death struggle. The Gaelic League had opened the eyes of the Irish people to the awful precipice which was before them, with the yawning chasm below of Anglicisation which, he said, was only another name for national extinction ... The philosophy of the Gaelic League, Dr. Hyde said, is that in every race there are certain racial distinctions, very subtle, but none the less very real, and the attempt to force one race into the groove cut out by another had never been a success in Europe, and never would be. In the case of no two races in Europe is there in temperament and racial nature so wide, real, and far-reaching a difference as between the Irish and English nations, and for Irishmen to attempt to compete with Englishmen on the lines that come naturally and instinctively to Englishmen, but the reverse to us, is folly and madness (applause).[28]

This report demonstrates the importance of print journalism in developing and promoting the concept of cultural nationalism in the opening years of the twentieth century. The reporter describes Hyde as 'impressive', indicating respect for his oratorical skills as well as his message, and is keen to inform readers that sections of Hyde's speech were greeted with applause.

By publishing reports on public speeches of this nature, the *Independent* and other newspapers played a pivotal role in spreading the revival campaign to a far wider audience than those in attendance at the event. This report also summarises Hyde's outlook on the new wave of thinking in relation to race and nationhood that was spreading through Europe at the time. Hyde's use of the terms 'race' and 'nation' lends weight to Ó Conchubhair's analysis of the influence of Darwinian theories and European philosophy on Irish revival activists:

[28] 'Killarney's welcome to Dr. Douglas Hyde. "The soul of an Irish nation."', *Irish Independent*, 8 May 1907, 8.

Ní dall, más ea, a bhí muintir na Gaeilge in Éirinn ná thar lear ar theoiricí an chros-síolraithe ná ar theoiricí thruailliú na fola mar a tuigeadh iad sa dara leath den naoú haois déag a léiríonn feabhas an chine Ghaelaigh i gcomparáid leis na ciníocha eile.

'Irish language supporters in Ireland and overseas were not blind to theories of cross-fertilization and blood corruption as they were understood in the second half of the nineteenth century which showed the excellence of the Gaelic race in comparison to other races.'[29]

The role of Irish in moulding the Gaelic nation is the dominant theme of Hyde's speech in Killarney, an ideological concept which far surpasses the role of Irish as a spoken or written language for communicative purposes. Examples of this kind illustrate how the 'Irish-Ireland' mindset was expressed through English in the public sphere, even though the saving of the language itself was often the main focus of the discussion. The *Irish Independent*'s dual-language approach reflects the bilingual forum in which the language revivalists themselves often functioned, as demonstrated by public events and orations of this kind.

Campaigns for compulsory Irish
This dual-language approach was echoed in letters to the newspaper by well-known *Gaeilgeoirí* or Irish language speakers who chose to debate important issues in English rather than Irish to reach a wider readership. Hyde adopted this approach in his response to Canon Peter O'Leary's[30] views on the controversial issue of compulsory Irish in the National University in November 1915. Canon O'Leary laid out his case against compulsory Irish in a letter published in the *Irish Independent* on 24 November 1915:

In fixing courses of study this inadequacy and inequality should be borne in mind, and the first step towards reform, in my opinion, should be the removal of compulsion regards Irish as a subject for matriculation. Make Irish an optional subject. Find a true standard.

[29] Brian Ó Conchubhair *Fin de siècle na Gaeilge: Darwin, an athbheochan agus smaointeoireacht na hEorpa* (Galway 2006) 79 (translation by author).
[30] For biographical information, see Peadar Ó Laoghaire (1839–1920), *ainm.ie*, https://www.ainm.ie/Bio.aspx?ID=210

Irish being optional, that true standard can also be a high one
without injustice to students or hardship to teachers.[31]

A similar view was expressed in the sub-leader 'Matters of Moment'
column of the *Independent* the following day.[32] Hyde did not agree and
was quick to defend the policy of compulsory Irish in the National
University in the face of recently published criticism by Canon O'Leary,
Shán Ó Cuív, Richard Foley and others. Hyde's defensive stance on the
issue was set out in a letter to 'Conor Mac Nessa' that was then published
in the *Independent*:

> Canon O'Leary (and Mr. O'Cuiv, if he agrees with him) stands, so
> far as I know, alone in the desire to undo a great national
> settlement. But, of course, if this campaign against the University
> and essential Irish be continued, no doubt the cry now raised will
> be taken up by every West Briton in Ireland.[33]

Another example of the ongoing discourse on the teaching of Irish at
third level can be found in an earlier article entitled 'The Gaelic League.
Essential Irish Question.' published in January 1910. This article reports
that Agnes O'Farrelly's[34] motion to continue the campaign for compulsory Irish in the National University was passed at a recent meeting of
the Gaelic League's Executive Committee:

> The Coisde Gnotha of the Gaelic League this week on the motion
> of Miss O'Farrelly, unanimously passed a resolution –
> Declaring that the claims of the country and the Gaelic League
> regarding essential Irish in the National University remain the
> same as ever, and confidently awaiting a favourable statement
> from the Board of Studies and the Senate.[35]

It is noteworthy that this report from the Gaelic League was published
in English by the *Irish Independent*, presumably in order to reach a wider

---

[31] 'Views of Canon P. O'Leary, P.P.', *Irish Independent*, 24 November 1915, 7. See also:
'Compulsory Irish', *Irish Independent*, 25 November 1915, 6.
[32] 'Compulsory Irish' in 'Matters of Moment', *Irish Independent*, 25 November 1915, 4.
[33] 'Essential Irish. Letter from Dr. Hyde', *Irish Independent*, 26 November 1915, 6.
[34] For biographical information, see Úna Ní Fhaircheallaigh (1874–1951), *ainm.ie*,
https://www.ainm.ie/Bio.aspx?ID=71
[35] 'The Gaelic League: essential Irish question', *Irish Independent*, 13 January 1910, 6.
O'Farrelly had previously been given a platform to express her views on this issue through
Ó Neachtain's Gaelic column in the series 'Ceist na hOllsgoile: aiste ó Úna Ní
Fhaircheallaigh', *Irish Independent*, 15 November 1907 – 20 November 1907.

readership. The *Independent* redoubled the League's efforts to promote the use of Irish at third level through the publication of such reports, though its comment section later questioned the initial success of the policy as seen above. The paper's columnist Eoghan Ó Neachtain had outlined the importance of incorporating Irish into the university system in his first article in January 1905 when he stated:

> Taobh amuigh de cheist na teangadh tá aon mhór-cheist amháin eile, 7 is cóir gan dearmad a dhéanamh uirri do láthair. Ní ceart dearmad a dheanamh uirri anois, ná feasta go dtí go mbeidh sí socruighthe. Is í sin ceist an árd-oideachais.

> 'Aside from the language question there is one other major issue, and it should not be forgotten right now. It should not be forgotten now, or ever until it is resolved. That is the question of higher education.'[36]

This view was also expressed through English in reports submitted to the *Irish Independent* by the Gaelic League:

> In addition, Irish should be a subject for matriculation, and should be adequately provided for throughout the whole college course, provision being made for instruction through the medium of Irish when so desired. The League in this, as in other phases of its propaganda, knows exactly what it wants, and nothing less than the concession of the demands outlined above will satisfy it.[37]

The League's view on the importance of including Irish in the National University had been put forward by Hyde in his evidence to the Royal Commission on University Education in 1902 when he declared that the aim of the Gaelic League was 'to bring about a revolution in the Primary Schools, and has been successful ... Now, as the Primary Schools feed the Intermediate, and the Intermediate the University, any new University must make the amplest provision for this'.[38] League members

---

[36] 'Árd-oideachas', *Irish Independent*, 2 January 1905, 4 (translation by author).

[37] 'The Gaelic League and the university question', *Irish Independent*, 8 February 1905, 7. See also 'The Irish language. (Special to the "Irish Independent")', *Irish Independent*, 11 January 1905, 3; 'The Irish language. (Special to the "Irish Independent")', *Irish Independent*, 23 February 1905, 7.

[38] 'Royal Commission on university education in Ireland', *Irish in university education: evidence given before The Royal Commission on university education, 1902: Gaelic League pamphlets, No. 29* (Dublin) 12.

wanted a new university which would be 'frankly and robustly national, in a spiritual and intellectual sense ... We want an intellectual headquarters for Irish Ireland'.[39]

Hyde's advocacy for compulsory Irish was not limited to higher education. He also campaigned consistently for the inclusion of Irish on the official school curriculum at primary and secondary level. A news report on an assembly held at the Rotunda in Dublin in February 1905 conveys the dissatisfaction of Hyde and other political and church leaders with the 'starvation policy' of the British administration in relation to education funding in Ireland:

> In an eloquent speech to the great educational meeting held in the Rotunda on Saturday night, Dr. Douglas Hyde scathingly indicted the Treasury and the National Board, more especially the latter. He pointed out that if the Board was responsive to Irish opinion, it would, with the means at its disposal, easily force the Treasury to disgorge the Irish money it had filched, and apply it to supplying the needs of Irish education.
>
> Mr. J.E. Redmond, M.P., pledged the services of his colleagues and himself to the Gaelic League.
>
> The correspondence included sympathetic letters from his Eminence Cardinal Logue and Most Rev. Dr. Walsh ... Dr. Douglas Hyde, who was received with a perfect storm of cheering, then proposed a series of resolutions which epitomise the entire case for the Gaelic League.[40]

This report illustrates the esteem in which Hyde was held, both in sharing a platform with Redmond and others and in receiving 'a perfect storm of cheering' from those in attendance. As this report shows, the Gaelic League tackled challenges facing the Irish education system as a whole, not just those directly connected to the teaching of Irish. Other League activists on the platform at the Rotunda meeting referred to above included Eoin MacNeill, Pádraig Pearse and Thomas O'Neill Russell. Prominent Catholic leaders such as Cardinal Logue and Archbishop Walsh who were unable to attend sent messages of support. While this news report informs readers of the support the Gaelic League received from nationalist politicians and from the Catholic hierarchy, it

---

[39] ibid.

[40] 'Starving the schools: treasury penury', *Irish Independent*, 27 February 1905, 5. Other examples include 'Hyde and intermediate education', *Irish Independent*, 25 June 1906, 6; 'Irish education: treasury and national commissioners', *Irish Independent*, 16 September 1909, 5.

clearly states that it was the League themselves who called this meeting
to discuss the issue of education funding in the public sphere.

The necessity of ensuring Irish was widely taught in schools and in
the National University remained a matter of priority for the Gaelic
League for many years and they continued to organise demonstrations
and public meetings to raise awareness of the issue. A letter from J. P.
Dunne published in the *Irish Independent* in September 1910 under the
title 'Appeal to Gaelic Leaguers' reminded readers of Young Irelander
Thomas Davis's statement on the importance of education:

> Sir – The Language demonstration to be held in Dublin next
> Sunday affords an opportunity to the members of the Gaelic
> League to show their sympathy with the educational needs of the
> democracy of Ireland. Will they arise to the occasion and advance
> the demand of higher education for the masses, thus linking the
> watchword of 'Tir agus teanga' with the motto of Thomas Davis,
> 'Educate that you may be free?'[41]

This linking of contemporary issues with the ideology espoused by
earlier Nationalists was invoked by Pádraig Pearse in his pamphlet
'Ghosts' published in 1915 and also in the 'dead generations' referred
to in the 1916 Proclamation.[42]

Contrasting visions of an 'Irish-Ireland'
Despite Hyde's theories on the need to de-anglicise Ireland and restore
the Irish language, he didn't seek to fully rid Ireland of the English
language. Rather, his vision was for a bilingual nation that would cherish
its rich literary past. In an address delivered to the Gaelic Society of
New York on 16 June 1891 – some two years before the foundation of
the Gaelic League – Hyde set out his objectives for preserving and
promoting the Irish language:

> I do not for a moment advocate making Irish the language of the
> country at large, or of the National Parliament. I do not want to be
> an impossible visionary or rabid partisan. What I do wish to see is
> Irish established as a living language, for all time, among the
> million or half million who still speak it along the West coast, and

---

[41] 'Appeal to Gaelic Leaguers', *Irish Independent*, 13 September 1910, 3.
[42] See Pádraig Bambury (ed.), *Ghosts* (1998, 2010). Cork, digital edition available
at https://celt.ucc.ie/published/E900007-010.html; 'Poblacht na hÉireann', National
University of Ireland, digital edition available at http://catalogue.nli.ie/Record/vtls
000276536.

to insure that the language will hold a favorable place in teaching institutions and government examinations. Unless we retain a bilingual population as large as we now have, Irish may be said to be dead, and with it nine-tenths of the glories of the past; for, with modern Irish once dead, adieu to all hope of translating, publishing or understanding that unique glory of our race – our vast Irish literature.[43]

Much of Hyde's rhetoric in relation to his vision for a truly Irish nation and with regard to achieving a bilingual Gaelic nation was echoed in the writings of D. P. Moran, first published as a series of essays in the *New Ireland Review* from 1898 to 1900 and then published in book form as *The philosophy of Irish Ireland* in 1905.[44] Like Hyde, Moran did not shy away from criticising the influence of 'West Britonism' on the Irish public. Though Moran declared the re-learning of Irish as the most important aspect of the 'Irish-Ireland' movement, his own writings were mainly in English. His goal was to see a 'bi-lingual people' in Ireland, rather than a monolingual Irish public, as he outlines below:

> We must retrace our steps, and take as much inspiration as possible from our own country and its history. We must be original Irish, and not imitation English. Above all, we must re-learn our language, and become a bi-lingual people. For the great connecting link between us and the real Ireland, which few of us know anything about, is the Gaelic tongue. A national language will differentiate us from the rest of the world, and keep us ever in mind that we are an entity of original and historic growth, not a parasite stuck onto the side of England because our own heart was too weak to keep the vital spark in us.[45]

These passages indicate that neither Hyde nor Moran envisaged the complete domination of Irish as being the ultimate aim of the language movement, unlike others involved in 'Irish-Ireland' activism at the time who sought to fully restore Irish as the only spoken language of the people of Ireland. An illustrative example of this mindset is the regular advertisement of the book, *Ireland Irish-speaking in 1921: Father Toal's phrase method handbook*, in the *Irish Independent* in 1919, the very title

---

[43] Douglas Hyde, *Óráid a tugadh do Chumann na Gaedhilge, Nua-Eabhrac* (16 June 1891). Quoted in Ó Conaire, *Language, lore and lyric*, 151–2.
[44] See D. P. Moran, *The philosophy of Irish Ireland* (Dublin 1905).
[45] Moran, *The philosophy of Irish Ireland*, 26.

of which gives the impression that Irish people could abandon English and make the switch to Irish within a couple of years if they only set their minds to it! This book was issued by the 'Phrase Method Committee' in Belfast. The advertisement informed readers that the first edition had already sold out and that the second edition was forthcoming, implying that there was a great demand for this instructional handbook.[46] The newspaper coverage afforded to works of this nature provide an insight into contrasting visions of 'Irish-Ireland' in the period before the foundation of the Irish Free State in 1922. They also denote how the mainstream press accepted advertisements with an almost propagandistic tone which promoted the language movement.

Divisions in the language movement were also reported by the *Irish Independent* in late 1919 in relation to the NUI Senate elections. An anonymous letter from 'Another Graduate' questioned the motivation of Eoin MacNeill who stood for election to the Senate against his Gaelic League colleagues, Douglas Hyde and Agnes O'Farrelly:

> Sir – It is pretty generally understood that a political ticket was prepared and a whip sent round to the Sinn Fein voters long before the election which was bound, in the present excited state of public opinion, to make the return of the Sinn Fein candidates a foregone conclusion. What the country would like to know now is why Eoin MacNeill opposed his colleagues of many years in the language movement, Douglas Hyde and Agnes O'Farrelly? Are they not 'national-minded' enough for him, or have they ever betrayed the interests of Ireland on the Senate? Why has he, of all others, undertaken this crusade?[47]

Another letter from Joseph Dolan places the blame for this division on those who voted for Sinn Féin candidates above all others. The extract below captures the disappointment of many 'Irish-Irelanders' that independent candidates including Douglas Hyde, Agnes O'Farrelly and Dr Sigerson who did Trojan work for the language movement lost out to their Sinn Féin counterparts: 'They stood before the Irish people as apostles of the most self-dependent national culture in education, industrial development, intellectuality and sentiment. In the circumstances, he regarded their displacement, in the name of nationality, an act of ingratitude which most Irish-Irelanders must feel a national humiliation.'[48]

[46] 'Advertisement', *Irish Independent*, 2 June 1919, 3.
[47] 'Use of the political ticket', *Irish Independent*, 14 October 1919, 4.
[48] 'A national humilation', *Irish Independent*, 15 October 1919, 7.

This correspondence indicates that divisions arose between Sinn Féin members and other language enthusiasts in relation to political objectives at times, despite their shared goals for the revival of Irish and other Gaelic customs. These letters show that the restoration of the Irish language took precedence over achieving political independence, according to some nationalists, while others placed the political aspirations above all else. The former position is supported by the writings of both D. P. Moran and Douglas Hyde, both of whom believed that Irish language and culture were central elements of Irish identity and therefore more valuable to the creation of a truly Irish nation than political concessions.[49]

McMahon has analysed various points of convergence within the revival movement through the lens of 'multivalence', claiming that: 'A critical component of the assimilative process is multivalence: those who declared allegiance to a specific ideology need not have understood that ideology in precisely the same way; indeed, it was unlikely that they would.'[50] This theory explains the differing visions of a Gaelic nation within the 'Irish-Ireland' movement and the competing priorities of its supporters. It is also important to note that although Hyde and Moran shared many common views on the devastating impact of British influence on Irish society and culture, Moran's writing was often sectarian in nature, particularly the opinions expressed in his own paper, *The Leader*, founded in 1900. Though Hyde was the son of a Church of Ireland rector, Moran's '*Leader* newspaper preached an Irish Irelandism which was Catholic and Gaelic', according to Elliott, who describes his 'mordant sectarianism' as stemming from earlier seventeenth-century Irish language writings: 'His barbed humour, insulting dismissal of Protestants as "sourfaces", "bigots", and "foreigners", and of fellow-travelling Catholics as "shoneens" (little Englishmen) and "West Britons", echoed what was already there in Irish-language sources.'[51]

Native amusements
The notion of fostering an 'Irish-Ireland' in all aspects of society and culture can undoubtedly be traced back to Douglas Hyde's 1892 lecture on 'The necessity for de-anglicising Ireland', as discussed earlier. D. P. Moran developed this ideology further in his *Philosophy of Irish Ireland*

[49] Moran, *The philosophy of Irish Ireland,* 98; Hyde, *Óráid a tugadh do Chumann na Gaedhilge, Nua-Eabhrac,* 151–2.
[50] Timothy McMahon, *Grand opportunity: the Gaelic revival and Irish society, 1893–1910* (Syracuse 2008) 6.
[51] Marianne Elliott, *When God took sides. Religion and identity in Ireland: unfinished history* (Oxford 2009).

manifesto which emphasised the need for creating a truly Irish nation
that would have 'a native colour in arts, industries, literature, social
habits, points of view, music, amusements and so on, throughout all
phases of human activity'.[52] From its foundation in 1893, strong links
were established between the Gaelic League and other nationalist
movements which came under the umbrella of the 'Irish-Ireland'
philosophy, such as the Gaelic Athletic Association, the Irish National
Theatre, the Irish Industrial Development Association, the Home Rule
movement, the Feis Ceoil and the Pioneer Association. Although the
League initially claimed to be an 'apolitical and non-sectarian' body, it
was of course heavily influenced by the Catholic church's teaching on
temperance and other social issues, including the censorship of so-called
'smutty' literature imported from Britain.

The Gaelic League's annual Oireachtas festival provided a platform
for the dissemination of the 'Irish-Ireland' philosophy on a large scale
and its success reveals that the Gaelic League was far more than a
language movement. The Oireachtas festival, established in 1897, set
out to re-gaelicise the country, not merely through its programme of
literary, social and cultural events but through the speaking of Irish in
the public sphere.[53] This approach was mirrored by other *feiseanna* and
aeraíochtaí held throughout Ireland during the early twentieth century.
Print media played a dual role in both publicising these events before
they took place and then reporting on them afterwards. Though such
events were commonly reported through English in the *Irish
Independent*, its readers were informed of ongoing efforts to develop
the use of Irish in the public space in the following report from
Blackrock, Co. Dublin in 1910. Hyde was in attendance, thereby
lending his support to the local teachers and their pupils:

> At the Frankfort Feis, Blackrock, whereat children from many of
> the primary schools in South Dublin competed, the evidence of
> solid progress due to sound teaching methods and keen interest on
> the part of the pupils was eminently gratifying to Dr. Douglas
> Hyde and the many other well-known workers in the Language
> movement who were present.[54]

In addition to coverage in English, Ó Neachtain regularly discussed
Gaelic amusements and entertainments through Irish in his Gaelic

---

[52] Moran, *The philosophy of Irish Ireland*, preface.
[53] See Proinsias Mac Aonghusa (ed.), *Oireachtas na Gaeilge 1897–1997* (Baile Átha
Cliath 1997).
[54] 'The progress of Irish', *Irish Independent*, 6 June 1910, 4.

column. For example, though he acknowledged that certain attendees felt the 1908 Oireachtas lacked some of the energy of previous gatherings, he was quick to point out that he heard more Irish spoken at that year's events than ever before:

> Facthas dá lán nach raibh an tOireachtas chomh fuinneamhail i mbliadhna 7 bhíodh sé bliadhanta eile. Ní raibh, dar leo, an oiread daoine ann ná an brígh i lucht na gcomórtas mar bhíodh bliadhanta eile. B'éidir sin, acht measaim gur leachtaighe focal Gaedhilge a chuala mé ann ná mar chuala mé ag aon Oireachtas roimhe.

> 'Many felt that the Oireachtas was not as energetic this year as it was other years. There wasn't, in their opinion, the same amount of people there or the same spirit among competitors as in other years. Perhaps this was so, but I believe I heard more Irish words there than I heard at any previous Oireachtas.'[55]

Though the competitions themselves may have lacked the energy and enthusiasm of previous events, Ó Neachtain homes in on the positive aspects in relation to the use of Irish among those attending. This shows the importance of using Irish in social settings and the development of the Oireachtas over time, as Mac Aonghusa reports that the earliest gatherings were conducted mainly through English.[56]

Central to the realm of 'native amusements' was of course the Gaelic Athletic Association founded in 1884 by Michael Cusack and others.[57] Indeed, what set the League apart from earlier language organisations such as the Society for the Preservation of the Irish Language and the Gaelic Union was its success at a grass-roots level. Its network of branches filtered down from national and regional committees to local groups, modelled along the same lines as the GAA club structure. Already in 1892 Hyde recognised the GAA as central to the re-Gaelicisation of Ireland:

> I consider the work of the association in reviving our national game of *camán*, or hurling, and Gaelic football, has done more for

---

[55] 'Críoch an Oireachtais', *Irish Independent*, 12 August 1908, 4 (translation by author). Other examples include 'Successful feiseanna: the Omeath gathering', *Irish Independent*, 26 June 1905, 6; 'Aonach Locha gCarmain', *Irish Independent*, 17 May 1909, 4.

[56] Proinsias Mac Aonghusa, 'Teacht Oireachtas na Gaeilge', in *Oireachtas na Gaeilge*, 5.

[57] See Mike Cronin, William Murphy and Paul Rouse (eds), *The Gaelic Athletic Association 1884–2009* (Dublin and Portland 1994).

Ireland than all the speeches of politicians for the last five years. Our games, too, were in a most grievous condition until the brave and patriotic men who started the Gaelic Athletic Association took in hand their revival. I confess that the instantaneous and extraordinary success which attended their efforts when working upon national lines has filled me with more hope for the future of Ireland than everything else put together.[58]

In the same fashion as the Gaelic League, which proved itself more than just a language movement, Cronin asserts that the GAA was 'not simply a sporting body, but rather a conduit for the creation and promotion of a national ideal'.[59] This correlates with Timothy McMahon's statement that the aim of the League's cultural and social activities was 'to popularize the ideas behind the language cause' and 'designed to "mobilize" their audiences through entertainments, not simply to educate them'.[60] Both organisations functioned under the umbrella of the 'Irish-Ireland' movement and its philosophy of creating a truly Irish nation, separate to Britain in all respects.

Conclusion

It is clear from this analysis that the *Irish Independent* played a significant role in fostering various manifestations of cultural and political nationalism in the years before the foundation of the Irish Free State, with a particular emphasis on the 'Irish-Ireland' ideology. The status of the Irish language and other revivalist campaigns were promoted, debated and reported in both English and Irish through national – and nationalist – daily newspapers. Given the extensive circulation of the *Irish Independent* at the time, considerable significance may be assigned to the examples discussed above, which are representative of the material provided to its readers in both languages during the revival period.

It would be unwise to assume that all nationalist supporters understood the aims of the movement in precisely the same way and this certainly seems to have been the case, even within the language movement itself. Some members such as Hyde and Moran placed the promotion of Irish language and culture above all other concerns, while others such as MacNeill and Pearse used the Gaelic League networks to develop and mobilise more militant factions. The importance of print

---

[58] Hyde, quoted in Ó Conaire, *Language, lore and lyrics*, 168.
[59] Cronin, Murphy and Rouse, *The Gaelic Athletic Association 1884–2009*, 223.
[60] McMahon, *Grand opportunity,* 167.

media in promoting both shared and contrasting visions of an 'Irish-Ireland' cannot be ignored. Mac Congáil has emphasised the vital role of national English-language newspapers in disseminating this revival ideology:

> Chuidigh siad [na nuachtáin Bhéarla] fosta le pobal na Gaeilge a thabhairt isteach i saol náisiúnta na tíre, na cruinne agus na haoise seo i gcoitinne in áit iad a fhágáil i saol dorcha cúng na seanaimsireachta paróistí nó i dtuilleamaí idé-eolaíocht na hAthbheochana.

'The English-language newspapers assisted in drawing the Irish-language community into the national life of the country, the world and this century in general rather than leaving them in the dark narrow world of parochial old-fashionedness or dependent on the Revival ideology.' [61]

Though the Gaelic League was founded as a non-sectarian and non-political organisation and though visions of an 'Irish-Ireland' were not always uniformly shared, Hyde acknowledged the central role of League members in the creation of a fully Gaelic nation in his St Patrick's Day address in 1903:

> Nílimid ag scrios ná ag leagadh ná ag milleadh aon rud ach táimid ag cur suas agus ag tógáil agus ag oibriú gach sóirt. Leanaigí den obair, tá sibh ag tógáil náisiúin; ná lig an uirlis as bhur láimh agus Bail ó Dhia ar an obair.

'We are not destroying or knocking or ruining anything but we are putting up and building and working all kinds of things. Continue with this work, you are building a nation; do not lay down your tools and may God bless your work.'[62]

AOIFE WHELAN

---

[61] Mac Congáil, 'Saothrú na Gaeilge ar nuachtáin náisiúnta Bhéarla, 169 (translation by author).

[62] Hyde, 1903, quoted in Proinsias Mac Aonghusa, *Ar son na Gaeilge. Conradh na Gaeilge 1893–1993: stair sheanchais* (Baile Átha Cliath 1993) 83.

DOUGLAS HYDE'S INTERNATIONAL IMPACT AND INFLUENCE: EVIDENCE FROM HIS POSTCARD CORRESPONDENCE AND MEMOIR

Introduction

On 23 June 1891 an address was given by Anna Ní Raghallaigh and Eibhlín Ní Bharclaidh, the two chairwomen of the event, on behalf of the ladies of the New York Gaelic Society to Douglas Hyde. The address was printed a month later on 11 July 1891 in the Chicago *Citizen* newspaper and stated:

> Is iomadh cuairteoir do tháinig chugainn as Eirinn le tréimhse; acht gidh go measamaoid iád go léir, is cinnte nach bh-fuil aon aca do thuill fáilte chomh mór, chomh teith no chomh dílis agus do thuill tusa i d-taoibh do shaothair air son sean-teangan ár sinnsear agus ár d-tíre. Is tú an cheud fhear ameasg aos óg na h-Eireann do chuir teagasg Thomáis Dháibhís i n-gníomh; óir is tú amháin do thóg air do ghúalannaibh an obair thíorthamhuil do thosuigh an deagh-fhear sin agus le'r fágadh í neamh-chríochniughthe tre a bhás ro-anabuidh. Mar do bhí seisean air feadh a bheatha gan mórán deisciobal 'san obair, do bhí tú féin mar an g-ceudna air feadh tamaill; acht buidheachas do Dhia, tá do shómpla-sa ag cur anma úir i n-Eirinn; tá cuid d'a h-aos óg fa dheireadh ag musgailt as an trom-shuan in ar luigheadar, agus tá siad ag adhmháil riachtanais na h-oibre in a raibh tusa ad'aouar ag saothrughadh le bliadhantaibh.[1]

'Many visitors have come from Ireland over the past years; and whilst we greet them all respectfully, certainly not one of them has deserved as big, as warm or as much and as proper a welcome as you have deserved for your work on the old language of our ancestors and our country. You are the first man amongst the youth of Ireland who has put the teachings of Thomas Davis into practice; for you are the only one who has taken on the national work that that good man started which was left unfinished before his very premature death. Throughout his life he didn't have many followers in the work, as you didn't yourself for some time; but thanks be to God your example is putting a fresh spirit into Ireland; some of its youth are finally awakening from the deep sleep in

---

[1] 'Address to Dr. Douglas Hyde', Chicago *Citizen*, July 11, 1891.

which they lay and they are acknowledging the necessity of the work in which you yourself were toiling alone for years.'

In 1893 Hyde became the President of the Gaelic League and throughout his life he was a pioneer for the Irish language, its cultivation and survival. Whilst he was a key figure in the revival movement in Ireland, Hyde was by no means a scholar and an influencer confined to Ireland alone. Over the years he maintained many and various relationships with friends, colleagues, and scholars on an international basis, sharing ideas and corresponding in many different languages. In this article the international impact and influence Hyde had in terms of his ambitions and ideology for the language will be analysed through the study of his memoir and postcards housed currently in the National Folklore Collection in University College Dublin (UCD).

Background of the memoir and postcards
In 2016 I began the digitisation of this project with the School of Irish, Celtic Studies and Folklore and the National Folklore Collection in UCD. The project was funded as part of the Irish language strand of the Ireland 2016 Centenary Programme in conjunction with An Teanga Bheo. The aim was to digitise and create metadata for the collection of postcards and memoir currently held in the National Folklore Collection in order to publish them on the UCD digital libraries website. In the National Folklore Collection the postcards are compiled into a folder similar to that of a photo album. There are roughly ninety postcards in total and they contain correspondence to and from friends, colleagues, and scholars from various parts of the world.

Hyde's memoir is arranged into four parts and contains personal and first-hand accounts of many significant events throughout his life. It was mostly written whilst he was sick in bed in 1918–19. The first part of the memoir is nine pages long and Hyde writes of the politicisation of the Gaelic League and his subsequent resignation as President. Part two is forty-four pages and discusses the Irish language movement and the resignation of Sceilg, the columnist J. J. O'Kelly, at *The Freeman's Journal* in 1905. Part three is twenty-one pages and Hyde discusses the politicisation of the Coiste Gnó, the Executive Committee of the Gaelic League, and his gradual loss of influence on said committee. Part four is nineteen pages and Hyde talks of his first encounter with Thomas O'Neill Russell and O'Neill Russell's grammatical attack on Michael Logan, editor and founder of the Brooklyn newspaper *An Gaodhal*.

Memoir

The international impact and influence of Hyde is evident in his memoir when he praises the Irish diaspora in the United States, notably Patrick Ford, editor of the newspaper the *Irish World*, and John Devoy, editor of the newspaper the *Gaelic American*. Both these men edited Irish-American newspapers which often contained material discussing Ireland and the Irish language. Hyde writes of their constant support for the Irish language movement and that because of their help it became 'impossible for the Irish Government [...] to kill off the language [...] by rules and regulations'. Hyde mentions Ford in the first part of his memoir in particular when he states that the $300 that Ford managed to raise for the League 'meant everything' to them, reiterating the positive impact the Gaelic League had overseas:

> for having won Forde[2] over there was no possibility of the Members of Parliament turning upon us and sending us, or at least of their openly disparaging us, once their own chief American ally had taken us up and given us his blessing. This was a distinct milestone in the early progress of the League.

Throughout the years of Hyde's presidency of the Dublin Gaelic League, and even prior to this, the Irish-American support was extremely influential in the early and later years of the language movement.[3] Irish-American print media and cultural organisations provided monetary support to the Dublin society, however their influence is likewise seen in the ideological and methodological similarities in the transatlantic

---

[2] Hyde spells it as 'Forde' in his memoir, however, in the *Irish World,* they note that the editor is 'Patrick Ford'.

[3] Fiona Lyons, '"Thall is abhus" – Irish language revival, media and the transatlantic influence 1857–1897' (PhD thesis, University College Dublin, 2021); Fiona Lyons, 'Irish diaspora, cultural activism and print media in transatlantic contexts between Ireland and North America c. 1857–1887', *Studi irlandesi. A Journal of Irish Studies* 9 (2019) 246-247. URL: https://doi.org/10.13128/SIJIS-2239-3978-25515; Regina Uí Chollatáin, '"Thall is abhus" 1860–1930: the revival process and the journalistic web between Ireland and North America', *Language identity and migration* (Oxford 2016); Regina Uí Chollatáin, 'Athbheochan thrasatlantach na Gaeilge: scríbhneoirí, intleachtóirí agus an fhéiniúlacht Éireannach,' *Litríocht na Gaeilge ar fud an domhain: cruthú, caomhnú agus athbheochan.* Imleabhar 1 (Baile Átha Cliath 2015) and Regina Uí Chollatáin, 'A new Gaelic League idea? The global context', this volume. See also the *Irish American*, 18 February 1895; the *Irish American*, 25 February 1895; *An Gaodhal*, April 1895; Úna Ní Bhroiméil, *Building Irish identity in America, 1870–1915: The Gaelic revival* (Dublin 2003); Dorothy Ní Uigín, 'An iriseoireacht Ghaeilge i Meiriceá agus in Éirinn ag tús na hathbheochana: an cúlra Meiriceánach', *Léachtaí Cholm Cille 28* (1998); Fionnuala Uí Fhlannagáin, *Fíníní Mheiriceá agus an Ghaeilge* (Baile Átha Cliath 2008).

approach towards the Irish revival. Ford in particular, having emigrated from Galway to the US in 1845, encouraged the Irish language cause despite never featuring an Irish language column in the Irish World newspaper he edited. Similar to his appreciation of Ford in his personal writings, Hyde made reference to the link between the US and Ireland with regard to the language in a public lecture he gave to the Gaelic Society of New York in 1891 on his return trip from Canada. Hyde spoke of how important the relationship between Ireland and the US was to the language movement and its progression, and without the help of the Gaels in the US much could not be achieved:

> We in Ireland owe a great deal to the Gaels of America; for if it were not for the help we get from them, the Irish Language movement would not have assumed the position it now occupies. We are both thankful and grateful to you for it. We are a people nervously sensitive to the least touch of sarcasm. It is sarcasm that has tended to root out the Irish language; but when we know that you in America, are admiring our efforts to revive it, that does more than anything else to keep the Irish language alive.[4]

Similar to the Irish-American aid the League received, Hyde also refers to the South African Boer War in the second part of his memoir as being a true stimulus for the Irish language movement. Although nobody had noticed it at the time, Hyde states that the war had been

> the first public happening since the foundation of the [Gaelic] League to give a real impetus to the language movement. It was something so wonderful so unexpected so unheard of that the English empire should be held up by a handful of farmers that it gave every Irishman a thrill – in most cases a thrill of joy! It was the first glimmering of a ray of hope that England was not all clothed in brass and triple steel, invulnerable and invincible ... For a couple of years the extraordinary courage and prowess of the Boers were steadily pumping hope and self-reliance into Ireland; and it was the language movement, which reaped most benefit from it.

Donal McCracken attests to the importance of the Boer War for the Irish language movement as he states that 'the Irish pro-Boer movement was the first effective example in modern times of solidarity of one colonially beleaguered people with another. Never before had the mass of the Irish

---

[4] 'Dr. Douglas Hyde', *Irish American,* 27 June 1891.

people espoused so fervently another nation's struggle against the British empire'.[5] Similarly, Cathal Billings in his recent studies of the Boer War, advanced nationalist politics, and the Gaelic League highlights that contributors and editors of *An Claidheamh Soluis* (the official newspaper of the Gaelic League) would often comment upon injustices occurring in other colonies around the world, the Boer War for example, as a means to draw readers' attention to the importance of retaining a national language in Ireland. The print media forum, therefore, was often used as a means to draw awareness to other international movements, as Hyde mentions, to advance various ideals and objectives.[6]

Whilst there is a focus in this article on the impact and influence of Hyde himself, the transatlantic and transnational impressions in terms of ideology *upon* Hyde in particular, which are reflected in his own work for the language and for the League cannot be dismissed. Many of the thought-processes and methodologies which Hyde practised and which were, in turn, reflected, in the work of the League and encompassed a global movement in which ideas, ambitions, theories, and approaches were shared and adopted.

In the final part of the memoir Hyde describes Thomas O'Neill Russell as a man 'with the most intense convictions … little things and great things bulked equally big before his eyes … and he expended his intense energy on the very smallest of them just as he might have done upon the very biggest'. O'Neill Russell was a Westmeath man whom Hyde had met during his time as a student in Dublin. O'Neill Russell was a member of the Dublin Society for the Preservation of the Irish Language alongside Hyde, and later attended the inaugural meeting of the Gaelic League in July 1893. In the 1880s O'Neill Russell was travelling across the United States as a corresponding member for the Gaelic Union. Along the way, O'Neill Russell would often stop by Irish language classes and events hosted by the Irish-American cultural societies. He would give lectures, aid in Irish classes, and in fact became the editor of the Gaelic columns in the Boston *Donohoe's Magazine* and Chicago *Citizen*. Despite his charitable disposition towards the Irish-American language movement, O'Neill Russell found himself involved in many arguments and disagreements with language enthusiasts in the States. This included Michael Logan in particular over Logan's supposed

---

[5] Donal McCracken, *Forgotten protest: Ireland and the Anglo-Boer War* (Belfast 2003 [second edition]) xiii.
[6] See Cathal Billings, 'Cogadh na mBórach agus an pholaitíocht fhorbartha náisiúnach i gConradh na Gaeilge', *Éigse: A Journal of Irish Studies* 41 (2020) 212–35; see also Billings's studies of the Boer War and advanced nationalistic politics and the Gaelic League in his forthcoming monograph.

improper use of grammar in his Brooklyn journal *An Gaodhal* in the latter half of the nineteenth century. The front page of *An Gaodhal* stated the aim of the journal, 'Leabhar-aithris míosamhal chum an Teanga Ghaedhilge a chosnadh agus a shaorthughadh agus chum Féin-riaghla Cinidh na h-Éireann' ('a monthly journal for the preservation and cultivation of the Irish language and the autonomy of the Irish nation'). *An Gaodhal* was set up in 1881 by Michael Logan in Brooklyn, a year before the establishment of *Irisleabhar na Gaedhilge* by the Gaelic Union in 1882.

O'Neill Russell began to discuss the grammatical inaccuracy of the Irish content present in *An Gaodhal* in the 1880s and found great fault with the grammatical structure on the front page of the paper in particular. O'Neill Russell was a fiery man with great intentions for the future of the Irish language and he was no stranger to creating debate, especially in regard to matters arising from the printing of the Irish language and subsequent grammatical fluency. O'Neill Russell began his argument with Logan in the Irish-American press as he believed that the genitive was to follow 'chum' instead of the word being in the nominative as was found on the front page of Logan's paper. Logan responded to O'Neill Russell's comments in *An Gaodhal* in the same article stating that:

> For many reasons we did not choose to adopt Mr. Russell's translation, and he seemed very much annoyed when we did not do so, and ever since he has not ceased, at the expense of ordinary courtesy and every manly principle, to try to injure the Gael because of this fancied slight. [...] Luckily, this evidence of his veracity and of his worthlessness as an authority has been preserved. [7]

The debate between Logan and O'Neill Russell raged throughout the 1880s–1890s in the Irish-American press. Hyde himself noted in his memoir that O'Neill Russell stated that if the grammar was to be so incorrect in *An Gaodhal* it 'would be better to see the Irish language dead than so profaned [and] far preferable would it be to have no Irish language at all'. It was similarly printed in *An Gaodhal* on January 1887 that O'Neill Russell 'said that he *sat down* on the Gael because it printed *bad* Irish'.[8]

[7] *An Gaodhal*, December 1882; Fionnuala Uí Fhlannagáin, *Mícheál Ó Lóchain agus An Gaodhal* (Baile Átha Cliath 1990) 113.
[8] *An Gaodhal,* January 1887.

Hyde's description of his character in his memoir attests to O'Neill Russell's impulsive nature to criticise, writing also that he was a man 'liable to fly off at some extraordinary tangent or to find a stumbling block of offense in something apparently perfectly innocent'. Hyde also referred to a verse a young Trinity College student, James Bartley Shea, once wrote entitled 'a Gaelic Leaguer's Paradise'. Hyde made note of the lines which 'hit off O'Neill Russell to perfection':

> And O'Neill Russell too was there
> With his Yanko – Franco – Celtic air
> Still speaking Irish wrong.

O'Neill Russell's negativity, challenging of relationships, and criticism which he was so often associated with, did in fact potentially hinder Hyde's international impact with scholars in the US, and with Logan in particular in later years. When Hyde visited New York in the summer of 1891 on his return from Canada there is no mention of him having visited Logan during this period in his diaries, despite him having visited Brooklyn and met other scholars such as O'Donovan Rossa, O'Neill Russell and Ford. Fionnuala Uí Fhlannagáin in her study of Logan and *An Gaodhal* accounts for his lack of acknowledgement towards Logan in his diaries as perhaps being due to the previous disagreements between Logan and O'Neill Russell. At any rate, Hyde never met Logan at this time.[9] This potentially highlights O'Neill Russell's influence on Hyde's US affairs and a subsequent impediment to his international impact and influence.

Postcards
Through the postcards in this collection, which were sent and received by Hyde from around the world, we can learn who Hyde was in contact with and what about, we also often see that he shared very similar ideologies and ideals with his correspondents. These postcards came from countries such as England, France, Germany, Hungary, Italy, Ireland and the United States. For this article in particular the focus will be on postcards sent from Germany, Hungary, Scotland and the United States.

[9] ibid. 21.

Germany

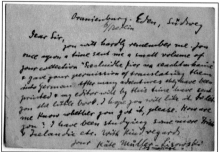
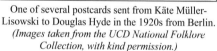

One of several postcards sent from Käte Müller-
Lisowski to Douglas Hyde in the 1920s from Berlin.
*(Images taken from the UCD National Folklore
Collection, with kind permission.)*

Two postcards in this collection were sent from Germany to Hyde by
Käte Müller-Lisowski. Müller-Lisowski was a scholar who studied Old
Irish at University College London and who worked on Irish manuscript
catalogues in the British Museum between 1913 and 1914.[10] She
translated Douglas Hyde's book *Sgéaluidhe fíor na seachtmhaine* into
German in 1920 and around this time she sent Hyde her postcards. In
the first postcard she sent, she writes how Hyde gave her his permission
to translate his work into German. She mentions that she has sent him
the finished copy and she hopes he will like it. Her second postcard in
1926 tells us that Hyde sent her *Lia Fáil* and that she mentions that she
was very pleased to have received it. *Lia Fáil*, published by the National
University of Ireland and now succeeded by the academic journal *Éigse*,
was founded with Hyde as its first editor in 1926 and is still published
today. In her postcard she sends her wishes to him and to 'his country'.
This postcard from Müller-Lisowski tells us of the international
relationship Hyde kept with other linguistic scholars, adding to his
overall international scholarly impact.

Another postcard in the collection comes from G. Lehmacher. Gustav
Lehmacher was a Celtic scholar and a student of the Old Irish scholar
Rudolf Thurneysen. He sent his postcard to Douglas Hyde in 1926 and
similar to Müller-Lisowski we see the relationships Hyde kept with
international scholars. In this postcard to Hyde Lehmacher writes of the
Irish language and its orthography. He observes that a team of Irish

[10] 'Life and Work of Käte Müller-Lisowski.' CELT: Corpus of Electronic Texts. 2014,
https://celt.ucc.ie//muellerlisowski.html.

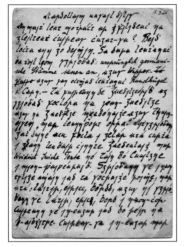

Postcard sent from Gustav Lehmacher to Douglas Hyde on 15 March 1926 from Bonn.
(Images taken from the UCD National Folklore Collection, with kind permission.)

speakers are writing a dictionary of Old and Middle Irish words and that Thurneysen is in charge. Entries are made on a list headed with a word in Irish in texts such as Táin Bó Cúailnge. In 1928, two years after this postcard was written, Lehmacher wrote a review on Dinneen's *Irish-English Dictionary*. In his review we see very similar criticisms of the language to those he refers to in the postcard he sent to Hyde. In his postcard he mentions that people today are writing words like they were when written previously in the literature, with spelling variations for example. In his review of Dinneen's dictionary he also makes reference to a similar point: 'Why, too, in words whose existence seems now to be purely literary, such spellings as *ósaic, iuidic, náit*, instead of *ósaig, iuidhig, náid* … Or is there evidence that in these words the original Latin value of the letters was restored?'[11] What is interesting in particular with this review is at the end when Lehmacher states that he has already given his opinion on this matter of the Irish language previously before and that:

---

[11] Gustav Lehmacher, 'Focloir Gaedhilge agus Béarla. An Irish-English dictionary by P. S. Dinneen,' *Studies: An Irish Quarterly Review* 17, no. 66 (1928) 323–5 (324). Accessed 2 December 2019, URL: http://www.jstor.org/stable/30094335.

I must mention my satisfaction when one of the most distinguished of living Irishmen wrote to me: 'Tá mé ar aon inntinn leat-sa. Caithfimíd aon teanga do bheith againn mar bhíonns i ngach tír shíbhialta is mar do bhí againn féin dá chéad bhliadhain ó shin.'[12]

'… I completely agree with you. We must have only one language such as those in all civilised countries do and as we had ourselves 200 years ago.'

Perhaps, therefore, the distinguished Irishman he is talking about is Hyde and that the quote Lehmacher refers to could have been the response Hyde sent back to him in their correspondence about the Irish language through postcards. If this surmise is correct, it highlights the influence in terms of ideology and aspirations for the language Hyde had on others on an international scale.

Hungary
The international influence and ideology associated with Hyde in terms of his work ethic and impacts can be seen in the postcard sent from John Th. Honti on 29 March 1934, from Budapest, Hungary. Honti was a

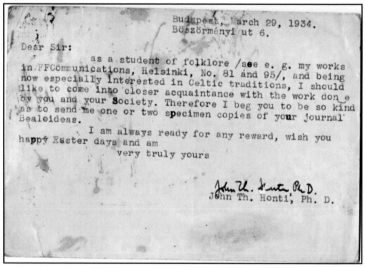

Postcard sent from John Th. Honti to Douglas Hyde on 29 March 1934 from Budapest.
(Image taken from the UCD National Folklore Collection, with kind permission.)

[12] ibid. 325. Accessed 14 July 2018.

scholar who studied Celtic studies and European folklore and in his postcard to Hyde he writes that he is 'a student of folklore' and is interested 'in Celtic traditions'. He continues and writes that he would like 'to come into closer acquaintance with the work done by you and your Society' and asks Hyde to send him on 'one or two specimen copies of your journal Bealoideas'. The Society I assume he is referring to is the Folklore of Ireland Society which was established in 1927 to 'collect, preserve and publish the folklore of Ireland' and of which Hyde was founding treasurer.[13] In 1934, the year Honti sends Hyde the postcard, Hyde had published two articles with the journal *Béaloideas*, 'An tseanbhean agus a tuaimín sméar' and 'Diarmuid agus Gráinne'. It is clear, therefore, that Hyde's work in folklore was familiar to scholars in Budapest at this time. It also shows that Hyde's international scholarly influence continued even after his resignation as President of the Gaelic League in 1915.

Honti wrote for the journal *Béaloideas* himself in 1936, two years after he sent this postcard to Hyde, publishing an article entitled 'Celtic studies and European folk-tale research'. In the article he mentions that 'Irish folklorists have set themselves the task of collecting the oral literature of their country, leaving the editing, arrangement, and comparative work to a later time, because the rapid decay of oral tradition urges them to save what still remains'.[14] Whilst there is no explicit connection between this statement and Hyde, it could be argued that he is referring to Hyde and the Irish language oral tradition which he was very passionate about. The quote also refers to Hyde's reasoning behind the publication of *Abhráin grádh chúige Connacht or love songs of Connacht*, published in 1893, which he viewed as necessary to preserve Irish language oral tradition, as one who had 'the wish to preserve what a score or so of years will find disappeared off the face of the earth'.[15] Similar to the German postcards, Hyde's influence can be seen in his role as a global advocate for cultural and linguistic preservation and survival.

---

[13] 'The Folklore of Ireland Society.' National Folklore Collection – Cnuasach Bhéaloideas Éireann, https://www.ucd.ie/irishfolklore/en/folkloresociety/.

[14] John Th. Honti, 'Celtic studies and European folk-tale research,' *Béaloideas* 6, no. 1 (1936) 33; Tadhg Ó Murchadha, 'Scéalta suathainseach ó Uibh Ráthach,' *Béaloideas* 3, no. 4 (1932) 502.

[15] Dominic Daly, *The young Douglas Hyde* (Dublin 1974) 61; Liam Mac Mathúna, 'An Craoibhín, "fóc-lór" agus stair chultúrtha na mothúchán', *Béaloideas* 78 (2010) 133.

Scotland

Postcard sent from Séamus Ó Dubhghaill, also known as 'Beirt Fhear', to Douglas
Hyde on 20 September 1913 from Dundee, Scotland.
(Images taken from the UCD National Folklore Collection, with kind permission.)

In 1913 Hyde received a postcard from 'Beirt F[h]ear', the pen-name
for Séamus Ó Dubhghaill. Séamus Ó Dubhghaill at this time was a
'teachtaire' or official representative on behalf of the Gaelic League in
Scotland, no doubt at the annual Mòd festival, which was held in
Dundee, 17–19 September that year. He sent Hyde a postcard on 19
September 1913, mentioning that he was the 'only representative from
Ireland' in Scotland at the time but was happy to be there as 'the Scottish
Gaels are extremely welcoming'. It echoes the interest and support the
diaspora routinely showed the language movement; a movement of
which Hyde was at its core.

Other postcards Hyde received from Scotland include those from
William J. Watson. Watson was a Scottish Gaelic scholar who studied
Scottish Gaelic place-names. As mentioned in a review of his book, *The
history of the Celtic place-names of Scotland*, Watson 'was especially
interested in the period from the second to the ninth centuries when the
population of Scotland was successively under the hegemony of the
Caledonians, the Picts, and the Scots or Irish'.[16]

Watson sent a postcard to Hyde on 25 March 1915. In this Watson
stated that he had received Neil Ross's book and had begun to read it.
Ross was another well-known Gaelic scholar in the late nineteenth, early
twentieth century. He was the President of 'An Comunn Gàidhealach',
an organisation which interpreted Celticism in the same manner as the
Gaelic League in Dublin, as 'cultural, non-political, and non-sectarian'.[17]

---

[16] E. L., reviewed work: *The history of the Celtic place-names of Scotland* by William
J. Watson', *The Geographical Journal* 70, no. 2 (1927) 170–1. Accessed 19 September
2018. URL: https://www.jstor.org/stable/1782183.

[17] 'Branch Reports', *An Gaidheal*, November 1931.

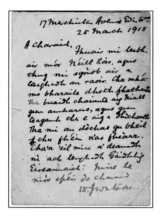

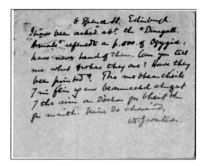

Postcard sent from W. J. Watson to Douglas
Hyde in 1915 from Edinburgh.
*(Images taken from the UCD National
Folklore Collection, with kind permission.)*

He also served as the editor of *An Gaidheal,* the newspaper of the Scottish Gaelic League. Watson goes on to mention that his impression of Ross 'isn't great yet' but he can confirm that he 'has a way with words and without a doubt he's doing his best'.

Watson, as a distinguished scholar in his own right, contributed frequently to the *Transactions of the Gaelic Society of Inverness*, which was founded in 1871 for 'cultivating the language, poetry and music of the Scottish Highlands and generally furthering the interests of the Gaelic speaking people'.[18] Watson was an office bearer of the Society for many years and contributed to the publication regularly.[19] Similarly, Ross was a member of the Scottish Gaelic League and also edited the Scottish League's newspaper, *An Gaidheal*, founded in 1923. Both Watson and Ross, the two scholars mentioned in this postcard, represented the ideology of the Gaelic League in Dublin and are reflections of Hyde in the work he did for the Irish language, as Ross and Watson did the same for Scottish Gaelic. The *Transactions of the Gaelic Society of Inverness* and *An Gaidheal*, both print media sources in Scottish Gaelic, incorporated the aims and objectives Hyde had in Ireland for the Irish language, namely its revival as a spoken and literary language. Watson and Ross are also echoes of Hyde and all three were members of cultural organisations, contributors to print media sources in their native language, and key figures in the promotion of their native language in society. Therefore, there was undoubtedly interaction and influence in relation

---

[18] 'A brief history of the Society', *Gaelic Society of Inverness – Comunn Gàidhlig Inbhir Nis*, 2015, http://www.gsi.org.uk/history/.

[19] Comunn Gàidhlig Inbhir Nis. *Transactions of the Gaelic Society of Inverness* (Inverness).

to similar goals and ideologies between Ross, Watson and Hyde, encompassing a language movement with inter-national influences and approaches from international sources, such as seen previously with the Boer War and the Irish-American newspaper editors.

The United States

Postcard sent from Douglas Hyde to Miss Ethel Chance, 26 February 1906, from San Francisco.
(Images taken from the UCD National Folklore Collection, with kind permission.)

In the postcards sent and received by Hyde from the US, the success of his tour around the US in 1905/06 is portrayed. He sent a postcard to Miss Ethel Chance on 26 February 1906, and stated that he had just 'been given the biggest banquet ever given anyone in California. The governor, mayor, archbishop [and] chief justice were present – over 500 guests'. In this postcard it is clear that the tour was well received and that there was great interest from the diaspora in it. Hyde found great success in the city of San Francisco in particular and managed to raise a significant amount of money for the League back in Ireland. When a fire raged through the city two months after his visit, following the great earthquake, Hyde decided to give back to the city the money he had received from his lectures there to help with the repair and reconstruction of buildings and infrastructure damaged. Dunleavy and Dunleavy describe this action:

> Some of the money he had raised in San Francisco had to be used to pay expenses. The small fees he received from his college lectures were supposed to be his own money; it had been John Quinn's idea to arrange these for that purpose, as a way to compensate Hyde for the eight months that he was devoting to the campaign. The rest was for the League. Calculating what these figures came to, Hyde estimated that he could safely return $5,000

for the relief of the people of San Francisco without danger of dipping into league funds or using them for expenses. He arranged with John Quinn for the money to be sent.[20]

Not only does this emphasise the positive and symbiotic impact and relationship between Hyde and the Irish diaspora, this postcard also highlights how Hyde would have been perceived abroad and we can see here how much he was appreciated and respected. Similarly, his act of kindness to repay back the money he had received from his lectures in the city to help with the damage and destruction caused from the disaster shows the respect Hyde had for the Irish abroad, strengthening his international impact and relationship with them.

Postcard sent from James D. Phelan to Douglas Hyde, 11 May 1914, from San Francisco. *(Images taken from the UCD National Folklore Collection, with kind permission.)*

In the second postcard from the US Hyde corresponds with James D. Phelan, the mayor of San Francisco at the time. Phelan wishes Hyde and his wife Lucy a pleasant year and thanks him for his Gaelic greetings. We can assume that Hyde previously sent Phelan a postcard and this was his reply and thanks. This was sent on 11 May 1914, eight years after

[20] Janet Egleson Dunleavy and Gareth W. Dunleavy. *Douglas Hyde: a maker of modern Ireland* (Berkeley/Los Angeles/Oxford 1991) 279–80.

Hyde's tour to San Francisco. It can be understood that Hyde kept in contact and maintained relationships with key figures he met throughout his tour. As both President of the League and a keen language enthusiast at this time Hyde, representing the ideology and objectives of the language movement, maintained many relationships internationally which would have created a greater platform for the progression of their aims and ambitions for the language.

Neilí Ní Bhriain and Fionán Mac Coluim also travelled to the US to raise funds for the League and to continue Irish language revival efforts.

Postcards sent from Neilí Ní Bhriain to Douglas Hyde from New York in 1914.
(Images taken from the UCD National Folklore Collection, with kind permission.)

The postcards sent from Neilí to Hyde whilst they were in the early twentieth century reiterate the success they had, particularly whilst they were in New York. Her postcards also, however, describe the struggle and hard work they undertook in raising funds for the League and this hardship is referred to in her first postcard in the collection dated 22 April 1914. She writes that 'the work has been very hard indeed getting everything started but I am sure we shall get on without killing ourselves after this work'. Another postcard she sent was on 12 May 1914, and she mentions that she 'had no time to write' as they were 'getting ready for a concert'. Similarly, in her final postcard to Hyde on 31 May 1914, she writes that 'its painfully dreadful that I haven't been able to write a proper letter where I was so glad to get yours. It's the running of a concert each week as well as the Exh. which makes such a rush but it's a pity not to do it when we make up to $100 each time'. Neilí's postcards reflect these tours' achievements in raising money for language efforts back home whilst noting that the diaspora was still showing great interest in tours and events organised by the Dublin Gaelic League. In one tour alone Mac Coluim, alongside another Gaelic League fundraiser an tAthair Ó Flannagáin, raised £3,000 for the League's efforts at home.[21]

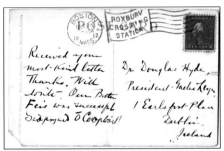

Postcard sent from Diarmuid Ó Cearbhaill to
Douglas Hyde on 28 November 1912, from Boston.
*(Images taken from the UCD National Folklore
Collection, with kind permission.)*

The next postcard in the collection sent to Hyde from the US is from Diarmuid Ó Cearbhaill. This was sent from Boston, describing the success of the Irish diaspora and their Boston feis in the year 1912. American cities hosted annual Irish cultural festivals known as a feis in which step dancers such as jig or reel dancers would compete against one another. They were open to the public and often used as a means to gather the Irish community together.[22] As Arthur Cleary wrote:

> Irish music is one of the most attractive parts of the League's work. Irish dancing has, however, made it more converts. Whether the traditional dancing of our country is really autochthonous is a matter of some dispute, but once acquired, and the simpler forms of it are not difficult to acquire, it is far livelier and healthier than most modern cosmopolitan dancing, and nevertheless embodies far more the expression of an artistic concept. For the young and vigorous it is the best dancing in the world. And the Gaelic League was not long in finding it a powerful instrument for making proselytes.[23]

[21] 'Fionán Mac Coluim', ainm.ie. 2017, http://www.ainm.ie/Bio.aspx?ID=0028.

[22] Marion Casey and J. J. Lee, *Making of the Irish American: history and heritage of the Irish in the United States* (New York 2006).

[23] Arthur E. Clery, 'The Gaelic League, 1893–1919', *Studies: An Irish Quarterly Review*, Vol. 8, No. 31 (Sept. 1919) 398–408 (at 403–4). URL: https://www.jstor.org/stable/30092777.

Events such as this were regularly reported on in the nineteenth century in Irish-American newspapers such as the *Irish Echo,* the *Irish-American,* and *An Gaodhal,* when the Philo-Celtic societies would often put on these events for entertainment purposes to increase a sense of nationality and community amongst the diaspora. In the same year Ó Cearbhaill sent this postcard to Hyde, there was an article published in the *Sacred Heart Review* on 16 November 1912. Printed just twelve days before Ó Cearbhaill sent his postcard to Hyde, this article states that a letter from Dr Douglas Hyde, the President of the Gaelic League in Ireland, was read at this feis. Amongst other things, Hyde said that:

> [...] there is really no better and no easier way of bringing home what we are doing to the minds both of Irishmen and Americans than the holding of a feis. The Gaelic League stands for a revival of Irish nationality through going back to its bed-rock principles. In other words, we are, as you know, reviving all through Ireland to-day those realities upon which nationality, as understood throughout Europe, is truly based, namely, the language, the music, the sports, customs and games that distinguish one nation from another.[24]

The continuity of Hyde's ambitions and ideologies for the language and for the League are communicated through the postcards from Ó Cearbhaill, Phelan and Ní Bhriain to Hyde. Whilst they focus on the missions of the League to raise funds internationally, the impact and influence Hyde had in the background is evident, showing that much of what the League portrayed was also believed, communicated, and understood by Hyde.

Conclusion
The international impact and the Irish ideology Douglas Hyde encompassed can be seen through his postcard correspondence and his memoir writings. His aims, objectives, and ideals were communicated globally amongst the diaspora and amongst those who were interested in Celtic literature, folklore, language, cultivation, and revival. His international impact is seen in the similarities of his own ideals in other people's work, international scholars' praise and respect for him as an intellectual, the eagerness of the diaspora to support and aid the revival movement in their attendance at his lectures or associated League events created to help raise funds for the future of the language movement, and

---

[24] 'Springfield's Gaelic feis', *Sacred Heart Review,* 16 November 1912.

in the similar aspirations Hyde shared with other enthusiasts for scholarship, learning, and teaching. The Irish language and cultural revival efforts of the Gaelic League were not confined to Ireland alone and its support transcended transnational boundaries which, as shown in this article through the medium of Douglas Hyde's writings and correspondence, created an international movement that positively impacted and influenced its various components Hyde was very much a key influence behind the Gaelic League until his retirement from the presidency in 1915, yet he remained just as passionate and as enthusiastic for the language movement after this and throughout his life. His ambitions and ideology for the language had as much an impact internationally as it did nationally and through the analysis of his postcard correspondence and memoir housed currently in the National Folklore Collection in UCD we can determine that there was more behind the man with the moustache than meets the eye.[25]

FIONA LYONS

---

[25] See Máire Nic an Bhaird, 'The man behind the moustache: meet the real Douglas Hyde', *RTÉ*, 15 May 2019, https://www.rte.ie/brainstorm/2019/0513/1049181-the-man-behind-the-moustache-meet-the-real-douglas-hyde/.

'THE APPLE DOESN'T FALL FAR FROM THE TREE':
THE CREATIVE INFLUENCE OF DOUGLAS HYDE AND
LUCY COMETINA KURTZ ON THEIR CHILDREN

Introduction

Douglas Hyde, An Craoibhín Aoibhinn (born 17 January 1860, died 12 July 1949), was founding President of the Gaelic League, first Professor of Modern Irish in University College Dublin (UCD) and first President of an independent Irish state (1938–45).[1] Douglas Hyde and his wife Lucy Cometina Kurtz (1861–1938) had two children, Nuala Eibhlín Hyde (1894–1916) and Mary Úna Hyde (1896–1977), known as Úna. Tragically Nuala died from tuberculosis at the young age of 22 in September 1916.[2] Mary Úna Hyde lived a long life, marrying Judge James Sealy (1876–1949). They had three children, Douglas (1929–2013), Christopher (1930–2017) and Lucy (1934–).

Douglas Hyde's grandson, Douglas Sealy, was a teacher, a critic and a translator who worked in both Irish and English creating poems and critical essays. He was a commentator and reviewer of cultural matters and the arts. He wrote for a wide range of publications, in particular *The Irish Times*.[3] His education took him to Sandford Park school, followed by St Columba's college, Dublin and then he became a student of Celtic Studies at Trinity College Dublin, where he was editor of the literary magazine *Icarus*.[4] An tOllamh Liam Mac Mathúna and I had the pleasure of visiting Douglas Sealy's widow Mary Sealy in her home in Howth, County Dublin in March and November 2019. She kindly gave us permission to view the personal collection of her husband, Douglas Sealy, new material which gives an insight into Douglas and Lucy Hyde's creative influence on their children.

In our effort to return to Douglas Hyde's roots our journey took us west, where Liam Mac Mathúna and I visited Michael Carty (1918–2019) in his home in Galway city in August and September 2018. A gentleman originally from Tibohine, County Roscommon, the young Carty knew Douglas Hyde, who was a neighbour when Michael Carty was attending school. When we spoke to Michael, he transported us back to his own childhood as he recalled looking up at Hyde and being struck

---

[1] Dominic Daly, *The young Douglas Hyde* (Dublin 1974) xv.

[2] Janet Egleson Dunleavy and Gareth W. Dunleavy, *Douglas Hyde: a maker of modern Ireland* (Berkeley and Los Angeles 1991) 346–7.

[3] 'Formidable critic and pioneering translator of Irish poetry', *The Irish Times*, 29 June 2013, 1.

[4] For biographical information on Douglas Sealy please see https://www.ainm.ie/Bio.aspx?ID=3079 [last accessed 11 January 2022].

by his impressive height and enigmatic character. During Michael Carty's recollections, the image that stood out most was his description of Hyde's moustache, 'Hyde had the biggest moustache of them all'.[5] Amongst Douglas Sealy's materials was his grandfather's passport. On this it states that he was 5ft 10 inches in height, though Michael's description of Hyde highlights his immense aura, 'Douglas Hyde was a very big tall man about 6 ft 4 inches'.[6] He was larger than life with a magnetic aura, whose features stayed in your memory long after meeting him, 'He always wore tweed suits and plus fours and long grey stockings and brown shoes about size 11'.[7] He had grey eyes and dark hair. This passport was issued in 1922 when Hyde was 62 years of age. Michael, in reminiscing of his childhood, at times spent in the company of Hyde, recalls that he was at least 6 ft 4. However, the memory of the child sees the adult as far more imposing than his actual height was. Hyde made such an impression on people he met, that perhaps it is not surprising that he was given an extra six inches!

Image 1: Douglas Hyde's passport from Douglas Sealy's personal collection (photograph and signature).

---

[5] Michael Carty, Michael Carty's interview with Liam Mac Mathúna and Máire Nic an Bhaird (Galway September 2018).

[6] ibid.

[7] ibid.

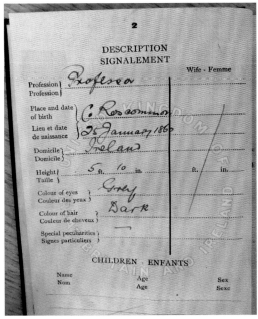

Image 2: Douglas Hyde's passport from Douglas Sealy's personal collection
(description).

From Galway to Co. Roscommon our journey took us to the homestead of Kevin Flynn.[8] Like Michael Carty, Flynn was also a native of Tibohine. With a keen interest in the preservation of history, he acquired the site of the old Ratra house in Tibohine, Co. Roscommon, where Douglas Hyde used to live with his family. In order to preserve and honour the life and work of Hyde, he painstakingly rebuilt the house using photos and recollections from locals who worked there in order to try and replicate the original abode. Kevin also has a personal collection of books and documents connected with Douglas Hyde. Hyde was a man who enjoyed documenting life and keeping notes. He was an adolescent of just fourteen years when he embarked upon his diary writing and continued this throughout and beyond his formative years,

[8] 'Douglas Hyde's home being rebuilt', *The Irish Times,* 18 August 2006. https://www.irishtimes.com/news/douglas-hyde-s-home-being-rebuilt-1.1039635 [last accessed 4 June 2020]: 'A modern version of Rathra House, the former home of Ireland's first president, Dr Douglas Hyde, which was demolished many years ago, is under construction on the site of the original near Ballaghaderreen, Co. Roscommon.'

completing his final diary volume in 1912. These diaries provide access to Hyde's inner thoughts and ideas which can be seen through his own pen in the thirteen volumes which are housed in the National Library of Ireland (MSS G 1036–48).[9] Using the personal collections of Douglas Sealy and Kevin Flynn, this paper will illustrate the artistic traits of the Hyde family and examine the creative talents that Douglas and Lucy bestowed on their two daughters, Nuala and Úna. The following material, meticulously preserved by Sealy and Flynn, will be central to the analysis:

- *My holiday record* owned by Lucy Hyde (1890), from the personal collection of Kevin Flynn
- Sketchbook owned by Úna Hyde (1914), from the personal collection of Douglas Sealy
- *Book of limericks* created by Úna and Nuala Hyde (1910–16), from the personal collection of Douglas Sealy
- Sketchbook owned by Úna Hyde (1916), from the personal collection of Douglas Sealy.

Nuala Hyde

Nuala Eibhlín Hyde, Douglas Hyde's elder daughter, was born in Ratra House, Co. Roscommon, on 26 August 1894. Nuala's birth is documented in Hyde's diary (1893–4)[10] in August that year, where he explains that the doctor who lived in Castlerea had to be reached by horse in the middle of the night. Castlerea was sixteen kilometres away and by the time the doctor arrived at Ratra House, Douglas comments that Lucy was in considerable pain, 'Bhí an creutúir bocht ag fulaing péine',[11] but gave birth to a strong, healthy girl the following evening. He further goes on to describe her baptism on 20 September 1894 and

---

[9] See National Library of Ireland (NLI) MS G 1040; cf. Dominic Daly, *The young Douglas Hyde*, 57. Hyde maintained a diary in Irish from 1874, when he was just fourteen, until 1912. This is in thirteen volumes, which are held in the National Library of Ireland as NLI MSS G 1036–48. They have been digitised and may be consulted online. For discussion of entries in the early diaries, see Máire Nic an Bhaird and Liam Mac Mathúna, 'Douglas Hyde (1860–1949): the adolescent behind the diarist', in *Literacy, language and reading in nineteenth-century Ireland*, eds. Rebecca Anne Barr, Sarah-Anne Buckley and Muireann O'Cinneide (Liverpool 2019) 28–50, and Máire Nic an Bhaird and Liam Mac Mathúna, 'Early diary insights into Roscommon's impact on Douglas Hyde, Ireland's first president', in *Roscommon: History and society*, eds. Richie Farrell, Kieron O'Conor and Matthew Potter (Dublin 2018) 515–37.

[10] See NLI MS G 1044, image 50.

[11] ibid.

writes in large letters 'DO BAISTEADH AN LEANBH NUALA EIBHLÍN' ('The child Nuala Eibhlín was baptised').[12] Hyde adopts the usage of large letters for important milestones, e.g. his wedding day and his daughter's baptism, 'LÁ MO PHÓSTA' ('My wedding day').[13] They celebrated the baptism in style with 'cúpla buideul mór seampéin' ('a couple of big bottles of champagne')[14] and time was also made for one of Hyde's favourite pastimes, fishing, where they caught six or seven young pike and one was three pounds: 'Fuaramar 6 no 7 de ghiosógaibh beaga, agus bhí ceann aca 3 púnta'.[15]

Tragically, Nuala died as a young woman of 22 years on 30 September 1916 after contracting tuberculosis and it was only fitting that she would be buried in the graveyard where her grandfather was once rector, Tibohine graveyard, Co. Roscommon. 'TB has always been associated with a high mortality rate over the centuries....'[16] Many members of the Hyde family have been buried in this graveyard – Douglas Hyde himself, Lucy Cometina Hyde, Elizabeth Hyde, Reverend Arthur Hyde, Nuala Eibhlín Hyde, John Cambreth Kane and Anne Hyde. The following is written on Nuala's grave:

Hic Jacet
Nuala Eibhlín Hyde
Filia Dilectissima
An Chraoibhín Aoibhinn.
Quae Viginti Duos Annos Nata,
Valde Defleta.
Trigesimo Die Septembris 1916.
Decessit.
Ameasg na
n-Aingeal.

'Here Lies / Nuala Eibhlín Hyde / the most beloved daughter / of An Craoibhín Aoibhinn. / Who was twenty-two years old. / Deeply regretted / Died On the thirtieth day of September 1916. / Amongst the Angels.'

---

[12] ibid. image 52.
[13] ibid. image 25.
[14] ibid.
[15] ibid.
[16] I. Barberis, N. L. Bragazzi, L. Galluzzo and M. Martini, 'The history of tuberculosis; from the first historical records to the isolation of Koch's bacillus', *Journal of Preventative Medicine and Hygiene* 58:1 (March 2017) 9–12, https://www.ncbi.nlm.nih.gov/pmc/articles/PMC5432783/ [last accessed 3 May 2020]).

Newspapers nationwide reported on the death of Nuala. The following was recounted in *The Dublin Daily Express*: 'Miss Eileen N. Hyde. The death is announced of Miss Eileen Nuala Hyde at Ratra House, Frenchpark, at the early age of 22 years. Miss Hyde was the eldest daughter of Dr. Douglas Hyde.'[17] The Gaelic League stated: 'On the motion of Mr. R. Foley, seconded by the Rev. P. O' Modhrain, the Coiste Gnotha of the Gaelic League passed a resolution deeply regretting the early death of Dr Douglas Hyde's daughter, Eileen Nuala. Revs. B. Crenan and M. Brennan were asked to represent the Coiste at the funeral.'[18]

The day after his beloved daughter died Hyde contacted a close friend, Mrs Jane Coffey née L'Estrange. She was born in 1857. Her father, Sir George Burdett L'Estrange (1796–1878), was a member of the British army, but when the family fortunes declined, he resigned from the British Army and became a land agent before working at Dublin Castle. George Coffey married Jane L'Estrange and their home at 5 Harcourt Terrace became a meeting place for the forerunners of the Celtic revival movement. Mr and Mrs Coffey were also members of the National Literary Society. Jane Coffey was one of the members of this committee which first met on 16 January 1899. Douglas Hyde had forged long-lasting ties with George Coffey when he was a student in Trinity College.[19] and it was fitting that their son Diarmid Coffey (1888–1964)[20] wrote the first biography on Douglas Hyde.[21]

News of the untimely death of Nuala is conveyed here in a handwritten letter in English from Douglas Hyde to Mrs Coffey:

> Ratra
> Frenchpark
> Oct 1 1916
> My dear Mrs Coffey
> You will be sorry to hear that dear Nuala died yesterday. Heart failure was the immediate cause, but it was brought on by the difficulty in breathing. She had two dreadful days fighting for breath but the end came quite peacefully. She was wonderfully brave and patient. Poor Lucy is quite broken down. She died just

---

[17] *Dublin Daily Express,* 2 October 1916, 3.

[18] *The Irish Independent,* 6 October 1916, 3.

[19] Dunleavy and Dunleavy, *Douglas Hyde: a maker of modern Ireland,* 108, 118.

[20] For biographical information on Diarmid Coffey, see https://www.ainm.ie/Bio.aspx?ID=415 [last accessed 10 January 2022].

[21] Diarmid O Cobhthaigh, *Douglas Hyde: An Craoibhin Aoibhinn* (Dublin 1917); second edition, Diarmid Coffey, *Douglas Hyde, President of Ireland* (Dublin 1938).

25 days from the time she got haemorrhage.

Hoping that you & Dermot are keeping well and with kindest regards from us all.

Yours very sincerely

Douglas Hyde[22]

It was no secret that Nuala had weak lungs. This was mentioned in Frances Georgiana Chenevix Trench's diary (published in Hillary Pyle's edition, *Cesca's diary 1913–1916*) when Hyde and Úna visited Cesca Trench on Saturday, 24 October 1914: 'Nuala is very fat just now after stuffing for a bad lung, and anyway she's not as interesting as Úna. Dr. Hyde was rather annoyed with me for Mór[23] not being there, as he wanted to compare her and Nuala.'[24] Unfortunately when Nuala died there was no real treatment for tuberculosis: 'It was not until 1944 that effective medicines were discovered (streptomycin and para-aminosalicylic acid).'[25] Douglas Sealy wrote the foreword to *Cesca's diary 1913–1916* and comments on Nuala's tuberculosis: 'The name Cesca meant nothing to me until I discovered that I had long known about her under the name of Sadhbh Trínseach, the artist who had supplied the frontispiece for Diarmid Cobhthaigh's book about Douglas Hyde, my grandfather, and who had also made a drawing of my mother's sister Nuala. Nuala had died not long afterwards, of TB, though that was never mentioned. Two years later Sadhbh herself was dead having succumbed to the Spanish flu.'[26] Cesca drew a portrait of Úna and Nuala during her stay with the Hydes mid-August 1916, shortly before Nuala's death. Douglas Sealy states that TB was never mentioned as the cause of Nuala's death. There was a certain stigma around tuberculosis during this period. In Ireland the tuberculosis death rate was still increasing in 1900. Tuberculosis sufferers and their families often felt stigmatised and many people chose to be discreet about the disease. In time this silence became common practice. The public felt that tuberculosis was associated with destitution and that it was also hereditary, which meant that entire families often entered into a collusion of silence. People were frightened of tuberculosis and they were also scared of how society

---

[22] See Death of Nuala: Coffey & Chenevix Trench Papers, NLI MS 46,302/3.

[23] 'Mór' was a nickname for her sister Margot, or Máighréad, who also had a bad lung, cf. Hilary Pyle, *Cesca's diary 1913–1916* (Dublin 2005) 168.

[24] ibid.

[25] M. D. Iseman, 'Tuberculosis therapy: past, present and future', *European Respiratory Journal* 20, Issue 36 (2002) 87–94, https://erj.ersjournals.com/content/20/36_suppl/87S [last accessed 3 April 2020].

[26] Pyle, *Cesca's diary 1913–1916*, xv.

would react if they knew tuberculosis was in the family. 'In 1912 Dr Woodcock of the National Association for the Prevention of Tuberculosis wrote "Tubercle is in truth a coarse common disease, bred in foul breath, in dirt, in squalor.... The beautiful and rich receive it from the unbeautiful poor ... tubercle attacks failures." This statement is from an educated doctor working in the field of tuberculosis which helps explain why a stigma was developed towards tuberculosis sufferers and their families.'[27]

The following is a description of Nuala's death by the Dunleavys: 'On September 5 Nuala Hyde suffered a hemorrhage. The diagnosis was tuberculosis; the prognosis was poor; the progress of the disease was rapid and devastating. Lucy and Hyde watched helplessly as day after day their once vivacious and beautiful daughter fought for breath. For Hyde all the horror of his boyhood when he had watched for months the suffering of his brother Arthur returned. Mercifully, Nuala's struggle was not so long. By September 30 – at the age of twenty-two – she was dead. In notes to friends Hyde spoke understandingly of Lucy's great sorrow. What he did not speak of was his own. Poised, articulate and gregarious, Nuala had been the daughter most like himself.'[28]

Douglas Hyde was stoic in his sorrow; to witness your daughter die from tuberculosis would have been an horrific ordeal and Nuala would have suffered greatly too: 'Pulmonary haemorrhage, besides being sometimes dangerous, and occasionally fatal, is always a terror to the patient.'[29] In a letter of October 1916 Douglas Hyde thanked Augusta Gregory for her note on the death of his daughter Nuala, described her death and funeral, and concluded, 'What a dreadful year this has been both public and private. Ireland seems in a hopeless muddle. So does everything, the Gaelic League included.'[30]

Úna Hyde

Úna was born on 19 June 1896 in Dublin, in Stillorgan in the Oldfields'[31] house as they had gone to England. This is documented in Hyde's diary

---

[27] Susan Kelly, 'Stigma and silence: oral histories of tuberculosis', *Oral History* 39, No. 1 (Spring 2011) 65–76.

[28] Dunleavy and Dunleavy, *Douglas Hyde: a maker of modern Ireland*, 346–7.

[29] Norman Bridge, 'Dangerous pulmonary haemorrhage in tuberculosis and its management', *Journal of the American Medical Association* 34, no.10 (10 March 1900) 579.

[30] Hyde to Gregory, 9 October 1916. NYPL, quoted in Gareth W. Dunleavy, 'The pattern of three threads: the Hyde-Gregory friendship', in *Lady Gregory, fifty years after*, eds. Ann Saddlemyer and Colin Smythe (Gerrards Cross, Bucks. 1987) 142, 413 n. 50.

[31] His maternal grandmother and unmarried aunts, Maria and Cecily, moved to Dublin after the death of Douglas Hyde's maternal grandfather, Dunleavy and Dunleavy, *Douglas Hyde: a maker of modern Ireland*, 20.

of the time (1896–1900).[32] Hyde stated that Lucy was in pain, but only suffered for about ten hours and their daughter Úna was born at 8.14 p.m. on 19 June 1896. He also documents that he went to Blackrock and to Dún Laoghaire too. He swam that morning, and he was sick then that afternoon.[33] On 20 June 1896 he notes that Lucy was doing well after giving birth the day before, but that he was not. He had a sore tooth and his tongue was swollen.[34] Úna was baptised 'Máire Úna' on 17 August 1896. Douglas's sister Annette joined them and they had champagne. He notes that it was a wet day.[35] Hyde also summarised the most important events of each year in his diaries; for 1896 he stated that the year left them pretty unscathed apart from the death of his brother John Oldfield Hyde who died in a private hospital in Dublin on 10 February after an illness of two or three months. He finished off the summary by saying that Lucy gave him another child, Máire Úna, on 19 June 1896 in Tigh Lorcáin, Stillorgan, Dublin.[36]

Úna is referred to as a 'charming person' in *Cesca's diary 1913–1916*, 3 February 1915: 'That evening Siobhán and Úna Hyde, a charming person of 18, came to sup with me and Miss West. We went to the Gaelic Service.'[37] The foreword to *Cesca's diary 1913–1916* written by Douglas Sealy states 'His daughter Úna, my mother, was 7 years younger than Sadhbh, but both came from families with a strong clerical background, both were talented artistically, and could speak Irish…. Úna was educated in Alexandra College, studied art at Miss Marsh's studio, went on a sketching trip to Brittany, illustrated (with K. Verschoyle) an Irish translation by Pádraic Ó Cadhla of *Alice in Wonderland* in 1923, and a book of Irish folktales … with her habitual reserve, which she inherited along with her artistic talent from Lucy'.[38] Both daughters were very creative. Nuala inherited her father's love of words and witty sense of humour and Úna inherited her mother's gift of art. Úna was not buried in the Tibohine cemetery like her sister and parents; she was buried beside her husband, Judge James Sealy in Saint Patrick's Churchyard Enniskerry, Co Wicklow.

Lucy Cometina Kurtz
Hyde's wife, Lucy Cometina Kurtz, an English woman with a German family background, was born on 30 June 1861, and was baptised in

---

[32] NLI MS G 1045, image 14.
[33] ibid. image 16.
[34] ibid.
[35] ibid. image 21.
[36] ibid. image 33.
[37] Pyle, *Cesca's diary 1913–1916*, 187.
[38] ibid. xvi.

Liverpool on 4 September 1861. She lived with her family in Orrell, near Liverpool. Her father Charles was a manufacturing chemist and her mother's name was Lucy Charlotte.[39] She married Douglas Hyde on 10 October 1893 in West Derby in St Nicholas Church in the Parish of Blundellsands.[40] On the marriage certificate Douglas Hyde's name is in Irish. From his diary account of his wedding day, we learn that he did this in order to 'get his own back' on the priest, as the priest didn't omit parts of the service as requested by Hyde.

LÁ MO PHÓSTA.

Tar éis ceudphroinn leis na Caröes, tháinig faoi 11 carráiste le mo ghlacadh-sa chum an teampoill i n-éinfheacht le Mrs Green, deirsiúr mná shean-Caröe bean an dheas. Cuadhmar le chéile agus d'imthigh an an [sic] carráiste ar ais i g-coinne Lúsia. Winslow an t-ainm do bhí ar an sagart. Phós sé sin[n] as láimh gan aon phonc de'n tseirbhís d'fhágbháil amach cidh gur iarr mé air é, acht bhain mise mo shásadh as nuair sgríobh mé m'ainm i nGaedheilg san registar [sic][41]

'MY WEDDING DAY.

After breakfast with the Caroes a carriage arrived by eleven to take me to the church with Mrs Green, a sister-in-law of old Caroe and a very nice woman. We went together and the carriage returned for Lucy. The priest's name was Winslow. He married us straight out of the book, without omitting any part of the service, although I asked him to. However, I got my own back on him when I signed my name in Irish in the register.'[42]

Lucy died on 31 December 1938 from pneumonia and then cardiac failure in Ratra house with Peter Morrisroe, Hyde's chauffeur and labourer by her side.[43] The following is written on her grave:

---

[39] Lucy Cometina Kurtz, Register of births: General Register Office UK, Year 1861, Quarter S, Vol. 08B, p. 375, West Derby and Toxteth Park.

[40] Lucy Cometina Kurtz and Douglas Hyde, marriage certificate: General Register Office UK, Year 1893, Quarter D, Vol. 08B, p. 489.

[41] NLI MS G 1044, image 25.

[42] Cf. Daly, The young Douglas Hyde, 165.

[43] Lucy Cometina Kurtz's death certificate, General Register Office Ireland, Irish Deaths 1864–1954. Details: Lucy Cometina Hyde Jan.–March 1939, Castlerea, Vol. 4, p. 85.

Hic Jacet
Lucy Cometina Hyde
Alias Kurtz
Uxor Dilectissima
An Chraoibhin Aoibhinn
Quae Prope Novem et
Septuaginta Annos Nata
Apud Ratra In Domo Sua
Ultima Die Anni 1938 Quievit

Here lies / Lucy Cometina Hyde / Alias Kurtz / The most beloved Wife / of an Craoibhín Aoibhinn / Who was almost 79 years old / At Ratra in her Home / On the last Day of the Year 1938.

As was noted in the papers at that time, Hyde did not attend the funeral of his wife, as the doctor had told him to stay at home due to illness. He abided by this advice and the private funeral was attended by his daughter Úna, her husband Judge Sealy, his sister Annette, Aide-de-camp to the President, Captain Éamon de Buitléar and other relatives. 'After a simple ceremony by the Rev. Canon Furlong, Mrs Lucy Cometina Hyde, wife of the President, was laid to rest to-day shortly after midday in Porthard Churchyard. The following were present. – The President's daughter, Mrs Sealy, and her husband Judge Sealy, Mrs Cambreth Kane sister of the President, and other relatives of the family. Captain E. Butler, Aide-de-Camp to the President, was also present. Acting on doctor's orders, the President, who has been confined to the house for the past few days with a chill, remained at home.'[44]

My holiday record
Kevin Flynn allowed us to examine an artist's travel record in his possession that Lucy kept in 1890. On the front page the following is written: 'Lucy Kurtz = Mrs Douglas Hyde. Married 1893. From the auction of Hyde effects and library at Ratra Park, Co. Roscommon 1949.' There was indeed an auction held to sell off Hyde's effects and library, but it was held in Little Ratra, in Phoenix Park 1949.[45] The front

---

[44] *The Irish Times*, 7 January 1939.

[45] The front cover of the auction catalogue reads as follows 'Catalogue of the library of Dr. Douglas Hyde (Decd.) for auction at "Ratra", Phoenix Park, Dublin, on 10th October, 1949, and following days, commencing each day at 11 a.m.', https://www.lotsearch. de/auction-catalogues/14-december-2010-rare-book-sale-109891?orderBy=lot-title&order =ASC&perPage=80&page=6 [last accessed 4 April 2020].

*Image 3: My holiday record in pen or pencil from the personal collection
of Kevin Flynn.*

page is titled 'My holiday record in pen or pencil' and Lucy has signed
her name L. C. Kurtz, Liverpool. The book was printed in London by
John F. Shaw & Co. 48 Paternoster Row. The following is written at the
start of the book: 'From Cousin Andrew January 1890'.

Lucy not only drew sketches in this travel record but she also kept a
brief diary account on the final page, where she writes as follows about
what she did on her holidays in the South of France from 10 January
1890–15 January 1890:

> Arrived at Cannes – Thursday January 10 in afternoon. Very fine.
> Splendid view of Esterel mountain on entering. Came to Hotel de
> la Grande Bretaigne very comfortable but people very unsociable.
> Friday walked from Cannet to Cannes – Town awfully smelly from
> drainage and very deserted. Very picturesque from the beach but

the odours too much for me. Saturday Took a donkey to Telegraph Hill. Fine birds' eye view of Cannes Grasse and Nice in far distance. Sunday – 13th Monday went to see Mrs Bernard Hall at Villa Mariposa. Very beautiful garden and view of Esterel mountains. Heliotrope, roses, narcissus, carnation and others all in full bloom. Had oranges from the trees. White sand. Tuesday 14th. Went by bus to Cannes. Took steamer to Isle of St Margaret. Met the Rev. and Mrs – very pleasant time spent.[46]

Villa Mariposa was situated in Rue Albert 1er[47] in Cannes. It is possible that Mrs Bernard Hall was a relative of Sir Douglas Bernard Hall who was one of ten children of Bernard Hall, a merchant, local politician and philanthropist, who was elected Mayor of Liverpool in 1879. His sister was Margaret Bernadine Hall (1863–1910) who was born in 1863 in Wavertree, Liverpool. She was an English painter who spent most of her career in Paris. She would have been of similar age to Lucy with parallel backgrounds and interests. Few of her works have survived, but she is notable for her 1886 painting *Fantine*, which hangs in the Walker Art Gallery, Liverpool, England. Telegraph Hill may be the name Lucy used for Le Suquet, in Cannes, which gives panoramic views of Cannes, Grasse and Nice are also visible from the top of the hill.

The *Travel record* shows Lucy's keen interest in art. She used either a charcoal wash or an ink wash to create her images. This method of capturing memories is not a common practice nowadays due to the popularity of smartphones and cameras. Lucy mindfully sketched glimpses of these special moments for herself as keepsakes as the camera wasn't sought after until 1900. She has recorded three images via sketches whilst on her holidays in the South of France in this travel record book. One has the title 'Morgen-Cannes' and is a landscape of Cannes, the second is a picture called 'Cathedral from the Hotel', where the Cathedral and the hills of Esterel are in the background. We know Lucy was staying in Le Cannet and consequently the Cathedral she sketched looks very similar to Eglise Sainte-Catherine. This church is situated on Rue Sainte-Catherine in Le Cannet and Lucy's sketches show us that the exterior of the church has not changed since her drawings in 1890. The third is a landscape of Cannes called 'Cannes from the Isle of St Marguerite'. This is a picture she drew when she was on 'Ile Sainte-

---

[46] Lucy's artist's travel record is part of Kevin Flynn's personal collection.
[47] Picture of Villa Mariposa from World War II, http://expos-historiques.cannes.com/a/3109/photographie-de-la-villa-mariposa-occupee-quartier-californie-rue-albert-1er-s-d-10fi945-/ [last accessed 4 April 2020].

Marguerite'. This island is situated about one kilometre out from the beaches of Cannes. She sketched Cannes in the background.

The first page of the travel record is also decorated with a well-dressed woman under an umbrella with her easel, drawing a country landscape of bridge and water. The presence of the small bird perched on the tree is reminiscent of an oriental scene. On the next page there is a space under the words 'Left home' where Lucy has written 'January 8. 90.' She didn't fill in the space below 'Returned home'. The third page has a poem by Mrs Barbauld:

> Sweet daughter of a rough stormy sire,
> Hoar Winter's blooming child, delightful Spring.[48]

This is decorated again by a bird and a tree. The imagery is reminiscent of spring, and the lyrics of the poem *An ode to spring* (1773) by Mrs Barbauld cleverly accompany the drawings. Anna Laetitia Barbauld (20 June 1743–9 March 1825) was a prominent English poet,[49] who had a successful writing career at a time when women rarely had the opportunity to write professionally. The decorative scheme and visual artistry along with the inclusion of Barbauld's work, indicates John F. Shaw & Co.'s willingness to celebrate the work of female artists of the time.

Lucy Hyde's sketchbook, Dresden 1893

The National Library of Ireland's collection houses a sketchbook created by Lucy Hyde from her time spent in Dresden, Germany in 1883.[50] Inscribed in pencil on front endpaper is Lucy Cometina Kurtz, Sidonien Strasse 13, Germany, April 1883. What is interesting to note is that Bertha Schrader (1845–1920), painter and graphic artist, lived in no. 14 Sidonien Strasse, Dresden. Schrader was born on 11 June 1845 in Memel, Lithuania. She studied with Carl Graeb's son Paul Greab (1842–92) in Berlin, and with Paul Baum (1854–1932) in Dresden. From 1882 to 1916 Schrader was a member of the Association of Berlin Artists where she exhibited her paintings. She was also a member of the Dresden Women Artists Association, serving as the chairwoman. She exhibited her work at the Woman's Building at the 1893 World's

---

[48] Robert Chambers, *Cyclopaedia of English literature: a selection of the choicest productions of English authors, from the earliest to the present time, connected by a critical and biographical history* (Boston 1853).

[49] Natasha L. Richter, 'Female writers in the 18th century: the power of imagination', *Inquiries Journal* 2, no. 10 (2010) 1.

[50] NLI PD 2024 TX.

Columbian Exposition in Chicago, Illinois. Schrader was well connected and may have introduced Lucy to others in artistic circles in Dresden at the time. Women were not allowed to study art in the University of Fine Arts Dresden until 1919 and it was 1907 before women could study art at the Royal Academy of Applied Arts in Dresden. However, it was not uncommon that ladies would take private art lessons from professors at the Dresden Academy. If Lucy did this there is no account of them in the University of Fine Art's files.

There are a total of nineteen drawings in this album, comprising pencil pictures of horses, dogs and bulls, as well as a view of Dresden. These sketches illustrate Lucy's skilful talent of line drawing. Reflecting the baroque style, a horse looks lifelike and strong. There is evidence of foreshortening and accurate observation skills. Lucy may have refined these skills under the guidance of an art teacher. Her impressive ability to attend to composition, depth, perspective, tone and shade would suggest she underwent some element of artistic training. Lucy's work gives the impression of studied attention and time taken in the execution of same.

Douglas Hyde's sketches in NLI

Douglas Hyde himself was also fond of sketching during his formative years. In many respects, the diaries that Hyde kept can be perceived as a social commentary, as they give us a fascinating picture of life in rural Ireland and in Roscommon in particular in the latter part of the nineteenth century. Nowadays, it may be disconcerting to observe a young teenager of fourteen years of age openly drinking and smoking tobacco, behaviour however that would not raise concern in 1870s Ireland. In fact, there are many references to alcohol throughout his 1874–6 diary.[51] Tobacco and whiskey were favourites of Hyde and his family, as is seen in his frequent entries related to them, e.g 'Pretty fine day. Connolly went to Boyle, and bought a canister of powder and brought a hamper with "an gallane d'isquebauch", potted ham, Worcester sauce, pickles etc. a heavy mist in the evening, went to Ratra and shot a fine rabbit with No 2 or 1 shot' (17 April 1874).[52] There are sketches of drinks, which he drew himself, dispersed through his first diary that he started in 1874.[53] At times Hyde illustrated his diaries, thus adding for a reader, and perhaps for himself, a greater sense of clarity to his commentary. For example, he uses sketches in this diary to describe

[51] NLI MS G 1036.
[52] ibid. 8.
[53] NLI MS G 1036.

how to set up a game of backgammon. There is a picture of the lamp, a candle and the game itself with instructions scattered across the diagram: 'How to set up backgammon Diagram.' 'Play towards the light, light on the left side.' Hyde has drawn two men and glasses on the table – one man is smoking tobacco and the other swigging from the top of a bottle. He would have seen his father play backgammon at home and clearly had a fondness for the game, thus spending time explaining how to set it up. Backgammon has often been called the aristocrat of popular games and it was considered a proper game for English gentlemen. This game therefore highlights the juxtaposition of the dual persona Hyde adopted during his adolescence. In Britain in the eighteenth century, backgammon was popular among the English clergy.[54] *A short treatise on the game of back-gammon* was published by Edmund Hoyle in 1743, in which the rules for the games were explained. Perhaps Hyde's father had this book in his collection?[55]

A sketchpad from a sixteen-year-old Douglas Hyde is available for consultation in the National Library of Ireland and is undated. However amongst the sketches is a drawing of three people fighting with sticks, which is dated 9 March 1876.[56] This involves two men on a bridge, hitting a third man, who is about to fall into the water. The paper label on the inside front cover states 'The Cambridge sugar paper sketch books A', Madderton & Co Ltd Loughton, Essex, London. There are five drawings in this sketchbook and they feature trees, a lake, a country landscape with mountains in the background and figures fighting with sticks on a bridge. They are charcoal and pencil and the pages measure 32.2 x 26.2 cm.

Hyde is also practising his cursive script on the top of the page with the alphabet. Shade has been created by the dark lines he uses under the bridge and the vanishing point helps the viewer focus on the action in the middle of the picture. As is documented in his 1874 diary on 28 March, boxing stoked the interest of the young Hyde, 'Had a fight with the gloves with Michael Lavin'.[57] This interest was further displayed in his own sketch of two boxers, as seen in the NLI collection.[58] Hyde's

[54] H. J. R. Murray, '6: Race-Games' in *A history of board-games other than chess* (London 1952).

[55] Sheila Allee, 'A foregone conclusion: fore-edge books are unique additions to ransom collection', https://web.archive.org/web/20060621093338/http://www.utexas.edu/support ut/news_pub/yg_foreedge.html [last accessed via The University of Texas at Austin on 1 March 2020].

[56] NLI PD 2185 TX.

[57] NLI MS G 1036, 3.

[58] NLI PD 2185 TX.

drawings are not as fluent or accomplished as Lucy's. What Hyde does show however through drawing, is his sense of humour, a personality trait evident in the limericks by Nuala and in the accompanying illustrations by Úna. Hyde's creativity is often imbued with a sense of mischievousness and irreverence, characteristic of the man himself.

Hyde recognised the artistic talents of his daughter Úna and he also understood the importance of how art could enhance folklore and storytelling. Úna was the artist who worked with Hyde on his books of folktales, *Sgeuluidhe fíor na seachtmhaine* (1935), producing beautiful drawings to help illustrate the narrative for the reader.

Úna Hyde's sketchbook 1914

The Douglas Sealy private collection also has a sketchbook from Úna which is undated, but has a drawing of Rathfarnham Castle and Park dated 23 June 1914. Rathfarnham Castle is a sixteenth-century fortified house in Rathfarnham, Dublin. Daytrips to Rathfarnham Castle would have been feasible, since Úna was then living only five kilometres away with her parents in 1 Earlsfort Place as Douglas Hyde was Professor of Irish in University College Dublin, which was then located in Earlsfort Terrace in Dublin city centre. The word 'private' is written on the canvas cover and Úna has drawn a mixture of portraits and landscapes. They are predominantly based in Dublin, with Rathfarnham Park featuring heavily. She has drawn landscapes, ducks, cows, sheep and cats. There is only one landscape which is made up of pencil and watercolour, all other sketches are black and white. There is one drawing titled Loch Gara where two people are fishing from a boat, a pastime which Douglas Hyde loved.

There is also a drawing titled Malahide and Lambay Island, where boats are seen on the water and Lambay Island is in the distance. Lambay Island lies in the Irish Sea, four kilometres off the coast of north Co. Dublin in Ireland.

There are also sketches of Douglas Hyde and Lord Ashbourne in this sketchbook. William Gibson held the title of Lord Ashbourne (16 December 1868–21 January 1942).[59] He was a keen Irish cultural revivalist, a member of the Gaelic League, whose cultural and religious views had caused him to be largely disinherited by his father. Ashbourne's death prompted messages of condolences for his French wife from the likes of Douglas Hyde and Eamon de Valera as well as a eulogy in the *Catholic Herald*, which told its readers that

[59] Cf. Timothy G. McMahon, 'All creeds and all classes? Just who made up the Gaelic League?', *Éire-Ireland* 37, no. 3–4 (2002) 118–68.

Ashbourne 'always wore the kilted Irish dress and was a picturesque figure. His green kilt, green stockings and belt with massive silver buckle always created unusual interest. Before the last war Lord Ashbourne created a mild sensation by appearing in the House of Lords in kilts and speaking in Gaelic'.[60] This style of clothing is evident in the sketches. These sketches seem to have been drawn by Miss L. Williams. Dublin born, Lily Williams (1874–1940) was first taught by May Manning and later went on to study at the Dublin Metropolitan School of Art. Well known for her Republican sympathies she fell out with her Protestant, Unionist family at the time of the Easter Rising 1916. Her portrait of Arthur Griffith is in the Hugh Lane Gallery collection. Additionally, she is well-known for her Irish stamp designs, having designed the Irish Free State's Cross of Cong stamp in 1922, a design which was used until 1968. She exhibited with the Royal Hibernian Academy annually from 1904–39 and became an associate of the RHA in 1929. On one sheet we have Lord Ashbourne sitting down and we see his side profile, Douglas Hyde's bust has also been sketched and he is wearing a cap. The following words are written in pencil beside the sketches. 'By Miss L. Williams Lord Ashbourne and Croahbin [sic]' On the following page we have a sketch of Lord Ashbourne seated at a table, having tea, with his full body on view. There is another of his side profile and finally a picture of An Craoibhín that has been scribbled out.

Úna Hyde's sketchbook 1916
When examining Douglas Sealy's personal collection, Liam Mac Mathúna and I found a sketchbook kept by Úna Hyde in 1916. These sketches further highlight Úna's creative ability, akin to that of her mother. 'Úna M. Hyde 1916 Oct' is written inside the front cover of the sketchbook. Úna began using this sketchbook shortly after the death of her beloved sister Nuala on 30 September 1916.

There is a special joy that comes from looking through an artist's sketchbook. Perhaps it is the sense of exclusive access that one gets into the inner workings of their mind and creative process, so often unseen by the public. Or is it because the pages are a physical extension of the artist themselves? Did Úna's artwork help her find some sort of solace after her sister's untimely death? Úna's sister had died just over two weeks before she began drawing in this sketchbook. There is a certain freedom for artists when using a sketchbook because the artist is not under pressure to produce a finished piece. Sketchbooks can be intimate as they are a private tool used to manifest one's thoughts and ideas in

[60] 'Lord Ashbourne: prominent figure in Gaelic League', *Catholic Herald,* 30 Jan. 1942, 7.

Image 4: Úna's sketchpad 1916 from the Douglas Sealy personal collection.

graphic form. The artist is able to self-reflect, and sketchbooks are a way to express this reflection. One could say that Úna's sketchbook feels as personal as a journal, due to the fact that it draws from her personal life, her family and her home. Artists of all genres express their emotions through their work. A sketchbook therefore can help a person experiencing loss on the journey through the grieving process. Art aids in processing grief and can sometimes help to identify or acknowledge feelings one is unable to express verbally. A sketchbook is a vehicle for an artist to authentically engage in this process, as an artist knows they will most likely not be hung in a gallery open to critique from the masses.

There are 27 sketches in this sketchbook – 26 are pencil on paper and one is watercolour. The majority are bust portraits; however, Úna has one still life and two sketches of her father's beloved cockatoo, Polly. Polly was a cherished pet in the Hyde household. When Douglas Hyde was in America fundraising for the Gaelic League and giving a lecture series across the United States in 1905–6 he sent postcards home to his children.[61] He collected more than £12,000 during his mission to

---

[61] These postcards are housed in the Aidan Heavey Collection in the Aidan Heavey Public Library, Athlone, Co. Westmeath, Ireland.

America.[62] The postcards are a striking visual representation of America at the time, but the words written by Hyde on them really evoke the father that he was. He says to Úna in February 1906 when he sent her a postcard from Minneapolis, Minnesota: 'Chuir mé cárda go Nuala cúpla lá ó shoin. Seo cárda agat-sa anois! Tá mé ann so indiú. Tá súil agam go bhfuil sibh go maith. Tabhair póg do Polly uaim. An Craoibhín. Feb 2, 06.' ('I sent Nuala a card a few days ago. Here's a card for you now. I am here today. I hope you're well. Give Polly a kiss from me. An Craoibhín. Feb 2, 06'). What is interesting to note is that he never signs off 'Dad' or 'Pa', he always uses 'An Craoibhín' to his children.

The sketches of busts are female and portray a sense of melancholy. The first sketch is dated 9 October, which was a little over a week since her sister's death. A lady is gazing into the distance and there is a sombre sadness in the pencil strokes. Bar two sketches, the watercolour and the sketch of three children in what seems to be a classroom setting – one reading, one leaving out the door and the other girl getting down her coat, these have an ease about them – all other sketches in this book have a sombre, unnerving quality. There is a hardness to the lines and the sketches are predominantly short quick snapshots of life – reminiscent of Nuala's short life. There appears to be a sketch of Lucy Kurtz; although untitled, the features of Lucy are to be seen. The lines in lips, eyes and the nose bear a resemblance to Lucy and this lady has a melancholic demeanour, which would be similar to Lucy's emotions during this time after the death of her beloved Nuala. The contrast between these sketches and the light-heartedness of Úna's drawing for the *Book of limericks* is immense. There is also a page with a sketch for a crib and details about the dimensions. Crib opening 13" high, 16" wide. Side wings 14" wide, 27" high.

A book of limericks

Hyde's cheeky nature, comedic quality and jovial wit were undoubtedly passed on to the next generation of Hydes. Thanks to the generosity of Mary Sealy, we saw evidence of this in Douglas Sealy's personal collection. In '*A book of limericks* written by Nuala Hyde and illustrated by Úna Hyde', created between 1910–16, the same dark mischievous humour peeps out. We see evidence of intergenerational continuity in creative flair. In this regard, we might well conclude that the apple doesn't fall far from the tree. Douglas Hyde's daughters, Nuala and Úna

---

[62] See Liam Mac Mathúna, Brian Ó Conchubhair, Niall Comer, Cuan Ó Seireadáin and Máire Nic an Bhaird (eds), *Douglas Hyde: my American journey* (Dublin 2019). The Foreword is written by President Michael D. Higgins.

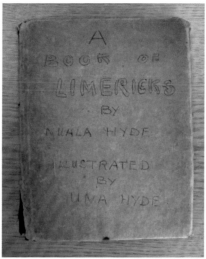

*Image 5: A book of limericks by Nuala Hyde and illustrated by Úna Hyde
(ca 1910–1916) from the Douglas Sealy personal collection.*

Hyde together created *A book of limericks*. This is a hard-backed book
covered in brown paper; the limericks are written by Nuala Hyde and
they are illustrated by her sister Úna. Hyde's daughters produced this
book when they were living in Dublin and it is placed sometime between
1910 and September 1916. Nuala would have been between 16–22 years
of age and Úna between 14–20 years of age.

The girls show understanding of using pun as a nonsense device and
the capability of treating language as a plaything that can be a source of
intellectual satisfaction. Hyde was working as Professor of Modern Irish
in University College Dublin, which was situated in Earlsfort Terrace at
the time. The following is written inside the brown cover of this book:
'Miss Una Hyde, 1 Earlsfort Terrace, Dublin.'

The limerick as a kind of verse appeared in England in the early years
of the eighteenth century.[63] Edward Lear (1812–88) was an English
artist, illustrator, musician, author and poet, now known mostly for his
limericks, a form he popularised. As an author, he is known principally
for his popular nonsense collections of poems. The first edition of these
was published by Thomas McLean on 10 February 1846. There were
altogether 72 limericks in two volumes. It was the convention at the time

[63] John Rieder, 'Edward Lear's limericks: the function of children's nonsense
poetry', *Children's literature* 26.1 (1998) 47–60.

for children's books to be published anonymously, so there was no mention of Lear's name in the book.[64] It eventually appeared in the third edition, published by Routledge, Warne & Routledge in 1861. This contained 112 limericks. Edward Lear wrote many iconic limericks. Among the most famous of these is the opening poem from *A book of nonsense*:

> There was an Old Man with a beard,
> Who said, 'It is just as I feared!
> Two Owls and a Hen,
> Four Larks and a Wren,
> Have all built their nests in my beard!'[65]

Here are two further examples of Lear's limericks:

> There was an Old Man with a nose,
> Who said, 'If you choose to suppose
> That my nose is too long, you are certainly wrong!'
> That remarkable Man with a nose.

> There was a Young Lady whose chin
> Resembled the point of a pin;
> So she had it made sharp, and purchased a harp,
> And played several tunes with her chin.

His drawings to accompany the limericks and 'nonsense poems' he wrote are definitely of a kind with Úna's, a sort of gauche but nonetheless capable and really charming line-drawing. The book by the Hyde sisters is called *A book of limericks*, a name reminiscent of Lear's title, *A book of nonsense*. It is full of nonsense and fun, not unlike Lear's work. It would make sense along a cultural timeline with the Hyde family that Lear could have been a potential influence and that they were exposed to his poetry and illustrations. The accompanying words tally with Lear's style as well. They are that 'ridiculous for the sake of being ridiculous' kind of humour which is so appealing to children to hear and for adults to compose. His work, mirrored by Úna and Nuala, is funny and strange and can fluctuate between harsh and cruel, or tender and poignant.

The limericks created by Nuala and Úna are dark and funny and show that the girls, like their father, had a very good sense of humour. An

[64] Matthew Potter, *The curious story of the limerick* (Limerick 2019).
[65] Edward Lear, *A book of nonsense* (Boston 1894).

upbeat, amusing postcard the sisters received from their father during his tour of America in 1905–6 reflected the ticklish Hyde sense of humour, also seen in their limericks. It was sent from 'An Craoibhín' to Nuala de h-Íde after he visited the Cawston Ostrich Farm in South Pasadena, California on 12 March 1906. The postcard was written the following day and shows a man on an ostrich with the following caption 'At the Cawston Ostrich Farm, South Pasadena, Cal.', and Hyde writes to the girls 'Nach deas an capall é seo! Chonnaic mé féin é! Tá mam go maith agus mé féin, buidheachas le Dia. Tá súil agam go bhfuil sibh-se go maith. An Craoibhín' ('Isn't this a fine horse! I saw it myself! Mum and I are well, thanks be to God. I hope you are well. An Craoibhín'). Cawston's ostrich farms supplied ostrich plumes to the public and they were also a tourist friendly business which made Cawston a considerable amount of money. Hyde visited the Cawston Ostrich Farm during his Californian tour in March 1906. He also sent a postcard to Úna from the Cawston farm dated March 13. 06. 'Cawston Ostrich Farm, South Pasadena, Cal. Bhí muid ann so indé, ag breathnughadh ar na h-éanacha[ibh] seo. Nach deas iad! Beannacht leat. An Craoibhín.' ('… We were here yesterday, looking at these birds. Aren't they nice! Blessings be with you. An Craoibhín'). He delivered a lecture in Los Angeles on 12 March and in St Vincent's College on 13 March 1906.

This collection of limericks is extensive and the girls produced thirty in all. Knowing Hyde's humour that he shared with his daughters, his postcards being an example of such mischief, one can understand how the Hyde sisters were inspired to do similar. The majority of the limericks focus on one male protagonist in a rural setting; there are six limericks featuring a female character and all limericks are based in Ireland except for one which is located in London and Dover. Nuala does feature one animal protagonist, which is typical of the children's literary realm, showcasing characters in nonsensical situations. There are three limericks situated in Dublin – in the areas of Dundrum, Foxrock and in the River Liffey, cf.

> There was a young man of Dundrum
> Who said to the people 'Just come
> And watch me perform!
> I'll raise such a storm
> As was never yet felt in Dundrum!'

Lough Glynn and Lough Gara are both place-names mentioned, which the girls would have known well from their childhood in Co.

Roscommon. Douglas Hyde rowed, sailed, went fishing and swam in Lough Gara.[66] Ratra House was situated exactly halfway between Lough Glynn and Lough Gara. These limericks are fine examples of the semantic level of language being used for humorous purposes. Twelve of the limericks are formed by two stanzas and the eighteen others stand alone with one stanza each.

Nuala has chosen to adopt the standard form of a limerick and created a stanza of five lines, with the first, second and fifth rhyming with one another. In lines one, two and five ca eight syllables were used. The third and fourth lines are shorter and also rhyme with each other, but have fewer syllables. The first lines of Nuala's limericks often adhere to tradition and introduce a person and a place, with the place appearing at the end of the first line and establishing the rhyming scheme for the second and fifth lines.

The limerick 'There was an old man of West Cork', created by Nuala and illustrated by Úna, is extended into two stanzas of five lines, and there is a lightness evident. A rural setting is portrayed and a slightly absurd scenario between a man and a dove is depicted through Nuala's humorous lines. Nuala and Úna would have been accustomed to imagery of this kind, having spent many years living the country life in Ratra House, Tibohine, Co. Roscommon. Nuala's personification of animals is antithetical to Lear's zoomorphic human beings, characteristic of his numerous picture-limericks. Likewise, the animals in Nuala's limericks are amiable and harmless, whereas Lear's creatures are often aggressive towards people.[67]

> There was an old man of West Cork
> Coming back from the field with his fork
> When he saw in the sky
> A dove flying by,
> The finest yet seen in West Cork.
>
> Then cried the old man to the Dove
> 'Come home, for I've nothing to love!'
> Said the Dove, 'if I do,
> I'll be made into stew
> And that is the thing that you love.'

---

[66] Dunleavy and Dunleavy, *Douglas Hyde: a maker of modern Ireland*, 26.

[67] Maria Tarnogórska, '"Funny" and "curious" verse: the limerick in Polish children's literature', *Bookbird: A Journal of International Children's Literature* 53.3 (2015) 37–45.

The pictures drawn by Úna are painted in a strong wash of primary colours – predominantly red and blue. 'The man of West Cork' has a frivolity and humour about him and is rotund, portraying a fondness for food. The first, second and fifth lines are rhyming with one another, and we can see that the first line adheres to tradition and introduces a person and a place, with the place appearing at the end of the first line and establishing the rhyming scheme for the second and fifth lines.

Another limerick called 'There was a man of Castlerea' shows the girls' affinity for their home county:

> There was a man of Castlerea
> Whose tennis made a fine display
> He jumped and ran
> – Oh bless the man! –
> And thought of nothing else all day.

Castelrea is ca sixteen kilometres from Tibohine and the girls depict a man playing tennis, a game which Douglas Hyde thoroughly enjoyed, having built a tennis court in his Ratra home in Co. Roscommon. Tennis is also mentioned in Hyde's diaries. When he returned from his academic teaching post in New Brunswick, Canada in the summer of 1891, he spent much of July 1891 playing tennis. There are references to tennis in Ratra, Frenchpark House and a tennis tournament in Boyle, Co Roscommon, cf.

> July 13th … bhí cluithche tennis le Seán agam.[68]
> July 14th Páirti tennis ag Dungar. Chuadhmar agus d'imir sinn a lán.… La an teith
> July 15th Lá an teith. … Tennis agus dinnéar ag Rátrá.
> July 16th Thiomáin me Annette go Mainistir go tournaméad tennis do bhí ann. Ann sin go dtí a 8.30. Abhaile faoi 'n 11.'
> July 21st Chuadhmar go Manastar go gcríochnóchainn an tennis. … Bhí droch-páirtnéar agam, Mrs Marsh éigin agus bualadh mé.[69]

> July 13th 'I had a game of tennis with Seán.'
> July 14th 'Tennis party at Frenchpark. We went and played a lot. A very hot day.'
> July 15th 'A very hot day. Tennis and dinner at Ratra'

[68] It is interesting to note that Hyde uses the word 'tennis', as 'leadóg' was not used until ca 1936 in the Irish language. It is noted to have been used in Achtanna Oireachtais in 1936 (Mac Mathúna 2020).

[69] NLI MS G 1043, 46–7.

> July 16th 'I drove Annette to Boyle to a tennis tournament. There
>   until 8.30. Home by 11.'
> July 21st 'We went to Boyle so we could finish the tennis. I had
>   a bad partner. Some Mrs Marsh and we were beaten.'

Therefore, both Nuala and Úna, in witnessing their father playing tennis,
and listening to dialogue around the game of tennis in their household
over the years, were inspired to feature the sport in one of their witty
limericks.

Another limerick reflecting their lived experiences is 'There was a
young man of Ratra', which also demonstrates the joyful collaboration
of Nuala's words and Úna's images. There are elements of this cartoon
and limerick that definitely speak to a specifically Irish audience. The
agricultural references are not metropolitan-life-focused as one might
experience with London contemporaries. There is a spirit of fun in this
limerick and in the accompanying pictures reminiscent of Julian Tuwim
(1894–1953), a Polish poet, who initiated nonsense poetry for children
in Poland. His poems (such as 'Słoń Trąbalski', 'O panu Tralalińskim',
and 'Lokomotywa') broke away from nineteenth-century didacticism
and brought into children's literature the spirit of pure fun, which
expanded boundaries of the material world and language.[70] This limerick
consists of two stanzas. The imagery produced by Úna for stanza one is
jovial. She illustrates a country scene and uses earthy colours – greens
and browns, to depict the man who is digging the pit in his work clothes
– boots, a shirt and braces. The facial expression is one of menacing
happiness and there is an ominous feeling lurking behind the man's
smile. In stanza two, Úna uses elegant colours in the man's suit. He is
well-dressed with a blue suit and handkerchief in the suit pocket. The
man is depicted jumping up in a happy, nearly absurd way, celebrating
his mother's fall from life into the pit. The imagery is ridiculous, yet
amusing to the reader, as the joy of the man is in contrast with the wide-
eyed bewilderment of his mother in the pit. It is interesting to note that
Hyde's own relationship with his mother, Elizabeth (Bessie) Oldfield,
was challenging, as he documents her bouts of illness in his 1874–6
diary;[71] cf. '… Bessie Hyde's long, debilitating illness, later diagnosed
as asthma continued. Day after day she stayed in bed or dragged herself
around…'.[72] Lucy Hyde was perhaps not as jovial as the girls' father,

---

[70] Maria Tarnogórska, '"Funny" and "curious" verse: the limerick in Polish children's
literature'.
[71] NLI MS G 1034.
[72] Dunleavy and Dunleavy, *Douglas Hyde: a maker of modern Ireland*, 75.

Douglas, which is evident in the sombre postcards that she sent to the girls when in America (1905–6). For example, she sent a postcard to Úna just after the San Francisco earthquake of 18 April 1906. Devastating fires broke out and lasted several days. 3,000 people died and 80% of the city was destroyed. Lucy's message to Úna on her postcard dated 26 April 1906 must have been hard for her to read and then share with her sister Nuala: 'The great recent earthquake and fire swallowed up these idols. We just escaped in time. You never would have seen us again if we had remained on. Everything was burnt up our grand hotel and all Chinese Town all burnt and lots of Chinese too. Save all post-cards all very valuable now. April 26.06, N. York, L.C.H.'[73] Therefore, one wonders if the contrasting personalities and maternal relationships of the Hyde family, had an influence on limericks such as 'There was a young man of Ratra':

There was a young man of Ratra
Who hated his odious Mamma:
So he digged a deep pit
Which he covered with grit,
To get rid of his odious Mamma.

Then did the young man of Ratra
Get rid of his odious Mamma,
For she walked o'er the grit
And fell into the pit –
The young man then shouted 'Hurreh!'

Úna's imagery for the limerick 'There was an old man of Tralee' shows an overweight bald man with a whip, wearing a pin-striped blue and white suit, alluding to the power 'the old man of Tralee' wields over the bee. The man is depicted as a businessman, which correlates with the local history of the time, as Tralee was a bustling market town in the early 1900s. The bee is colourful with yellow and black stripes; however, he seems to be struggling to fly with the weight of the man and the man's use of his whip is ominous. The second image nods towards Zoosadism where the man seems to be gaining pleasure from killing the bee. There is a subtle, joyful smile creeping across his face and this is certainly a nod towards the obscenity associated with limericks. Again, we see Nuala has played with two stanzas and that the main protagonist is male.

---

[73] See Hyde's postcard collection housed in the Aidan Heavey Collection, Athlone, Co. Westmeath, Ireland.

Gershon Legman, the American limericks expert, believed that the true limerick as a folk form is always offensive. From a folkloric point of view, the form is essentially transgressive, involving a violation of moral or social boundaries which is seen in the final stanza of 'There was an old man of Tralee' – violation of taboo is part of its function:

> There was an old man of Tralee
> Who rode on a very large bee;
> But the man was so fat,
> That he squashed the bee flat,
> Which annoyed that old man of Tralee.

> 'Now' said the old man of Tralee
> 'How shall I get rid of this bee?'
> Then he went for his knife
> And ended its life,
> Which pleased the old man of Tralee.

It is wonderful to delve into the lived experiences and the artistic life of a family across two generations, each member having a particular area of interest, but in no way considering art, poetry or storytelling to be the exclusive realm of one individual. These limericks created by Nuala and Úna are a superb example of collaboration amongst siblings, in order to create a unique book which with some minor edits and censoring[74] would be a fantastic publication for children today.

Conclusion
Douglas Hyde and Lucy Hyde were both creative individuals. They had a flair for the arts – Douglas for the written and spoken word and Lucy for the visual arts. Their two children also possessed their creative abilities, Úna being an artist like her mother, and Nuala relishing the written word like her father. Douglas Hyde possessed a determination and self-belief, personal characteristics needed to enact an artistic life. Douglas Hyde and Lucy Hyde found the time to pursue their creative pursuits, a luxury which their circumstances in life afforded them. To be creative professionally takes luck and circumstance. To be creative in life, requires you to make it a priority. The girls and their parents associated with many talented, intelligent people, who shared their

---

[74] Cf. Máire Nic an Bhaird, *Cleachtadh na cinsireachta, próiseas na heagarthóireachta agus lucht léitheoireachta na Gaeilge ó 1922–1972*, PhD thesis (University College Dublin 2012).

propensities and skills, and their creativity was nurtured – 'Children are like tiny flowers; they are varied and need care, but each is beautiful alone and glorious when seen in the community of peers'.[75] There is a hereditary and environmental nature of creativity. Creativity like tiny flowers, needs the correct environment to thrive and flourish.[76] The creative style of Douglas and Lucy has been seen in their children, grandchildren and in their great-grandchildren. The following was written about Hyde's great-granddaughter, the artist Una Sealy, at her fourth solo exhibition in 2000: 'The fourth solo exhibition of work by Una Sealy opened this week at the Ashford Gallery in the Royal Hibernian Academy in Ely Place. Úna Sealy is the great granddaughter of Douglas Hyde, whose wife, Lucy Cometina Kurtz and daughter Una Hyde were both "keen amateur painters. That would have influenced me."'[77] This paper explores aspects of two generations of the Hyde family, with a particular focus on the connection of Douglas and Lucy Hyde with their daughters Nuala and Úna. It affords the opportunity for the reader to realise the impact creativity, the arts specifically, had on the Hyde children. Judging by the legacy Douglas and Lucy left, clearly the apple is still falling.

MÁIRE NIC AN BHAIRD

---

[75] Bruce Watson, *Words of Friedrich Fröbel* (1997) http://www.froebelweb.org/fblquote. html [accessed 11 January 2022].
[76] Maria Konnikova, 'What makes a family of artists', *The New Yorker*, 15 August 2014. https://www.newyorker.com/science/maria-konnikova/makes-family-artists [last accessed 10 June 2020].
[77] Catherine Foley, '"Paint all over"', *The Irish Times*, 8 July 2000, https://www.irishtimes.com/news/paint-all-over-1.290808 [last accessed 3 April 2020].

PRESIDENT HYDE, PROFESSOR POKORNY AND IRISH REACTIONS TO THE HOLOCAUST

The Holocaust is a huge stain on European history.... It showed us the horrific story that unfolds when genocide is unleashed, and allowed to become state policy and the consequences of such a silence as becomes complicity. It also shows us the dangers of looking the other way, of denial or of simply 'not wanting to know'. – President Michael D. Higgins, 29 January 2012.[1]

When the ninth President of Ireland made the above remarks on the first occasion he officially attended the National Holocaust Memorial Day Commemoration, many Irish people may not have been aware that President Higgins's initial predecessor, President Douglas Hyde, stands accused of 'looking the other way', despite appeals for assistance from a close friend, Professor Julius Pokorny, whose life was put in extreme peril by the Nazi Holocaust.

This article examines whether the response in Áras an Uachtaráin to the treatment by the Nazi regime of Professor Pokorny was ungenerous and primarily motivated by a desire not to do anything that would give rise to controversy or cause the Germans offence. In a broader context, this article also examines Douglas Hyde's attitude towards the Jewish faith and explores wider Irish reactions to the Holocaust.

Pokorny was ultimately assisted in his plight by the intervention of the then Taoiseach, Eamon de Valera. Keogh has argued that Pokorny's case is illustrative of 'the willingness of de Valera's government to help scholars who found themselves the victims of Hitler's racial laws', but the case of Pokorny is also of note because it shows an extremely rigid and unfeeling adherence to neutrality in the Áras, which, in this instance, at least, was far more inflexible than the attitude of the head of government.[2]

Julius Pokorny was born on 12 June 1887 in Prague, but he was brought up in Austria. He was appointed 'Lektor' in Irish in Vienna University in 1912 and became 'Dozent' in Celtic philology in 1914.[3]

---

[1] Remarks by President Michael D. Higgins at the National Holocaust Memorial Day Commemoration, 29 January 2012; available at http://www.president.ie/speeches/holocaust-memorial-day-commemoration/ [accessed 16 June 2019].

[2] Dermot Keogh, *Jews in twentieth-century Ireland: refugees, anti-Semitism and the Holocaust* (Cork 1998) 103.

[3] Aideen Breen, 'Pokorny, Julius', in *Dictionary of Irish biography: from the earliest times to the year 2002*, vol. 8, ed. James McGuire and James Quinn (Cambridge 2009) 197.

Pokorny was a leading academic authority on Old Irish and he developed political sympathies with the Gaelic League and Irish nationalism. He had first visited Ireland in 1908 and had befriended Douglas Hyde.[4] In that same year and again in 1910, he taught courses in the School of Irish Studies in Dublin, where he 'acquired the nickname "Póigín" 'Little Kiss' from his fondness for the affection of young ladies'.[5] Pokorny had supported moves towards Irish self-determination and in 1916, at the time of the Easter Rising, he published *Irland*, a German language history of Ireland. In 1920, following on from the death of Kuno Meyer, Pokorny succeeded to the chair of Celtic at the University of Berlin. During Ireland's War of Independence, Pokorny played a valuable role in Irish publicity efforts in Germany and edited *The Bulletin*, a pro-Irish independence newsletter, which was distributed to Berlin newspapers, the German provincial press and other key influencers. George Gavan Duffy who, along with Sean T. O'Kelly, was coordinating the Irish campaign to counter British propaganda in continental Europe about events in Ireland described Pokorny as 'one of the best and keenest friends' of Ireland. Pokorny was subsequently a translator of Patrick Pearse's work and he was name-checked in James Joyce's *Ulysses*.[6] On 23 October 1925 Pokorny received an honorary doctorate from the National University of Ireland for 'distinguished services in the field of Celtic research' with his citation being read by Dr Douglas Hyde in his capacity as Dean of the Faculty of Celtic Studies.[7] According to Pokorny's biographer, Ó Dochartaigh, from 1920 until 1935, he was 'arguably the most important figure in Celtic Studies on the European mainland, as well as a propagandist on Ireland's behalf'.[8]

Though Pokorny was a Roman Catholic and 'a German Nationalist who had little difficulty with Nazism',[9] Pokorny's difficulties began in

---

[4] Pól Ó Dochartaigh, 'Professor Pokorny of Vienna: Austrian Catholic, German nationalist, Celtic Professor and Jew', *History Ireland*, issue 1 (Spring 2000), vol. 8.

[5] Breen, 'Pokorny, Julius', 197.

[6] The relevant paragraph in *Ulysses* reads: 'Eternal punishment, Haines said, nodding curtly. I see. I tackled him this morning on belief. There was something on his mind, I saw. It's rather interesting because Professor Pokorny of Vienna makes an interesting point out of that.' Mervyn O'Driscoll, *Ireland, Germany and the Nazis: politics and diplomacy, 1919–1939* (Dublin 2004) 23; Brian P. Murphy, *John Chartres: mystery man of the treaty* (Cambridge 1995) 35–9; Ó Dochartaigh, 'Professor Pokorny of Vienna'; Breen, 'Pokorny, Julius', 198, James Joyce, *Ulysses* (Dublin 1922) 234.

[7] *Irish Times*, 24 October 1925.

[8] Pól Ó Dochartaigh, *Julius Pokorny 1887–1970: Germans, Celts and nationalism* (Dublin 2004) 15.

[9] Ó Dochartaigh, 'Professor Pokorny of Vienna'.

1933 within months of Adolf Hitler becoming Chancellor. In a letter to Douglas Hyde, on 5 May 1933, Pokorny wrote:

> You know I have always been a good German patriot, from my Christian parents and educated in a Benedictine convent. This Easter I got a form from the Government, asked to give particulars about my grandparents. To my astonishment my father informed me, that my mother's father had not been 'Aryan'. He had died long before I was born and I had never known it. According to a new law, everybody, one grandparent of whom is a Jew, is looked upon as Jew and to be dismissed from his office, except if he has fought in the war or been in office before August 1914. Though a lecturer since April 1914, I have been suspended from office.[10]

Pokorny continued by informing Hyde:

> Mr MacCanley [official in the Irish legation in Berlin] has written to Dublin, full particulars, in order to bring about a diplomatic intervention on my behalf, pointing out, that my person was an important link between Ireland and Germany. I have given your name as a reference. Perhaps you could help me with the Foreign Office. But please remember that any anti-German propaganda may ruin me. When writing to me, please do so through the Irish legation in Berlin.[11]

On the same date, Pokorny wrote in almost identical terms to Richard Best, the Director of the National Library of Ireland.[12] Pokorny was clearly living in fear. It is unclear what steps Hyde or Best took – if any – but, by December 1933, Pokorny had been restored to his position. De Valera had made informal representations in August 1933, via the Irish legation in Berlin, to have Pokorny reinstated. In a subsequent letter to Best, Pokorny attributed his job being saved to 'the intervention of the Irish Government'.[13] This was however to be a short return to office for Pokorny.

Despite the precarious nature of his own position in 1933, Pokorny had shown immense moral courage in speaking out against the imprisonment of a Jewish colleague from the University of Berlin, Ernst

---

[10] National Library of Ireland (NLI), Letters to Douglas Hyde, letter from Pokorny to Hyde, 5 May 1933, MS 17,996.
[11] ibid.
[12] Keogh, *Jews in twentieth-century Ireland*, 103.
[13] O'Driscoll, *Ireland, Germany and the Nazis*, 100; Keogh, *Jews in twentieth-century Ireland*, 103.

Lewy, a Professor of Comparative Linguistics. Though this brought unwanted Nazi attention on Pokorny and he became the target of police investigations, he continued to support Lewy publicly and helped to secure his release in early 1935.[14] Following the adoption of the Nuremberg Laws in September 1935, Pokorny was once again suspended from the University of Berlin, in November, before being formally removed from his position that December.

Following his dismissal from his academic post, Pokorny chose to remain in Berlin and lobby the Nazi authorities for his reinstatement. Lewy, upon his release, had chosen a different course. He had quickly left Germany for England and, in 1937, he settled in Ireland.[15] In 1938, de Valera sought Lewy's assistance in the establishment of an Institute of Celtic Studies in Dublin and the Taoiseach personally intervened to ensure that Lewy's daughter was granted a visa for admission to Ireland.[16] It is likely that Lewy also availed of his relationship with de Valera to offer assistance to Pokorny. In May 1938, de Valera made efforts through the Department of External Affairs to have Pokorny reinstated to his post in Berlin.[17]

Pokorny may also have been heartened at this time by the fact that his friend of thirty years was about to become President of Ireland. Though he was neither the first choice of Fianna Fáil or Fine Gael, on 21 April 1938, after a meeting of plenipotentiaries from both parties, Douglas Hyde, the founder of the Gaelic League and a retired Professor of Irish at UCD, emerged as an agreed candidate for the presidency. He was formally elected on 4 May 1938. On 15 June, ten days before his inauguration, Hyde wrote to Pokorny from his Roscommon home pledging his support. Hyde wrote:

> I am very sorry to hear so bad an account about you, and you may be certain that I shall do all I can to get the matter remedied. But I am not president yet, and shall not be, until I take the oath, at the close of the month, and then I must wait until 'I find myself', like

---

[14] ibid.; Breen, 'Pokorny, Julius', 197. Cf. Ó Dochartaigh, 'Professor Pokorny of Vienna'.

[15] Gisela Holfter, Siobhan O'Connor and Birte Schulz, 'Resources relating to German speaking refugees in Ireland, 1933–1945 – some initial thoughts and results', in Andrea Hamill and Anthony Greenville (eds), *Refugee archives: theory and practice* (Amsterdam 2007) 43.

[16] Keogh, *Jews in twentieth-century Ireland*, 127.

[17] This May 1938 intervention by de Valera was a further attempt on the Taoiseach's behalf to have Pokorny restored to his post. In November 1935, following Pokorny's suspension de Valera had also instructed the Irish legation in Berlin 'to make unofficial representations' to the German Foreign Office in Pokorny's favour. O'Driscoll, *Ireland, Germany and the Nazis*, 176; Ó Dochartaigh, *Julius Pokorny 1887–1970*, 113.

Kipling's ship, for I shall be new to everything, but I expect I shall
be seeing the foreign minister [de Valera, the Taoiseach and
Minister for External Affairs] soon, and then will be my time.[18]

Pokorny's biographer has observed of this letter that 'whether Hyde did
indeed speak to de Valera on this matter is not recorded. There is no
written documentation relating to the twelve months after Hyde sent this
letter to Pokorny'.[19] In fact, a confidential file maintained by Michael
McDunphy, the Secretary to the office of President, sheds far more light
on Hyde's dealings with Pokorny and shows that, in office, Hyde
gradually distanced himself from Pokorny's plight.[20]

Prior to the outbreak of war in 1939, Hyde did make some efforts to
assist Pokorny, but subsequently he ignored Pokorny's increasingly
desperate pleas for assistance. At the same time, the available evidence
shows that de Valera, who did not share the same personal bonds with
Pokorny, was much more flexible in his approach and that the
Taoiseach's assistance ultimately saved Pokorny's life and secured his
escape from Germany in 1943.

On 24 June 1938, the day prior to Hyde's inauguration, Pokorny
wrote to Hyde from Berlin detailing the deteriorating anti-Semitic
situation in Germany. In this letter, which McDunphy put on file in Áras
an Uachtaráin, Pokorny noted:

[My] prospects here become worse and worse. It is proposed to
confiscate 'Non-Aryan' property and to force 'Non-Aryans' to live
only in Jewish houses. This would mean everybody would know
one's descent at once. So far I have had in spite of everything a
comparatively easy life, since nobody suspects my descent I can
move socially wherever I like. Fact is, I have very little 'Jewish
blood' in me, but according to the law I am reckoned as a Jew….
In the last year, I have come by inheritance into some money, so I
could live quite comfortably together with my pension – but the
new measures threaten confiscation of my property since I am
looked upon by law as a Jew.[21]

In a direct plea to Hyde to intervene on his behalf, Pokorny also
intuitively recognised the Nazi sympathies of Charles Bewley, the Irish
Minister in Berlin. Pokorny wrote:

[18] ibid.117.
[19] ibid.
[20] National Archives of Ireland (NAI) 2002/7/4.
[21] NAI, 2002/7/4, letter from Pokorny to Hyde, 24 June 1938.

If there would be a way in which the German Government could be induced to let me live in peace and to treat me as an ordinary Christian and German, I could go on working and should be quite satisfied.... Foreign opinion is the only thing that matters to them, and since I am politically beyond reproach, it is only my grandparents that stand against me. I am quite sure, you could help me, if some personal action from your side could be added to those of President [sic] de Valera. If you would allow me a suggestion, it is my opinion that Mr Bewley is not enough personally interested in my fate and that any action through the Berlin ambassador alone would be perhaps too colourless and impersonal.[22]

There is no record of Hyde replying to this letter, however, in September 1938, in a letter to John Glyn Davies, the retired head of the Department of Celtic Studies at the University of Liverpool, President Hyde alluded to a rather tepid appeal he had made on Pokorny's behalf. On 16 September 1938, Hyde wrote:

Many thanks for your kind letter about Pokorny. I am very sorry for him. I took occasion when the German Ambassador called on me the other day to mention his name as if accidentally, and to say that we appreciated his work here in Ireland.[23]

Davies's original letter to Hyde, on 11 September, had recognised, given the treatment of the Jews in Germany, that Pokorny's life was in danger. Davies wanted to create a refuge for Pokorny under the auspices of the University of Liverpool, as a lecturer of Irish, and asked for Hyde's help in getting the Irish Government to support this initiative. Davies wrote:

I can see that he stays in Germany at his peril, and my feeling that something should be done for him in Great Britain prompted me to ask him to let me suggest one scheme to you. Eighteen months ago I discussed with the late Professor Garmon Jones the possibility of getting Pokorny to Liverpool. Garmon Jones, one of the shrewdest men in the University thought my plan feasible, if it was backed by the Government of the Free State. I have set forth my views in the enclosed statement.[24]

---

[22] ibid.
[23] NAI, 2002/7/4, letter from Hyde to Davies, 16 September 1938.
[24] NAI, 2002/7/4, letter from Davies to Hyde, 11 September 1938.

Hyde's reply to this proposal was stunning in its insensitivity and does his reputation little credit. Oblivious to or ignoring the threat that Pokorny's continued stay in Nazi Germany posed to his safety, Hyde's reply was rooted in academic politics, it was dismissive of Pokorny's abilities as an Irish teacher (even to the extent of suggesting another individual for the post) and it crucially gave no undertaking to attempt to source funding from the Irish Government. Hyde wrote:

> All the same, do you think he would be a man who would bring in students to Manchester or Liverpool? I don't think he could enthuse the Irishmen, and I am afraid they want to be enthused. If Father Kelleher could attract 50 or 60 students, I do not think Pokorny could do the same. I really don't know what to say for I don't know anyone now in Liverpool or Manchester, and have no knowledge of where to go to look for money. Of course, I understand the Government in Germany never took Pokorny's salary from him. I think he branched off into a number of un-Celtic avenues which would hardly arouse enthusiasm.[25]

Later, in the same month in which Hyde and Davies had corresponded, Pokorny briefly visited Dublin. On 21 September 1938, he was received by President Hyde at Áras an Uachtaráin. Pokorny's focus was still on remaining in Germany and being restored to his position in the University of Berlin. Pokorny presented President Hyde with a personal memorandum which suggested that

> perhaps a personal, non-official intervention, such as a letter from An t-Uachtarán or An Taoiseach to the Secretary of Foreign Affairs in Dublin would be of immense value. I would add that I have proved to the German Government that I had myself been an active fighter for their present nationalistic principles since 1916, being particularly active in fighting the Czechs in Sudetenland. All I want is to be left in peace in order to be able to continue my research work into the Celtic Past, which of course is very difficult under the present circumstances, not having any citizen's rights whatever. I can do so only if I get exempt from all repressive measures against the Jews, to whose community I do not belong, myself and my parents being Catholics.[26]

---

[25] NAI, 2002/7/4, letter from Hyde to Davies, 16 September 1938.
[26] NAI, 2002/7/4, Pokorny memo, 21 September 1938.

McDunphy's note of this meeting was curt and hardly sympathetic. He recorded:

> The President saw Prof. Pokorny today. The latter was anxious that the President should assist him in some way, either to get him restored to his former post of Professor in the Berlin Unvy. [*sic*] from which he had been removed on the grounds that he was of Jewish ancestry, and/or to get restored to him his property in Germany of which he had been dispossessed for the same reason. The President told him that he could not interfere in this matter affecting the internal administration of another country.[27]

Hyde had moved quite a distance from his promise to Pokorny, made shortly prior to his inauguration as President, that he would 'do all I can'. Whether Hyde felt constrained by his office or whether McDunphy was exerting influence on him is debatable, but, with the President a political greenhorn, the Secretary to the office of President was very much the power behind the throne in the Áras. Hyde's lack of knowledge of his role is clear from an account that McDunphy has given of one of his first meetings with the President. McDunphy recalled:

> Scarcely were we seated than he asked me what were his powers as President of Ireland. It was not a question to be answered briefly, amid the din of a public restaurant and to a man who had no previous interest or experience in politics but I did my best to the detriment of the meal. I told him that apart from ceremonial duties involving no authority the powers and duties conferred on him by the Constitution were to be exercised by him on the advice of the Government, although there were a limited few which he could exercise in his absolute discretion, and I told him what they were.[28]

Hyde heavily relied upon his Secretary, a talented and experienced civil servant, who had previously served as an Assistant Secretary in the Department of the Taoiseach. McDunphy had played a key part in the drafting of Bunreacht na hÉireann and he took a very conservative view of the President's role. McDunphy believed that one of his own main functions was to build a sense of dignity around the new constitutional office and, even more importantly, to keep it removed from controversy.[29]

[27] NAI, 2002/7/4, McDunphy memo, 21 September 1938.
[28] Janet Dunleavy and Garret Dunleavy, *Douglas Hyde: a maker of modern Ireland* (California 1991) 395.
[29] NAI, PRES 1/P350, undated McDunphy memo.

McDunphy appears to have enjoyed very good relations with the German Legation. He was a keen hiker and he had regularly holidaycd in Germany, Austria and Switzerland since the 1920s. As a result, he spoke very competent German.[30] From the mid-1930s, McDunphy was a regular guest at social events hosted by the German Legation.[31] Shortly after the announcement that McDunphy had been appointed Secretary to the office of President, he attended a German Christmas celebration at the Gresham Hotel in December 1937. The *Irish Times* printed a list of those present, naming McDunphy, who was the most senior Irish civil servant at the function, and reported that those in attendance were asked

> to rise and salute the Leader and Chancellor of the Reich. With right arms raised in the Nazi salute, the gathering sang Deutschland uber alles [the German national anthem], the Horst Wessel Lied [the official marching song of the Nazi Party] and the Soldier's Song [the Irish national anthem].[32]

In fairness to McDunphy, it should be pointed out that this should not be taken as an indication that he had any sympathy for the Nazi regime and, in a long career, he served the Irish State with ability and integrity. Hyde and Eduard Hempel, the head of the German Legation in Dublin, were also personally friendly. Both the President and the German Minister shared an interest in literature, regularly exchanged books and Hempel wrote of 'the unfailing friendly kindliness' Hyde always displayed towards him.[33]

Irrespective of the harmonious relations between the Phoenix Park and Northumberland Road (the site of the German Legation), there may have been a feeling in the office of President that with the clouds of war hovering – and Irish neutrality well flagged in advance of the hostilities commencing – that nothing should be done by the Head of State that could put him at odds with any foreign government. Certainly, McDunphy's attitude to Pokorny's difficulties was defined not by any trace of empathy, but rather by a strict sense of protocol and bureaucratic propriety. This was very evident in April 1939 when Liam Gógan wrote to the Secretary to the office of President, presumably with a view to

---

[30] 'Experience and Qualifications of Michael McDunphy', copy of document in the author's possession.

[31] *Irish Independent*, 8 October 1934; *Irish Independent*, 2 May 1935; *Irish Independent*, 7 February 1936; *Irish Independent*, 21 May 1937.

[32] *Irish Times,* 20 December 1937; Gerry Mullins, *Dublin Nazi no.1: the life of Adolf Mahr* (Dublin 2007) 64–6.

[33] NAI, PRES 1/P519, undated letter from Hempel to Hyde.

McDunphy briefing the President on the up-to-date position with
Pokorny.

Gógan, like Pokorny, was a scholar of Old Irish and he was the
Keeper of the Art and Industrial Division in the National Museum.[34]
In his letter, on 1 April, Gógan explained that a friend of Pokorny's
had visited Dublin to obtain letters from other scholars requesting a
re-consideration of Pokorny's case.[35] Gógan said that these letters
would form the basis for an 'approach through a Reichminister not
unfavourable to such cases' and that, in this instance, it had been decided
that letters from the President and Taoiseach were 'not actually
requisite'.[36] Gógan's letter did not request anything from Hyde bar
discretion. Gógan wrote that Pokorny 'regards it of great importance
that neither the German Ministry here nor the Nazi group should know
anything about these démarches'.[37] This particular request seemed to
draw McDunphy's hostility and he annotated beside it, on 4 April 1939,
that 'Mr Gógan apparently suggests that the President should be
associated with activities in regard to a German citizen, of which the
accredited representative of the German Govt. in Ireland would not be
prepared to approve'.[38] This comment was clearly a reference to a phone
call McDunphy had received from Gógan, on 3 April, following up on
his earlier letter. In this conversation, Gógan asked McDunphy to ensure
that Hyde received a Mr Lisner, an Attaché of the German Foreign
Office in Berlin, who Gógan must have believed was well disposed
towards helping Pokorny.[39] A memo McDunphy wrote on 4 April 1939
regarding the requested Lisner meeting said:

> The object of the suggested interview was that the President should
> make some representations or take some other action which would
> move the German Government to reinstate Prof. Pokorny in his
> former post, or restore him to his property.[40]

Despite the previous warning that nothing about Pokorny should be
disclosed to the German Legation in Dublin, McDunphy's memo of 4

---

[34] Eoghan Ó Raghallaigh and Lesa Ní Mhunghaile, 'Gógan, Liam Seosamh', in
Dictionary of Irish biography: from the earliest times to the year 2002, vol. 4, ed. James
McGuire and James Quinn (Cambridge 2009) 122–3.
[35] NAI, 2002/7/4, letter from Gógan to McDunphy, 1 April 1939.
[36] ibid.
[37] ibid.
[38] NAI, 2002/7/4.
[39] NAI, 2002/7/4, McDunphy memo, 4 April 1939.
[40] ibid.

April indicates that this was exactly what he did. This memo also seems to underline that in this matter at least, McDunphy leaned more favourably towards the German authorities than those trying to help Pokorny. McDunphy noted:

> I informed Mr Gógan that it would not be proper for the President to intervene in a matter of this nature. I pointed out moreover that I understood it to be the wish of the German Legation here that any German seeking to be received by the President should be introduced by the German Minister. It was a matter of surprise to me that with an official of the German Government such a procedure should be overlooked. Mr Gógan informed me that he had anticipated my reply and that he has already caused Dr. Eoin MacNeill to speak to the President on the same matter. I must say that I found Mr Gógan lacking in a proper sense of respect due to the President.[41]

MacNeill was another venerable Gaelic scholar, a former Government Minister and a lifelong friend of the President, yet his intervention did not move Hyde. Lisner was not received at the Áras and, instead, on 12 April, McDunphy sent a sharp warning to Gógan that 'you do not appreciate that it would not be proper for the Head of State to do anything which might, even in the remotest manner, be capable of being construed as interfering in the internal affairs of another country'.[42] Gógan's efforts had so irked McDunphy that he noted on 20 April that

> there is a personal file for Mr Liam Gógan, who as will be seen from the attached file has endeavoured to get the President to intervene on Prof. Pokorny's behalf. While Mr Gogan's activities in this regard are perfectly legitimate, his attitude to the Head of State is so peculiar and so irresponsible that I have made it the subject of a separate note on his file.[43]

In effect, what this meant was that Gógan was being blacklisted by the Áras.

As the effective decision-makers in the office of President, Hyde and McDunphy may have genuinely believed that it was prudent not to intervene in Pokorny's case given the State's policy of non-alignment

---

[41] ibid.
[42] NAI, 2002/7/4, McDunphy to Gógan, 12 April 1939.
[43] NAI, 2002/7/4, McDunphy memo, 20 April 1939.

in the fraught international situation in the run-up to the war. However, their actions (or lack thereof) contrast with those of de Valera, the main architect of war-time neutrality, who was prepared to temper this policy with compassion for Pokorny's predicament. On 17 August 1939, with war now almost inevitable, Joseph Walshe, Secretary to the Department of External Affairs, wrote to the Department of Justice making it clear that de Valera wanted Pokorny to be issued with an Irish visa. Walshe wrote:

> Although Professor Pokorny is of Jewish origin, the Minister for External Affairs [de Valera] feels that in view of his outstanding position in the world of Celtic studies the Legation at Berlin should be authorised to grant a visa to Professor Pokorny at any time he desires to visit this country.[44]

In January 1940, the Irish Legation in Berlin was authorised to issue a visa to Pokorny. Pokorny however seemed reluctant to leave his home in Germany. His biographer has noted:

> Pokorny's behaviour in this period is still contradictory. On the one hand, he acquired an Irish visa, suggesting that he wished to leave the country. On the other hand, he continued his academic research, trying for all the world to behave as if nothing had changed.[45]

In this period, President Hyde was conscious of Pokorny's ongoing research in the field of Celtic studies. In May 1940, in honour of Eoin MacNeill, the Three Candle Press finally published an acclaimed 593-page Festschrift, *Féil-sgríbhinn Eóin Mhic Néill: essays and studies presented to Professor Eoin MacNeill on the occasion of his seventieth birthday, May 15th 1938*, edited by Hyde's former pupil Rev. John Ryan. Hyde himself authored the preface for this book and Pokorny contributed an essay on Irish pre-history entitled 'Ériu and the coming of the Goidels'.[46] Meanwhile, in August 1940, Pokorny again featured on the radar of the office of President when McDunphy received correspondence from Frederick Boland, the Assistant Secretary in the Department of External Affairs. In an effort to pre-empt himself being

---

[44] Ó Dochartaigh, *Julius Pokorny 1887–1970*, 120.
[45] ibid. 123.
[46] *The (Clonmel) Nationalist*, 15 May 1940; John Ryan, *Féil-sgríbhinn Eóin Mhic Néill: essays and studies presented to Professor Eoin MacNeill on the occasion of his seventieth birthday, May 15th 1938* (Dublin 1940).

taken away from his own academic research and forced to work for the
Nazi war effort, Pokorny wanted the Irish Legation in Berlin to furnish
him with a letter saying that he was working on an important Celtic
research project at President Hyde's request. On 2 August 1940, Boland
wrote to McDunphy:

> Dr Julius Pokorny, formerly Professor of Celtic Studies at Berlin
> University, has informed [the] legation at Berlin that, at the request
> of An Uachtarán, whom he saw during his last visit to Ireland in
> 1938, he is at present compiling a Celtic etymological dictionary.
> He has asked the legation to give him confirmation of this, in
> writing, for presentation if necessary to the German authorities.
> Professor Pokorny's purpose in asking for some such document is
> that he thinks that it would be of some use to him should, as is
> sometimes suggested, all persons who are not of full 'Aryan'
> descent be forced to work in munition factories, particularly those
> who are not already otherwise engaged in important work.[47]

Boland continued by asking McDunphy to ascertain Hyde's views on
this matter while, at the same time, managing to both downplay
Pokorny's concerns and to suggest that, in any case, there was little Irish
officials could do to help him. It was a diplomatic washing of hands
from which the office of President would ultimately take its lead. Boland
wrote:

> I would be glad if you would be good enough to inform me at your
> earliest convenience, whether or not An Uachtarán actually did
> request Dr Julius Pokorny to prepare a dictionary. I am to add, for
> your private information, that the Legation is of opinion that Dr
> Julius Pokorny's fears of being sent to work in a factory are based
> entirely on rumour. Work of that kind would be a great hardship
> on him, but in spite of his services to Irish learning, the Legation
> does not see how it could assist him.[48]

As Pokorny's biographer has noted, Boland's suggestion to McDunphy
that Pokorny's fears might be exaggerated was stunningly inaccurate. Ó
Dochartaigh wrote:

---

[47] NAI, 2002/7/4, Boland to McDunphy, 2 August 1940.
[48] ibid.

On 4 March 1939 the president of the Nazi Employment Office, Friedrich Syrup, had decreed that unemployed Jews could be press-ganged into heavy work in factories. This practice had begun immediately. It seems impossible that the Irish Legation in Berlin was unaware of this nearly eighteen months later. As a 'Jew' without work, Pokorny was eligible. Contrary to Boland's assertion, the threat of forced labour was very real indeed.[49]

This threat became even more menacing when, in October 1941, the deportation of German Jews from Berlin commenced. By this stage, the Irish Legation had largely lost sight of Pokorny and he was most likely living an underground existence in Berlin.[50] Pokorny had not been ultimately helped by Hyde in his ruse – to keep the Nazi authorities off his back – that he was working on a Celtic dictionary at the behest of the President of Ireland. McDunphy's response to Boland's query, while not hostile, refused to bend the truth to fit Pokorny's perilous position. McDunphy's letter, dated 7 August 1940, read:

> While it would not perhaps be strictly accurate to say that the President commissioned or even definitely requested Dr Pokorny to compile a Celtic etymological dictionary, a proposal to this effect was discussed by the Doctor with the President and was then, and still is, regarded by the President as a commendable project. The President has a high regard for the services rendered by Dr Pokorny to the Irish language.[51]

In Hyde's defence, it should be pointed out that, given Boland's less than critical assessment of the danger to Pokorny, the President may not have felt morally obliged to tell a white lie to assist Pokorny. The President's refusal to confirm that he was the instigator of Pokorny's research project put paid to any hopes that Pokorny may have harboured that letters from distinguished Irish friends would save him from the Nazis. Two days after McDunphy's response to Boland, the Department of External Affairs drew up a memo noting that it would not be true to say the President had commissioned Pokorny's research and instructing that 'the Legation should inform Dr Pokorny that it is not possible to comply with his request'.[52]

---

[49] Ó Dochartaigh, *Julius Pokorny 1887–1970*, 122.
[50] Ó Dochartaigh, 'Professor Pokorny of Vienna'; Ó Dochartaigh, *Julius Pokorny 1887–1970*, 124.
[51] NAI, DFA 438/146, McDunphy to Boland, 7 August 1940.
[52] Ó Dochartaigh, *Julius Pokorny 1887–1970*, 122.

Though Pokorny must have felt let down by his old friend, President Douglas Hyde, he would have reason to be grateful to the Irish Taoiseach. Pokorny was, in the words of his biographer, 'one of those [German Jews] who held out in what they saw as their own country until they finally had no option but to flee (or were deported to a death camp)'.[53] In September 1942, Pokorny had reappeared at the Irish Legation in Berlin looking for his visa to be renewed. In October 1942, the Taoiseach sanctioned the renewal of Pokorny's Irish visa and, following a subsequent tip-off that the Gestapo were looking for him, Pokorny eventually managed to escape out of Germany.[54] De Valera's generosity played no small part in securing Pokorny's safety. Ó Dochartaigh wrote that 'this visa probably saved his life: when he fled to Switzerland in July 1943, the Swiss authorities were turning back thousands of refugees and only a valid visa for a third country was likely to secure legal entry'.[55]

Initially, Irish diplomats were unaware of Pokorny's escape. In early September 1943, William Warnock, the Irish chargé d'affaires in Berlin, believed that Pokorny was still in Germany. He informed Joseph Walshe in a coded telegram that the 'visa did not help him. Police are averse to letting anybody out of Germany; they are afraid that information might leak out'.[56] Warnock's reply gave solace to Walshe's belief that, despite de Valera's earlier granting of a visa to Pokorny, such gestures were futile and should not be encouraged. In an earlier coded telegram to Warnock in Berlin and to Sean Murphy, the Irish diplomatic representative in Vichy France, Walshe was clear in setting out his viewpoint that providing Irish visas to 'prominent Jewish personalities to get out of German occupied territory' was pointless. Walshe wrote: 'Our understanding is that there is no prospect of such persons being able to get German exit permits in present circumstances.'[57] Walshe's

[53] Pokorny's wish to hold out as long as possible is apparent from his correspondence with Richard Best. In the aftermath of Kristallnacht in November 1938, the Nazi regime issued 40,000 arrest orders for Jews and non-Aryans, including '"intellectuals'. Forewarned of the arrests, Pokorny 'had gone away for a few weeks', but then returned to Berlin. In a letter to Best in 1939, Pokorny articulated his predicament: 'I still have not given up hope and shall try to remain in Germany as long as possible. But, I am afraid, the changes grow worse from day to day, and in the end I shall probably be obliged to leave the country as a scoláire bocht ['poor scholar']!' O'Driscoll, *Ireland, Germany and the Nazis*, 238–9; Ó Dochartaigh, *Julius Pokorny 1887–1970*, 124.

[54] Ó Dochartaigh, *Julius Pokorny 1887–1970*, 125.

[55] ibid. 17.

[56] Coded telegram from Warnock to Walshe, 3 September 1943, Michael Kennedy et al. (eds), *Documents on Irish foreign policy 1941–1945,* vol. vii (Dublin 2010) 333.

[57] Coded telegram from Walshe to Warnock and Murphy, 25 August 1943, Kennedy et al. (eds), ibid.

viewpoint may explain Hyde and McDunphy's reluctance to push for a visa for Pokorny. While McDunphy's personal relationship was poor with Maurice Moynihan, the Secretary to the Government, he held Walshe in high regard and regularly consulted with and was guided by the advice of the Secretary to the Department of External Affairs on matters pertaining to the presidency and diplomatic relations.[58]

Walshe's assessment was erroneous in regard to the case of Pokorny insofar as that, though the Nazi regime were unwilling to sanction Pokorny or other people of a Jewish background with exit permits, his possession of an Irish visa was enough for the Swiss authorities to allow him passage into their territory. As a refugee in Switzerland, Pokorny's position was uncertain and he was financially destitute. On 21 September 1943, Liam Gógan wrote to McDunphy that Pokorny was 'badly out of funds, that he is trying to make his way to this country and asking me to convey his greetings and kind regards to the President'.[59] Hyde's response was a shameful abandonment of Pokorny to his predicament. McDunphy was on holiday when Gógan wrote his letter, but on his return he wrote in relation to it: 'Seen. President has also seen. No action necessary.'[60] On 16 January 1944, Pokorny again appealed to his old friend, the President, for financial assistance. In a telegram addressed to 'Douglas Hyde President of Éire Dublin', Pokorny wrote 'Am refugee at Berne please send money through Irish Legation Switzerland'.[61] This telegram may have pricked Hyde's conscience because McDunphy was given instructions by the President to contact the Department of External Affairs for advice on the matter. McDunphy, however, was clearly unhappy with the Pokorny telegram. The following day, he wrote by hand on Pokorny's telegram, 'this is very indiscreet. Spoke to Boland, Asst Sec. Ex Affairs. He will wire today to Irish Legation at Switzerland for a report'.[62] Ultimately, it was Joseph Walshe who advised on the Pokorny telegram. Walshe had already earlier that month heartlessly rejected an appeal from Gógan for funds for Pokorny. Walshe had written:

> It is quite clear that Pokorny has no friends here and we have no benevolent society for the relief of foreign professors of Celtic Languages. The general feeling seems to be that as foreigners take

---

[58] Brian Murphy, *Forgotten patriot: Douglas Hyde and the foundation of the Irish presidency* (Cork 2016) 225–6.
[59] NAI, 2002/7/4, Gógan to McDunphy, 21 September 1943.
[60] NAI, 2002/7/4.
[61] NAI, 2002/7/4, Pokorny to Hyde, 16 January 1944.
[62] NAI, 2002/7/4.

up Celtic languages as a study subject, and a means of livelihood, there is no reason why they should be supported by us as if they were Irishmen.[63]

Walshe gave similarly callous advice to McDunphy in regard to Pokorny's telegram. On 15 February 1944, in a memo which McDunphy entitled 'Wire of 16th January not to be answered', the Secretary to the office of President noted:

> I consulted with the Secretary [of the Department of External Affairs] on the matter today and he expressed the opinion that it would be better to take no action on the wire, and in fact to ignore it. Prof Pokorny has made similar appeals to others in Dublin, and addressing this appeal to the President in a time of crisis like the present, is a type of indiscretion which should be rigidly discouraged.[64]

McDunphy's memo betrays a concern with the President not being seen to do anything which the German Government might disapprove of and this was clearly ranked by him far ahead of Pokorny's welfare. Hyde chose to take Walshe's advice. He never did respond to Pokorny's telegram which appears to have been the last ever communication between the two men. It is unclear whether Pokorny felt let down in his time of need by President Hyde. However, his appeals to others in Dublin appear to have borne some fruit, particularly, in the case of the Taoiseach. Pokorny was given 'special treatment' in the Swiss refugee centre after being furnished with a letter of introduction from Eamon de Valera.[65] Pokorny was subsequently granted asylum in Switzerland and he maintained thereafter that this was because of the efforts of de Valera. Pokorny lived a long and productive academic life, teaching in universities in both Zürich and Berne. After the war, he was central to *Zeitschrift für celtische Philologie* being 'revived and denazified' with financial support from de Valera's short lived 1951–4 administration.[66] Pokorny died in Zürich in 1970, aged eighty-two, after being involved in a road traffic accident.[67] The then President of Ireland, Eamon de Valera, was represented at Pokorny's funeral by Frank Biggar, the Irish

[63] Ó Dochartaigh, *Julius Pokorny 1887–1970*, 17.
[64] NAI, 2002/7/4, McDunphy memo, 15 February 1944.
[65] NAI, 2002/7/4, Report of the Irish Ambassador to Switzerland, April 1970.
[66] *Irish Times*, 22 July 2003 (letter by Pól Ó Dochartaigh).
[67] Breen, 'Pokorny, Julius', p. 198.

Ambassador to Switzerland. Biggar reported that the eulogy at Pokorny's funeral was delivered by Professor Hubschmidt, who in his remarks 'attributes to the intervention of President de Valera the decision of the Swiss Government to grant asylum to Professor Pokorny'.[68]

In the case of Pokorny, it is hard not to arrive at the conclusion that de Valera, despite the constraints of neutrality that the head of government may have felt, showed much more flexibility and decency than President Hyde. Douglas Hyde is an underrated, but outstanding figure in Irish history. As an academic and an activist, he played a phenomenal role in preserving the Irish language. As President, he was an unassuming and popular first citizen whose personality did much to secure broad acceptance of his office. However, Hyde's inconsiderate treatment of Professor Pokorny, a victim of the Nazi's racial laws and an individual desperately struggling to escape the horrors of the Holocaust, is an ugly blot on an otherwise distinguished record of service to Ireland.

In fairness to Hyde, though he was remiss in his conduct towards Pokorny, it should be noted that prior to the war (and, indeed, just prior to his presidency), Hyde had provided some assistance to another family seeking sanctuary from Nazi Germany. Käte Müller-Lisowski was a scholar of Celtic Literature, who had collaborated with Hyde in past academic projects. In 1920, *Irische Volksmärchen*, her translations of Irish folk songs and fairy tales, which had been collected and edited by Hyde and others was published in Berlin. Another volume of *Irische Volksmärchen*, this time edited by Müller-Lisowski herself, appeared in 1923 with a preface by Julius Pokorny.[69] Müller-Lisowski and Hyde remained in contact with each other sporadically over an extended period and, by 1926, there was an affectionate tone to their correspondence with Müller-Lisowski sending Hyde a family photo of her son, and also informing Hyde that 'Prof. Pokorny told me lots of good from you and your country. I was so glad of it'.[70]

By 1935, Müller-Lisowski and her family were 'suffering Nazi persecution', primarily on account of her husband's membership of the Social Democratic Party and his willingness to allow their family home to be used as 'a meeting place for anti-Nazis of various parties calling

---

[68] NAI, 2002/7/4, Report of the Irish Ambassador to Switzerland, April 1970.

[69] Gisela Holfter and Horst Dickel, *An Irish sanctuary: German-speaking refugees in Ireland 1933–1945*, (Berlin 2017) 28.

[70] National Folklore Collection, UCD, postcard from Müller-Lisowski to Hyde, 29 January 1926. See also an earlier postcard in the same collection from Müller-Lisowski to Hyde, 16 November 1920. I am indebted to Dr Fiona Lyons for providing me with this information.

themselves the "Winkel Group"'.[71] The Müller-Lisowskis made a number of trips to Ireland in 1936, preparing for emigration, meeting Hyde and also enrolling their only son in boarding school in Waterford. On 20 November 1937 the Müller-Lisowski family were officially registered as immigrants in Ireland. Fleeing Germany, they had, in Käte's words, 'left behind much of our money and property', but her contacts with Douglas Hyde had made Ireland 'a suitable destination' for them to seek refuge.[72] Only a very small number of refugees were given permission to reside in Ireland in this period – according to the research of Holfter and Dickel this figure may have been as low as 52 persons between January 1933 and October 1938 – so sway was clearly important.[73] Käte Müller-Lisowski remained friendly with Hyde on his elevation to the presidency and the *Irish Times* noted her name, alongside others, as having sent Hyde a message of sympathy on the death of his wife, which occurred on the last day of 1938.[74]

Despite his failure towards Pokorny, it should not be argued that Douglas Hyde was in any way anti-Semitic in his views. In fact, Hyde greatly admired the achievements of the Jewish people in protecting their culture and in working to revive the Hebrew language. In his landmark address, 'The necessity for de-anglicising Ireland', delivered to the Irish National Literary Society in November 1892, Hyde made positive reference to the Hebrew revival, which was growing apace alongside the rise of Jewish nationalism in late nineteenth century Europe, as an example to Irish language enthusiasts, noting:

> We can also insist, and we shall insist, that in those baronies where the children speak Irish, Irish shall be taught, and that Irish-speaking schoolmasters, petty sessions clerks, and even magistrates be appointed in Irish-speaking districts. If all this were done, it should not be very difficult, with the aid of the foremost foreign scholars, to bring about a tone of thought which would make it disgraceful for an educated Irishman – especially of the old Celtic race, MacDermotts, O'Conors, O'Sullivans, MacCarthys, O'Neills – to be ignorant of his own language – would make it at least as disgraceful as for an educated Jew to be quite ignorant of Hebrew.[75]

[71] Holfter and Dickel, An Irish sanctuary, 29.
[72] ibid. 27–9.
[73] ibid. 30.
[74] *Irish Times*, 5 January 1939.
[75] Douglas Hyde, 'The necessity for de-anglicising Ireland', November 1892, reprint of pamphlet in possession of author.

Hyde's admiration for the work of Hebrew revivalists was enduring and, in July 1934, in his opening address to the Celtic Congress, held in Dublin, he remarked:

> It is certain that English speaking children can be made Irish speaking again all over Ireland. Our schools are giving children the teaching wanted for the expression of their thoughts and their needs, and if they do not speak it, it is for want of a healthy spirit of nationalism such as the Jews and the Welsh have.[76]

Hyde's knowledge of Jewish cultural nationalism was informed by a long-running correspondence he maintained with Loeb Jaffe, a poet and a friend of Isaac Herzog, the Chief Rabbi of Ireland from 1921 to 1936. Jaffe visited Ireland in the early years of the Irish Free State and befriended Hyde. Jaffe described Hyde in his private journal as 'an Irish Ben Yehuda', who is regarded as the father of modern Hebrew and was primarily responsible for reviving that language and forging it into a modern and viable instrument of communication.[77] After his initial meeting with Hyde, Jaffe recorded:

> He talks a great deal about the uphill fight for the renaissance of Gaelic…. Three hundred years ago Gaelic was the only language spoken. One hundred years ago, it was still the principal language. Today it is spoken by just a few. Hyde tells me that Gaelic is today part of the school curriculum but he adds, with regret in his voice, that the teachers themselves do not know it well…. I told him that the revival of our tongue was an accomplished fact. Hebrew was the language of instruction in schools, the vernacular of our children, of the street, of the Jewish population. Hundreds of Hebrew books appeared every year, covering every field of literature and science. 'I have been told,' said Hyde, 'that barely a few dozen years ago, only two boys spoke Hebrew in Jerusalem, and now it has become your living tongue. How did you work this miracle? You are greater patriots than we.'[78]

On Hyde's inauguration as President of Ireland, Jaffe sent Hyde a copy of his collected poems in English translation and was pleased to receive in return an Irish poem, which Hyde suggested 'shows how much our

---

[76] *Irish Times*, 10 July 1934.
[77] Gabriel Fallon, 'Eretz Israel and the Irish revival', *Irish Times*, 23 May 1969.
[78] ibid.

two nations have in common'.[79] In the same letter, President Hyde wrote about 'how impressed' he had been by a speech made by Chaim Weizmann, President of the Zionist Organisation, in November 1936, at the Royal Commission of Inquiry to Palestine, headed by Lord Robert Peel, who had been appointed by the British Government to investigate the causes of unrest among Palestinian Arabs and Jews.[80]

Weizmann's tour de force, two and a half hours long speech, delivered without a prepared text, referenced the prejudice, hatred and intolerance in Germany, Poland, Austria, Romania and Latvia, which would ultimately lead to the Holocaust. He testified that 'there are in this part of the world six million people pent up in places where they are not wanted, and for whom the world is divided into places where they cannot live, and places into which they may not enter'.[81] Weizmann maintained that 'there should be one place in the world, in God's wide world, where we [the Jewish people] could live and express ourselves in accordance with our character, and make our contributions towards the civilized world, in our own way and through our own channels'.[82] Hyde's stated approval for this speech, which laid before the Commission the permanent principles of the Zionist movement, underlines that he was in no way anti-Semitic and was, in fact, in sympathy with Jewish aspirations for their own nation-state.

In his often-quoted conversation with a Trinity College contemporary, W. M. Crook, which concluded with Hyde's wonderful assertion that 'I dream in Irish', Hebrew was one of eight languages that Hyde suggested he had a good working knowledge of.[83] At the time of Hyde's graduation from Trinity in the late 1880s,[84] the revival of Hebrew as a modern, living language was very much in its infancy. When Ben Yehuda and his wife had a son in 1882, they vowed to only speak Hebrew to him.

[79] ibid.
[80] ibid.
[81] John Mann, *Antisemitism: the oldest hatred* (Oxford 2015) 169–76.
[82] ibid.
[83] 'You do know a lot of languages, Hyde. How many do you know? English, German, Hebrew, Latin, Greek and French, I suppose?'
'Yes, and I can read Italian; but the language I know best is Irish.'
'"Irish!" I exclaimed in astonishment; "do you know Irish?" "Yes," he said quietly, "I dream in Irish."'
Conversation between Crook, a classical scholar, and his fellow student, Douglas Hyde, quoted in Diarmid O Cobhthaigh, *Douglas Hyde: An Craoibhín Aoibhinn* (Dublin 1917) 11.
[84] Hyde was awarded the LL.B. in December 1887, and, in April 1888, the LL.D. with first class honors. Paper in possession of the author by Mary Robinson, President of Ireland, 'Douglas Hyde (1860–1949): the Trinity connection', *Quatercentenary discourse*, Trinity College Dublin, 11 May 1992.

Therefore, Itamar Ben-Avi became the first native speaker of Hebrew in almost 2,000 years. Initially, however, as de Barra has pointed out, Ben Yehuda's efforts bore little fruit and 'while he was successful in making Hebrew the language of his home, he only managed to convince a few other families in Jerusalem to copy his example'.[85] Hyde, thus, acquired a good knowledge of Hebrew at a time when it was hardly 'anyone's first language', though it had retained a ceremonial use and many Jews would have had some familiarity with the language through learning Jewish prayers and reading the Torah.[86] As a student in Trinity's Divinity School up to 1885, Hyde would have encountered texts in Hebrew, but his strong knowledge of the language suggests a broad-mindedness, an interest and an empathy with Jewish culture.

Such empathy was not commonplace in late nineteenth and early twentieth century Ireland. Jim Larkin's *Irish Worker* paper published anti-Semitic verses and cartoons, the novelist William Bulfin racially stigmatized a Jewish character in his bestselling book *Rambles in Eirinn*, Arthur Griffith published derogatory articles about Jews in his *United Irishman* and *Sinn Féin* papers before 1907 and even the socialist *Harp*, edited by James Connolly, referred to some non-union immigrants as 'Jew scabs'.[87]

There is no evidence of Douglas Hyde making any anti-Semitic utterances throughout his long public career. However, he did prominently join with Griffith and other well-known literary figures in protesting against the actions of members of a British-Israelite sect in Ireland. Between 1899 and 1902, the British-Israel Association of London, founded by Edward Wheeler Bird, a retired Anglo-Indian judge, engaged in a series of exploratory digs at the Hill of Tara. The British-Israel Association believed that the Anglo-Saxon race was descended from the Lost Tribes of Israel, the wandering biblical Hebrews, and one of their bizarre theories, deduced from a 'strange mixture of early Irish history, genealogy and Old Testament rhetoric' was that the Ark of the Covenant was buried beneath the ancient and ceremonial hill in County Meath, the traditional inauguration place and seat of the High Kings of Ireland.[88] The crude digging up of Tara was facilitated by Gustavus

[85] Caoimhín de Barra, 'Hebrew's revival has lessons for the Irish language', *Irish Times*, 15 March 2019.

[86] ibid

[87] Colum Kenny, 'Anti-Semitic prejudice in Edwardian Ireland', *Irish Times*, 6 June 2016; Keogh, *Jews in twentieth-century Ireland*, 22.

[88] According to the Hebrew Bible, the Ark of the Covenant was constructed by the ancient Israelites, while they were camping out in the Sinai Desert, after they fled Egypt, and contains tablets engraved with the Ten Commandments. Mairead Carew, *Tara and the Ark*

Villiers Briscoe, 'a bankrupt Meath squire and ex-Imperial Yeoman, who owns the greater portion of the hill'.[89] Briscoe had reportedly been 'bought' by the British-Israelites and 'sat by heartlessly drinking whiskey as the zealots began their crazy "excavations"'.[90]

On 24 June 1902, at the behest of Maud Gonne, Hyde, Griffith, William Butler Yeats and George Moore, decamped from Dublin to Tara with a view to taking direct action against the excavation work of the British-Israelites. The quartet were 'rather astonishingly equipped with a shotgun' and 'they meant to shut it [the dig] down'.[91] Ultimately shots were not fired. Hyde's involvement in this foray, which had the potential for violence, was not motivated by any religious animosity against the British-Israelites, but rather by enflamed nationalist passions and also by outrage at what he saw as an act of cultural vandalism. Gonne had claimed that 'the diggers planned to present the Ark to Edward VII' and, in doing so, 'they would reconfirm the colonial relationship between England and Ireland and the imperial power from which their project had sprung'.[92] This would have been anathema to an Irish-Ireland nationalist like Hyde. On returning from Tara, Hyde, Yeats and Moore (but curiously minus Griffith), penned an angry letter to the *Times* newspaper. The letter stated:

> We have just returned from a visit to the Hill of Tara, where we found that the work of destruction, abandoned a year or two ago, has begun again. Labourers are employed to dig through the mounds and ditches that mark the site of the ancient Royal duns and houses. We saw them digging and shovelling without any supervision, hopelessly mixing the different layers of earth and altering the contour of the hill. This is not being done through any antiquarian zeal, but, apparently, that the sect which believes the English to be descended from the Ten Tribes may find the Ark of Covenant. We are assured that the Commissioners of Public Works in Ireland can do nothing in this case, for by the Ancient

of the Covenant: a search for the Ark of the Covenant by British Israelites on the Hill of Tara (Dublin 1986) 11; Eileen Battersby, 'The Ark at the seat of kings', *Irish Times*, 19 April 2003.

[89] Boston College Library, *The Sacred Heart Review*, vol. 28, number 1, 5 July 1902, 'The destruction of Tara', 13.

[90] Battersby, 'The Ark at the seat of kings'.

[91] Aby Bender, 'British Israelites, Irish Israelites and the ends of an analogy', in Aidan Beatty and Dan O'Brien (eds), *Irish questions and Jewish questions: crossovers in culture* (New York 2018) 18–20.

[92] ibid.

Monuments Protection Act of 1882 they can only interfere when
the 'owner' has himself 'constituted' them 'the guardians of such
monument.' All we can do under the circumstances is to draw the
attention of the public to this desecration. Tara is, because of its
associations, probably the most consecrated spot in Ireland, and
its destruction will leave many bitter memories behind it.[93]

This letter contains no religious animus against the British-Israeli sect
and the clear concern of Hyde and his co-signatories is the destruction
of Irish national heritage. Any suggestion that Hyde's involvement in
the Tara escapade was motivated by disdain for Judaism, or what some
wrongly interpreted as the pseudo-Judaism of the British-Israeli sect, is
wholly undermined by remarks Hyde made earlier that year. In a lecture
in Athlone on 25 January 1902, which was subsequently reprinted in the
Irish Catholic, Douglas Hyde strongly voiced his respect for Jewish
culture and for Jewish people and he lauded their efforts to revive
Hebrew as an example to Irish nationalists. Hyde said:

Do you know how the Jews, the most marvelous people in the
world, keep alive their nationality? They would be as scattered as
the mist were it not that the Jewish child is taught from his infancy
his own language along with any other he may have to learn. In
the future I hope the Irish child will have on one side of the book
his own language and English on the other, and thus be treated as
well as the child of the Jew.[94]

Given Hyde's consistently stated admiration for Jewish people over a
lengthy period, his later lack of support for Pokorny is all the more
inexplicable. It is not beyond the bounds of possibility that Hyde
privately raised the issue of Pokorny with de Valera, away from the gaze
of McDunphy, who had a tendency to be a domineering advisor.
However, none of the available archival material shows or hints at
communication between the President and the Taoiseach on this matter,
but this does not conclusively prove that Hyde did not directly speak to
de Valera on Pokorny's behalf. Unless new material comes to light

[93] The letter's mention of the 'Ten Tribes' is a reference to the British-Israel theory, which
asserts that the British nation is the 'lost' ten tribes of Israel. The ten lost tribes were ten
of the Twelve Tribes of Israel that were said to have been deported from the Kingdom of
Israel after its conquest by the Neo-Assyrian Empire circa 722 BC, *The Times*, 27 June
1902.
[94] Bender, 'British Israelites' 22.

documenting such an appeal, this will remain very much in the realms of speculation. The correspondence currently available to scholars hardly paints Hyde in a good light. Hyde had a longstanding reputation for being personally parsimonious and his lack of response to a desperate Pokorny's plea from a refugee camp for funds seems heartless and inconsiderate.

A mitigating factor for Hyde's reputation may be his own personal lack of knowledge of the horrors being inflicted on European Jewry by Hitler's regime. How much the Irish Government knew about the Holocaust and the Nazis' systematic murdering of Jews remains contentious, but there is little doubt that de Valera and some leading figures in his administration had a strong indication of the perilous position of Jewish people in Nazi-occupied Europe.[95] It is however very much a matter of conjecture how much President Hyde knew of Nazi efforts to exterminate Europe's Jewish population. De Valera's war-time administration operated on a needs-to-know basis and there was an ingrained culture of secrecy and censorship. Ó Drisceoil's study of this period notes that war news was 'neutralised', newsreels were banned, expression of opinions on the war, neutrality and much else of vital importance were disallowed – all 'for the purpose of securing public safety and the preservation of the State'.[96] For the same reason, all information received regarding the activities of belligerent powers during the conflict, especially if it was likely to provoke hostile reactions amongst the populace, was tightly managed and not widely disseminated, even within government, and treated as classified material. De Valera made a point of keeping President Hyde regularly briefed on government policy, in accordance with Article 28.5.2 of the Constitution, meeting him once a month for this purpose, however, these meetings took the form of private conversations between the Taoiseach and Hyde. Notes were not kept.[97] Given the layers of confidentiality de Valera wrapped around Irish government intelligence on the wartime activities of the countries involved in the conflict, it is unlikely that de Valera shared the extent of his knowledge of the Holocaust with the elderly and infirm President. Official records from Áras an Uachtaráin for the period of the whole war, including top-secret files maintained by McDunphy,

[95] Michael Kennedy, 'Irish foreign policy: 1919 to 1973', in Thomas Bartlett (ed.), *The Cambridge history of Ireland: Volume 4, 1880 to the present* (Cambridge 2018) 619; Robert Fisk, *In time of war: Ireland, Ulster and the price of neutrality 1939–45* (London 1983) 419; Keogh, *Jews in twentieth-century Ireland*, 174.
[96] Donal Ó Drisceoil, *Censorship in Ireland, 1939–1945: Neutrality, politics, and society* (Cork 1996).
[97] Murphy, *Forgotten patriot*, 228.

who was an inveterate chronicler of any information he received, even
if this had been relayed to him on a confidential basis, make no reference
to the Nazi's wholescale assault on European Jews.[98]

Hyde's abandonment of Pokorny remains disappointing, even today,
for our first President's many admirers, but there are further extenuating
factors. As well as the President's lack of knowledge of the Holocaust,
it should be noted that Hyde was a political novice, reliant on the ultra-
conservative McDunphy for advice. McDunphy's point of guidance in
regard to refugee policy were his senior civil service counterparts,
Stephen Roche, the Secretary of the Department of Justice, and, of
course, Walshe at the Department of External Affairs. In contrast to de
Valera, who was sympathetic to the plight of Jewish refugees and
responded positively to overtures to assist specific Jews, on occasion
overruling the Departments of External Affairs and Justice, Walshe and
Roche, in particular, were hostile to admitting Jewish refugees, citing
difficulties of assimilation and fears of exacerbating domestic anti-
Semitism.[99] Most certainly, McDunphy would have been reluctant to act
in contravention of the official advice received from senior civil service
colleagues in regard to refugee policy. McDunphy and Hyde would also
have been conscious of the need for the office of President not to be seen
as acting in conflict with the policy emanating from government
departments. When the office of President came into existence, arising
from the ratification of the 1937 Constitution, a persistent fear from
opponents of the Government was that the office could be a stepping-
stone to a dictatorship. Hyde was acutely aware of this viewpoint and
was determined to quell it. Accordingly, the office of President in its
formative years took pains not to be perceived as an alternative
government and to be seen, at all times, its discretionary constitutional
powers apart, to be acting on the advice of the Government, as per the
President's mandate under Article 13.9 of the Constitution.[100] Pokorny
may have been a friend, but Hyde would have felt compelled not to act
in contradiction of the direction of government departments regarding
refugee policy.

[98] NAI, S10332B, 'Ireland and World War II, 1939–1945, Conversations with Mr
Michael McDunphy'.
[99] Diarmaid Ferriter, *The transformation of Ireland 1900–2000* (London 2004) 387;
Keogh, *Jews in twentieth-century Ireland*, 189–91.
[100] Article 13.9 of Bunreacht na hÉireann states: 'The powers and functions conferred on
the President by this Constitution shall be exercisable and performable by him only on
the advice of the Government, save where it is provided by this Constitution that he shall
act in his absolute discretion or after consultation with or in relation to
the Council of State, or on the advice or nomination of, or on receipt of any other
communication from, any other person or body.'

The fear of overstepping his powers, breaching protocol or, worse still, compromising Ireland's neutral stance, which had overwhelming public support at that time, may all have influenced Hyde's abandonment of Pokorny, but physical factors also cannot be ruled out. In April 1940, Douglas Hyde suffered a serious stroke and, although his mental prowess remained undiminished, from this point forward, the ailing President did not have the same vigour as of old and would not have had the stamina for the intra-departmental manoeuvrings necessary to alter, subvert or side-step government policy on refugees.

In a wider context, maybe the question should be not why did Hyde, a man of compassion and tolerance, who was never anti-Semitic, not do more to aid Pokorny, but rather why did the Irish State not do more to save the Jews? In 2012, the then Minster for Justice, Alan Shatter, suggested that 'the doors of this State were kept firmly closed to Jewish families' during the Nazi era.[101] Keogh's fine historical study is more tempered and highlights de Valera's personal sympathy and occasional interventions on behalf of Jewish refugees, while noting that 'Irish policy towards the Jews remained reactive rather than proactive throughout the war'.[102] Though de Valera saw his primary responsibility as protecting the State's neutrality as a means to safeguard and insulate the Irish people from the ravages of World War Two, Ireland's illiberal policy towards Jewish refugees was '"a vast lost chance" to save many lives'.[103] In the final analysis, undoubtedly, our first President should have done more to assist Julius Pokorny and most certainly should not have 'looked the other way' when his old friend sought assistance in escaping from the Hitler regime, but, equally the entire Irish State could have and should have done more to provide shelter to Jewish people fleeing from the evils of Nazism.

During World War Two, Hyde maintained cordial relations with Eduard Hempel, the German Minister in Dublin, who was a welcome guest at Áras an Uachtaráin.[104] Debate still rages as to the extent of Hempel's Nazi sympathies, if any. Sean MacEntee, a minister in de Valera's wartime government, insisted in a 1974 interview that 'Hempel was not a Nazi, he was an honourable man'.[105] Hempel had joined the diplomatic service of Saxony in 1920, which was incorporated into the

---

[101] Address by Alan Shatter TD, Minister for Justice, Equality and Defence, National Holocaust Memorial Day commemoration, Mansion House, Dublin, 26 January 2014. http://www.justice.ie/en/JELR/Pages/SP14000021 [accessed 16 June 2019].

[102] Keogh, *Jews in twentieth-century Ireland*, 193.

[103] ibid. 194.

[104] Murphy, *Forgotten patriot*, 214

[105] Michael McInerney, 'The Sean MacEntee story', *Irish Times*, 25 June 1974.

German foreign service. In 1928, he joined the German People's Party, a national liberal party, whose members were increasingly subjected to harassment by the Nazis until the party's dissolution post the Enabling Act of 1933, which gave Hitler's cabinet the power to enact laws without the involvement of the Reichstag. Duggan, in his 2003 study of Hempel, suggests that Hempel was a career diplomat and 'only a nominal member of the Nazi Party'.[106] McMenamin, however, while accepting that Hempel was 'pressured into joining the Nazi Party in 1938' and that he was 'not a strict doctrinaire Nazi', still contends that Hempel 'was more than willing to carry out [Nazi] party policy'.[107] Hempel's Nazism is debatable, but there is no doubting the Nazi predilections of Dr Hans Hartmann and Professor Ludwig Mühlhausen, both of whom were on good terms with Douglas Hyde.

Hartmann, who had joined the Nazi Party in 1933, moved to Ireland in April 1937 to study the Irish language and folklore.[108] Hartmann initially worked for Dr Adolf Mahr, an Austrian archaeologist, who was Director of the National Museum of Ireland, while at the same time holding the position of head of the Nazi Party in Ireland, which he had helped to establish.[109] Hartmann also regularly socialised in Dublin with Helmut Clissmann, an Abwehr agent, who would be involved in the preparation of Operation Sea Lion, the Nazi's plan to invade Britain. Though the Irish intelligence service officers from G2 kept a watching brief on Hartmann, his interest in Ireland was 'purely academic' and Mahr organised for Hartmann's transfer to the Folklore Commission, then based at University College Dublin in Hyde's old academic stomping ground of Earlsfort Terrace.[110] The Director of the Folklore Commission was Professor Séamus Ó Duilearga, a long-time friend and academic collaborator of Hyde. Ó Duilearga had been a student of Hyde and was subsequently, in 1923, appointed assistant to Hyde, in his capacity as Professor of Modern Irish in UCD.[111] In 1927, Ó Duilearga was a founding member of the Folklore of Ireland Society, which elected

[106] John P. Duggan, *Herr Hempel at the German Legation in Dublin 1937–1945* (Dublin 2003).

[107] Marc McMenamin, *Codebreaker: the untold story of Richard Hayes, the Dublin librarian who helped turn the tide of World War II* (Dublin 2018) 30.

[108] David O'Donoghue, 'State within a state: the Nazis in neutral Ireland', *History Ireland*, issue 6 (Nov./Dec. 2006), vol. 14.

[109] Mullins, *Dublin Nazi no.1.*

[110] David O'Donoghue, *Hitler's Irish voices: the story of German radio's Irish propaganda service, 1939–1945* (PhD Thesis, Dublin City University 1995) 56–7.

[111] Eoin Mac Cárthaigh, 'Ó Duilearga, Séamus (James Hamilton Delargy)', in *Dictionary of Irish biography: from the earliest times to the year 2002,* vol. 7, ed. James McGuire and James Quinn (Cambridge 2009) 436–7.

Douglas Hyde its treasurer. Hyde was also Chairman of the State's complementary organisation, the Irish Folklore Institute, from 1930 to 1934, which paved the way for the Folklore Commission, formally established in 1935, shortly after Hyde's retirement from academia to Ratra, Frenchpark, Co. Roscommon, under the leadership of Ó Duilearga.

At the Folklore Commission, Hartmann worked closely with both Ó Duilearga and Máire MacNeill, another former student of Hyde and also a daughter of Eoin MacNeill, a co-founder of the Gaelic League with Hyde.[112] It was, most likely, through this axis that Hartmann was introduced to Douglas Hyde. Hartmann left Ireland in September 1939, eight days after Britain and France declared war on Germany, but dedicated a book he authored, *Über Krankheit, Tod und Jenseitsvorstellungen in Irland* ['*Sickness, death, and concepts of the hereafter in Ireland*'], published in the German city of Halle in 1942, 'to the President of Ireland, Douglas Hyde'.[113]

Hartmann's book emanated from his PhD thesis, which was based on folklore material he had collected whilst living in Ireland, and was supervised by Professor Ludwig Mühlhausen at Berlin University. Mühlhausen, who had served in the German infantry in World War One, had a long track record in extremist politics. Shortly after being demobbed from the German Army, he first joined an 'ultra-right wing party' in 1919.[114] A profile of him authored by G2, Irish military intelligence, claimed that Mühlhausen had been associated with pre-Nazi fascist groups, such as the German National People's Party and their paramilitary wing The Steel Helmet organisation. With the emergence of Adolf Hitler, he became an 'enthusiastic' Nazi, who had joined the Nazi Party in 1932, nine months before Hitler had come to power. By this stage, Mühlhausen's wife, Else, was already part of 'the inner circle of the Nazi Party in Hamburg'.[115] In 1933, the same year that the Sturmabteilung (the SA), the Nazi Party's paramilitary wing, were instrumental in organising a national boycott of Jewish businesses, Mühlhausen joined this intimidatory, brownshirted force and his military background saw him begin to rise through the ranks.[116] From 1935, Mühlhausen was also closely associated with the Abwehr, German military intelligence.[117]

---

[112] Maureen Murphy, *Béaloideas* 72 (2004) 7–8.
[113] O'Donoghue, *Hitler's Irish voices*, 56–7, 363.
[114] Kevin Magee, 'Nazi sa Ghaeltacht', BBC 2 Northern Ireland television documentary, 26 July 2020.
[115] O'Donoghue, *Hitler's Irish voices*, 36.
[116] Magee, 'Nazi sa Ghaeltacht'
[117] ibid.

Mühlhausen undoubtedly benefitted from all of these political associations. After Pokorny was dismissed from his post in Berlin University in 1935 on the grounds of his Jewish ancestry, the Nazi Party ensured that Mühlhausen got Pokorny's job in preference to two other candidates.[118] Mühlhausen's appointment was 'very controversial' in academic circles, as, though he spoke fluent Irish, was 'well versed in folklore' and had founded the Department of Celtic Studies at Hamburg University in 1928, he had published very little at this stage of his career. Detailed research in the 1990s by Joachim Lerchenmüller indicates that a significant number of mediocre academics in the field of Celtic Studies, such as Mühlhausen, had opportunistically advanced their careers during the Hitler era in Germany through having Nazi party links.[119] Mühlhausen had studied the Irish language on various trips to Ireland from the late 1920s to 1937. He was an accomplished linguist, but his later visits, especially one to Teelin, Co. Donegal, from August–October 1937, were not just about achieving fluency in the Irish language and indulging his fascination with Irish folklore. Mühlhausen was a spy and compiled intelligence reports, including analysis of Irish economic and social mores and Irish attitudes to National Socialism, for the German military authorities. Photographs that Mühlhausen took in Ireland, particularly in Donegal, in the 1930s later appeared in a German military handbook prepared to assist a top secret invasion of Ireland codenamed Operation Green.[120] Mühlhausen had spent 'a prolonged

---

[118] This was not the first time that Mühlhausen had landed a plum job because of his Nazi connections. In 1933, the Nazis had sacked the Jewish director of Hamburg's Commerce Library, Dr Rosenbaum, to make way for Mühlhausen. In the same year, when Pokorny suffered his initial suspension from Berlin University, Mühlhausen had made 'a determined effort' to acquire Pokorny's post. In 1935, following Pokorny's ultimate dismissal, Mühlhausen's Nazi credentials were central to him getting the job. See O'Donoghue, *Hitler's Irish voices*, 34–6; O'Driscoll, *Ireland, Germany and the Nazis*, 100.

[119] Magee, 'Nazi sa Ghaeltacht'; O'Donoghue, *Hitler's Irish voices*, 34; O'Driscoll, *Ireland, Germany and the Nazis*, 100.

[120] Mühlhausen had a background in espionage, having worked as a spy in southern Belgium (Wallonia) for a period in World War One. At least three photographs taken by Mühlhausen in Teelin appeared in a 1941 German manual entitled *Military geographical data on Ireland*, which was prepared for the use of troops in the event of an invasion of Ireland. Excellent research in Dr David O'Donoghue's doctoral thesis and in Kevin Magee's BBC television documentary detail Mühlhausen's espionage activities in Ireland. In 1937, Mühlhausen spent about six weeks in Teelin, a small Gaeltacht fishing village, in Co. Donegal. He took hundreds of photographs in the area and was especially interested in Teelin harbour – according to one account even measuring the depth of the sea there. Mühlhausen's reports were scathing of the inefficiency and wastefulness of the Irish economy, but he was also focused on the topography of the countryside, especially in maritime areas. On leaving Teelin, Mühlhausen met with Adolf Mahr in Dublin. Mühlhausen's activities in Teelin were the cause of some suspicion locally and León Ó Broin, a distinguished Irish civil servant and author, who briefly shared accommodation with Mühlhausen reported his behavior to the Irish Army. G2 files show that they were

period of time in Ireland in 1937, collecting folk tales in the Gaeltacht and doing research in Dublin' and, depending on the source, became 'acquainted' or developed a 'friendship' with Hyde.[121]

When, or even if, Douglas Hyde actually met Mühlhausen remains uncertain, though Mühlhausen, as will be seen, sought to imply that there was a bond of friendship between them. Mühlhausen's visit to Teelin had been organised by Séamus Ó Duilearga, who had put Mühlhausen in touch with Seán Ó hEochaidh, a local folklore collector employed by the Commission. In early October 1937, after his six-week stay in Donegal where he had spent as much time intelligence-gathering as folklore gathering, Mühlhausen spent some time as a guest in Ó Duilearga's family home in Dublin, before returning to Germany. It is conceivable that Ó Duilearga would have sought to introduce the visiting German Celtic scholar to Hyde, arguably the most renowned Celticist in the world at that time. Ó Duilearga's Folklore Commission was based in Earlsfort Terrace and St Stephen's Green, which were close to Hyde's (former) Dublin home and the two men regularly socialised together, though by October 1937 Hyde was living out his soon to be interrupted retirement in Roscommon and his visits to Dublin were less frequent. Of course, Ó Duilearga could also have first introduced Hyde to Mühlhausen on an earlier visit, as Mühlhausen and Ó Duilearga had first struck up a friendship in July 1932, when the German national had visited Cornamona, Co. Galway, to study the local folklore.[122]

keeping tabs on Mühlhausen and an Irish Army intelligence report, dated 17 June 1943, described him thus: 'Enthusiastic Nazi, most energetic worker. Approves of Irish whiskey, can be very genial, but can fly into a violent temper.' Magee, 'Nazi sa Ghaeltacht'; O'Donoghue, *Hitler's Irish voices*, 34-40.

[121] Mark. M. Hull and Vera Moynes, *Masquerade: treason, the Holocaust and an Irish imposter* (Oklahoma 2017) 72; Christopher Hutton, *Linguistics and the Third Reich: mother-tongue fascism, race and the science of language* (London 1999) 127. A small amount of formal scholarly correspondence between Mülhausen and Hyde (variously dated 1921, 1926, 1932) has recently come to light in the Douglas Hyde Papers, National Library of Ireland, MS Accession 3,213.

[122] Mühlhausen was accompanied on his 1932 visit to Galway by 'a German professor of geography' who took a great number of photos of Lough Corrib and the Aran Islands. In January 1937 Ó Duilearga stayed at the Mühlhausen family home in Hamburg and Mühlhausen showed his visitor 'the thousands of photographs, drawings and plans' he had made in Ireland. Mühlhausen's trip to Donegal later that year involved further photographing of Irish terrain. It is not possible to pinpoint when Ó Duilearga first had doubts as to whether Mühlhausen was interested in Ireland solely for academic and linguistic reasons, but eventually he would compile a report for G2 on Mühlhausen's activities in Ireland. In an undated memo (thought to have been written in early 1940), Ó Duilearga noted of Mühlhausen: 'he has – I believe – a very sincere regard for Ireland and the people, but thinks that German culture would be good for us, and our country better run by Germans than by either the British or ourselves'. O'Donoghue, *Hitler's Irish voices*, 37, 357.

Hyde's potential personal connection with Mühlhausen, Pokorny's successor at Berlin University, may have been a factor in Hyde's reluctance to immerse himself in efforts to restore Pokorny to his position. Another layer to the Pokorny-Mühlhausen rivalry emerged in 1939 when *Zeitschrift für celtische Philologie*, a distinguished academic journal of Celtic studies, was 'Nazified by the removal of Pokorny [as editor] and appointment of Mühlhausen' to this role, a departure that would not have been missed by Hyde, a keen follower of academic affairs.[123] Nevertheless, on 7 November 1939, two months after the outbreak of war, following Hitler's invasion of Poland, President Hyde wrote to Mühlhausen acknowledging receipt of a book the latter had edited, entitled *Zehn irische Volkserzählungen aus Süd-Donegal ['Ten Irish folk tales from south Donegal']*. In this same correspondence, Hyde shared with Mühlhausen his experiences in collecting fairy tales, 'Märchen', and publishing them.[124] In 1940, Mühlhausen wrote a flattering essay on Hyde's life in a volume edited by Ruth Weiland, entitled *Irische Freiheitskämpfer: Biographische Skizzen [Irish freedom fighters: biographical sketches]*, commissioned by Scherl, a major Berlin publishing house.

The introduction to this German language book was penned by the Irish writer Francis Stuart, who had taken up a position in Berlin University and also had connections with the IRA and the Abwehr. In his introduction, Stuart explains that the volume takes the term 'freedom fighters' in its 'widest sense' by including pieces about 'noncombatants Charles Stewart Parnell and Douglas Hyde'.[125] The other lives covered in essays in the book are those of Roger Casement, Maud Gonne MacBride, Padraig Pearse and Eamon de Valera. Hull and Moynes argue that the book makes 'subtle suggestions of fraternity' between Irish nationalism and Nazi Germany and that the 'the book belongs within the wider context of a German state siding with a nation that had been the victim of English imperialism'.[126]

By the time he had written his biographical sketch on Hyde for the above-mentioned volume, Mühlhausen was deeply immersed in the Nazi propaganda machine. O'Donoghue has noted that Adolf Mahr

> drew up a top secret radio propaganda blueprint for Nazi Foreign
> Minister Ribbentrop aimed at converting Irish communities around

---

[123] *Irish Times*, 22 July 2003 (letter by Pól Ó Dochartaigh).
[124] NLI, Private Accessions 1997–2002, 99/43, Letter to Dr Ludwig Mühlhausen, Professor of Celtic Studies, University of Berlin from the President of Ireland, Dr Douglas Hyde, November 1939.
[125] Hull and Moynes, *Masquerade*, 72.
[126] ibid.

the world to the Nazi cause. From the outbreak of the Second World War on 3 September 1939, radio propaganda had a high priority in the capital of the Third Reich. So intent was the Nazi leadership on making sure that its message got through, not only to its opponents but also to neutrals and minorities within states, that by the summer of 1940 Germany's national broadcasting company (the Reichsrundfunkgesellschaft or RRG) was putting out programmes in 31 languages. These included the three Baltic tongues of Latvia, Lithuania and Estonia, the language of the Faroe Islands, in addition to Icelandic, Flemish and Irish. Berlin's weekly radio talks in Irish were inaugurated in December 1939 by the noted Celtic scholar, Professor Ludwig Mühlhausen.... From 1939 to mid-1941 German radio propaganda to Ireland comprised first weekly then twice-weekly talks in Irish by Mühlhausen and his academic protégé, Hans Hartmann.[127]

From December 1939 to June 1941, Ludwig Mühlhausen was in charge of the German Radio's Irish service – the Irland-Redaktion – which in this period was answerable to Goebbels' Propaganda Ministry. From November 1941 to May 1945, the Irish service was run by Adolf Mahr and Hans Hartmann on behalf of Ribbentrop's Foreign Office.[128] According to O'Donoghue, the Irland-Redaktion followed the Propaganda Ministry's basic broadcasting formula and this included:

> anti-British and anti-Jewish talks (Hans Hartmann says that anti-Jewish material was 'kept to a minimum' at his insistence when he took over the service in December 1941....); laudatory remarks about Hitler; war communiqués from the German Army's High Command; and, from 22 June 1941 onwards, anti-Bolshevik talks.[129]

Mühlhausen was an accomplished propagandist and, in order to give his broadcasts a local dimension, he regularly sent his Irish acquaintances personal greetings over the airwaves. When Mühlhausen sent Christmas greetings to Seán Ó hEochaidh in December 1939 it placed the Teelin folklorist in, in his own words, 'a spot of trouble', as the Irish authorities thought he might be 'a German fifth columnist'. Ó hEochaidh was subjected to Garda Special Branch surveillance and this only came to an end when Ó Duilearga assured the Department of Justice of

---

[127] O'Donoghue, *Hitler's Irish voices*, 3.
[128] ibid. 13.
[129] ibid. 25.

'the innocent relationship' between Mühlhausen and Ó hEochaidh.[130] Transcripts of Irish-language broadcasts by Ludwig Mühlhausen and Hans Hartmann are now 'few and far between' and, at this remove, it is unclear whether either of the Nazi propagandists ever sent greetings to (or even mentioned) their acquaintanceship with the President of Ireland, Douglas Hyde, in their war-time broadcasts. However, the Irish Army of which President Hyde was the nominal Commander-in-Chief closely monitored the broadcasts of Irland-Redaktion, seeing the station as a threat to Irish neutrality.[131] That the two most prominent broadcasters on Irland-Redaktion were acquaintances and admirers of Hyde, one having penned a short biography of him and the other having dedicated a book to him, must have been a source of great embarrassment to the Irish President, especially given the crude pro-Nazi and anti-Semitic nature of the propaganda work of Mühlhausen and Hartmann.

This embarrassment would have been accentuated if it was known that, in the midst of the war, Mühlhausen was touting his links to the Irish President, as he sought advancement in the Nazi hierarchy. Mühlhausen departed Irland-Redaktion and the Reich Ministry of Propaganda in the summer of 1941 and, after having previously been in the SA, he volunteered for the Schutzstaffel (the SS), the organisation most responsible for the genocidal killing of the Jews during the Holocaust, as well as millions of other victims of war crimes and crimes against humanity in World War Two. In summer 1942, Mühlhausen took over the management of an SS-controlled section dealing with Celtic ancestry, the Office for Celtic Ethnological Research. Mühlhausen also worked with the SS in France, forging links with pro-Nazi elements in the Breton nationalist movement. Mühlhausen did not forget Ireland or Douglas Hyde in this period. In September 1943, Mühlhausen was the signatory on a message of congratulations sent by the German Society for Celtic Studies to the Gaelic League, delivered via the German Minister Eduard Hempel, to mark the golden jubilee of the foundation of Conradh na Gaeilge with Hyde as the organisation's first President.[132]

---

[130] Hugh Byrne, a Teelin fisherman, who had provided lodgings to Mühlhausen during his time in Donegal, was also questioned by Gardaí when the German began his radio broadcasts. See O'Donoghue, *Hitler's Irish voices*, 25, 39, 241.

[131] ibid. 243.

[132] The German Society for Celtic Studies was founded in January 1937 at Berlin University. Séamus Ó Duilearga, on a visit to Germany, attended its inaugural meeting. The founding members of the society included a number of committed Nazis, such as Mühlhausen and Adolf Mahr, as well as Helmut Clissmann, the Abwehr agent. *Irish Times*, 20 September 1943; *Irish Times*, 25 January 1937.

In 1943, Mühlhausen was formally recruited into the SS. The SS considered themselves to be the ultimate defenders of the so-called 'Aryan' race and Nazi ideology and, before beginning his work for the SS, Mühlhausen completed a comprehensive curriculum vitae on 3 May 1942, which was placed on his Nazi Party file. In this CV, Mühlhausen detailed his research work in Ireland and claimed in German that these journeys 'gave me the opportunity to establish close relationships with the leaders of the Irish independence movement. I formed a personal friendship with the current President, Dr Douglas Hyde'.[133]

Given the scant evidence of direct contact between Ludwig Mühlhausen and Douglas Hyde, it is hard not to construe Mühlhausen's claim of a personal friendship with the President of Ireland as an exaggeration or embellishment designed to inflate Mühlhausen's own standing. In addition, Mühlhausen's comments about being on good terms with 'the leaders of the Irish independence movement' and his shoehorning of Hyde into this category are incongruous. Though Hyde was a leading figure in the cultural nationalism movement, he did not play a significant role in the movement for political independence and Mühlhausen may well have been not only exaggerating his relationship with Hyde, but also misrepresenting it. This did not do Mühlhausen any harm within the SS hierarchy. Mühlhausen was ambitious and by November 1943 he had achieved the rank of Untersturmführer, a commissioned officer rank equivalent to second lieutenant.[134]

In the immediate aftermath of the war, Mühlhausen again sought to highlight his relationship with President Hyde for his own advantage. In spring 1945, in the closing phase of World War Two, Mühlhausen was taken prisoner by American troops near Ulm, in south-western Germany, and he was eventually moved to a prisoner of war camp in Naples. In July 1945, Mühlhausen sent at least two letters from this place of internment to Ireland. One of these letters was to Dr Joseph Healy, a talented linguist and lecturer in University College Cork's Department of Spanish. Healy had undertaken postgraduate work as a student in the late 1920s in Hamburg and had become friendly with Mühlhausen, who was at this stage lecturing Celtic Studies at Hamburg University. In this

---

[133] This extract from Mühlhausen's CV was displayed in Kevin Magee's documentary 'Nazi sa Ghaeltacht'. I am grateful to Professor Liam Mac Mathúna for assistance in translating this extract into English. Mühlhausen's full CV from 1942 is located at the Federal Archive, Berlin.

[134] Paul R. Bartrop and Michael Dickerman (eds), *The Holocaust: an encyclopedia and document collection* (Santa Barbara 2017) 582; Magee, 'Nazi sa Ghaeltacht'; Perry Biddiscombe, *The SS hunter battalions: the hidden history of the Nazi resistance movement* (Gloucestershire 2006) 289.

same period, Muhlhausen often visited and stayed with Healy's family during summer trips to Cork and Kerry, including the Blasket Islands, to perfect his Irish. By the 1930s, Mühlhausen and Healy had gone 'their separate ways'.[135] Healy had little sympathy with Mühlhausen's fascist beliefs and at the outbreak of World War Two he was seconded into the Irish Army, with the rank of lieutenant, as a linguistic expert to the Army's Reserve Officer Corps. Throughout the war, Healy vigorously inter-rogated German spies that were apprehended in Ireland. When Mühlhausen began broadcasting to Ireland in December 1939, Healy compiled a report for Colonel Dan Bryan, the Head of G2, on his former friend. By July 1945, Healy had returned to his job in UCC when he received correspondence from Mühlhausen informing him that he was being detained in Naples. Healy did not reply and forwarded the correspondence to Army Intelligence.[136]

Mühlhausen's correspondence to Healy was surprising given the chasm that had developed between them, but his letter to the UCC professor may have been an attempt to alert his captors, who scrutinised (and often censored) all outgoing prisoner mail, of his international academic credentials. Even more surprising was a second letter Mühlhausen wrote from detention in Naples. The recipient of this letter, dated 9 July 1945, was the now retired President of Ireland, Douglas Hyde, whose term of office had ended two weeks earlier, on 24 June 1945. Writing in Irish, Mühlhausen adopted a conversational tone and told Hyde:

> You will be amazed to hear, friend, that I am a prisoner of war of
> the English, – but that's how it is. However, I am well; I am still
> in excellent health. I have no cause for complaint at the moment,
> apart from the terrible heat; one has to be satisfied, because nothing
> can be done about it. – It is an awful pity I haven't received any
> word from my family for ages: My wife and my older daughter
> are in a small town near Ulm am Donau.... I hope to God that they
> are well. (It is the Yanks who are there.)[137]

---

[135] O'Donoghue, *Hitler's Irish voices*, 244–6

[136] O'Donoghue, *Hitler's Irish voices*, 244–6, 264.

[137] Letter from Mühlhausen to Hyde, 9 July 1945. This letter is contained in the National Irish Folklore Archive, 'foreign correspondence' file, in UCD. I am grateful to Kevin Magee for bringing this letter to my attention, to Dr Críostóir Mac Cárthaigh, UCD, for providing me with access to this letter and to Professor Liam Mac Mathúna for assistance in translating this document into English. Mühlhausen's suggestion that he was a prisoner of the English seems a little incongruous, given that he was captured by American troops and the envelope he addressed to Hyde was stamped 'US Army Examiner', indicating that the correspondence had been examined by American military censors.

Mühlhausen's correspondence to Hyde does not contain any evidence of a close relationship between the Irish President and the German prisoner of war. Indeed, Mühlhausen's letter seems to place an emphasis on reminding Hyde of his interest in Irish folklore. Mühlhausen also name-dropped other Irish academics and folklorists, possibly either as an attempt to bolster his own credentials as a scholar with President Hyde or again with the camp authorities who he knew would scrutinise his letter. Mühlhausen wrote:

> My books are there [in Ulm] as well and all the other things relating to Celtic studies as for example around 80,000 'slips' relating to the folklore of Ireland, a collection of photos etc. May God grant that these things are safe, as they are the heart of my work! – I have every hope to God that you yourself are well. I would be delighted to hear for example from Professor Ó Duilearga in Dublin and my loyal friend Séamus Ó Caomhánaigh MA in Cork and Joe Healy MA and from 'Tórna' in Cork as well. – Understandably, it is a great pity that there is not a single Irish book to be had here. It would be a great, a very great pastime to read the old stories. But one must be satisfied and I must be patient – and I am.[138]

Mühlhausen did not ask Hyde to do anything for him, but he would have been astute enough to realise that such a request would not have escaped censorship by his captors.

Mühlhausen's correspondence was, however, designed to prick Hyde's conscience by informing him that a fellow Gaelic scholar was in difficulty while, at the same, alerting Mühlhausen's captors that their prisoner had influential international political and academic connections. This scheming did Mühlhausen little good. He remained incarcerated until 1948 and emerged from this experience 'a broken man' and 'a complete wreck'.[139] Hyde never did reply to or even acknowledge

---

[138] Letter from Mühlhausen to Hyde, 9 July 1945. Mühlhausen's reference to 'Joe Healy MA' actually highlights the long breach in the relationship between the two men. Healy had been conferred with his PhD as far back as 1936.

[139] Mühlhausen never regained his full health, following his incarceration, and he never returned to Ireland. He died in April 1956 after a heart attack. Mühlhausen's protégé, Hans Hartmann, fared better in the postwar world. Hartmann managed to escape imprisonment, despite being the subject of 'heated debate' between the Russian and Western Allies occupying Germany. The British charged that Hartmann was 'notorious during the war period for his books on Nazism and the superiority of the German race'; nevertheless, the Russians briefly installed Hartmann as the editor of a newspaper, the *National-Zeitung*, in the Soviet zone in Berlin. In 1948, Hartmann became a lecturer in Celtic Linguistics at

Mühlhausen's correspondence, though, unlike Healy, he does not seem to have passed the correspondence from the Nazi prisoner of war on to the Irish security services. It is perhaps not surprising that Hyde suppressed Mühlhausen's correspondence, as it was a potential major source of embarrassment to the Irish President. Mühlhausen's correspondence was sent in the immediate aftermath of the international furore begun by de Valera's condolences on the death of Hitler. Had international news organisations picked up on the fact that an imprisoned SS officer was in communication with the President of Ireland, this would have further exacerbated the situation and inflicted more reputational damage on Ireland. If Mühlhausen was a genuine friend of Hyde's (and this seems dubious), he was certainly not a very considerate one. From his prisoner of war camp Mühlhausen was unlikely to be aware of the international controversy stemming from de Valera's Hitler condolences; however, it is still true to say that he gave little thought to how his correspondence could impact on his 'friend'. At a time when Nazi Germany had been vanquished in the war and the full scale of the Holocaust was emerging, it was certainly not an act of discretion on Mühlhausen's part to post a letter to the President of Ireland with a clearly visible return to sender address on the outer envelope that read 'SS Untersturmführer, Ludwig Mühlhausen, AA 074 170 – SS, 216 PW Camp, Naples, Italy.'[140] Hyde would have surely been eager not to do anything to encourage the arrival of further such correspondence.

the University of Göttingen and in 1953 he was appointed Professor of Comparative Linguistics at the University of Hamburg. In 1952, Hartmann made his first return visit to Ireland since before the war, when he journeyed to West Kerry to undertake a study of the syntax of modern Irish. He made numerous further trips to Ireland up until his death in 2000. Despite his controversial war record, Hartmann was largely welcomed back into the fold of the Celtic studies community. In October 1964, he was even received at Áras an Uachtaráin by President de Valera to discuss a Western European language research project, studying speech in the south-west Galway Gaeltacht, which was being led by Hartmann and Dr Tomás de Bhaldraithe, Professor of Modern Irish at UCD. Not everyone was willing to set aside Hartmann's wartime propaganda work on behalf of the Nazi regime. O'Donoghue recorded that 'on one occasion at a social function in Dublin, someone introduced the German to Professor Dan Binchy, with the words "Have you met Dr Hartmann?" Turning on his heels, Binchy replied: "No, but I heard his voice."' Binchy had served as the Irish Minister Plenipotentiary to Germany from 1929 to 1932, as Germany descended towards fascism. He remained for the rest of his life 'a fervent anti-Nazi'; see O'Donoghue, *Hitler's Irish voices*, 264–74, 421; Magee, 'Nazi sa Ghaeltacht'; *Irish Press*, 23 September, 1952; *Belfast Newsletter*, 29 April 1948; *Irish Independent*, 4 September 1964; *Cork Examiner*, 24 October 1964, Maurice Manning, 'The lives of Daniel Binchy: Irish scholar, diplomat, public intellectual by Tom Garvin review', *Irish Times*, 18 June 2016.

[140] Envelope from Mühlhausen letter to Hyde, 9 July 1945. This envelope is contained in the National Irish Folklore Archive, 'foreign correspondence' file, in UCD.

As this author's monograph has explored, Hyde was appended to de
Valera's controversial action in visiting the German legation to express
condolences upon the death of Adolf Hitler, as World War Two drew to
a close.[141] De Valera always maintained that it was his personal respect
for Hempel, as well as a proper adherence to the protocols of neutrality,
that influenced his decision to visit the German Minister on the death of
Hitler.[142] Similar reasons motivated what has only in recent times come
to be seen as one of the most controversial aspects of Hyde's presidency
– his decision to extend his condolences to the German Minister.

The background to this controversy was Hitler's suicide in Berlin on
30 April 1945. After this news reached Ireland, on 2 May 1945, de
Valera, accompanied by Joseph Walshe, visited the German Minister.
The following day's main newspapers all reported that the Taoiseach
had 'called on Dr Hempel, the German minister, last evening, to express
his condolences'.[143]

In 2005, a newspaper story claiming that President Hyde had also
visited Hempel upon Hitler's death made international headlines.[144] It
was claimed that Presidential protocol records newly released at this
time, for the years 1938–1957, suggested that Hyde had personally
called to Hempel's residence and that this event occurred on 3 May
1945, the day after the Taoiseach's visit.[145] These protocol records state
that the President did not send an official letter because 'the capital of
Germany, Berlin, was under siege and no successor had been
appointed'.[146] The records however make clear that it was, in fact, the
Secretary to the President who called upon Hempel on 3 May 1945. The
protocol records in relation to the death of Hitler state:

Call on Diplomatic Representative of State Concerned.

(a) Representative of the President – Secretary to the President
(b) On whom he called – His Excellency the German Minister,
     Dr. Hempel
(c) Date of call – 3 May 1945

---

[141] Murphy, *Forgotten patriot*, 215–26.
[142] Earl of Longford and Thomas P. O'Neill, *Eamon de Valera: a biography* (London
1970) 411.
[143] *Irish Times*, 3 May 1945; *Irish Press*, 3 May 1945; *Irish Independent*, 3 May 1945.
[144] *Irish Independent*, 31 December 2005; *The Guardian*, 31 December 2005; *Los Angeles
Times*, 31 December 2005; *Sarasota Herald Tribune*, 31 December 2005.
[145] *Irish Independent*, 31 December 2005; NAI, 2005/163/5, 'Deaths of Heads of State',
book of protocol records from Áras an Uachtaráin 1938–1957.
[146] NAI, 2005/163/5, 'Deaths of Heads of State', book of protocol records from Áras an
Uachtaráin 1938–1957.

(d) Response to call, with date – The German Minister called on the Secretary to the President on 3 May, 1945.[147]

These records plainly show that it was McDunphy, not Hyde, who called on Hempel and that Hempel returned the courtesy, on the same day, by calling to the Áras. The more sensationalist story that Hyde actually visited Hempel is based on a misunderstanding or a misrepresentation of these protocol records by a news syndicate service. Contemporary newspapers from 1945 also attest that it was McDunphy, on the President's behalf, who called on Hempel and this meeting took place not in Hempel's residence, as the 2005 news story suggested, but at the German legation. The *Irish Times* on 4 May 1945 reported that 'Mr McDunphy, the Secretary to the President, called on the German Minister yesterday to express condolence on behalf of the President'.[148] This story was reported in almost identical wording in the *Irish Independent* and the *Irish Times*, suggesting that the information had come from government sources and had been cleared by the censor.[149] McDunphy's records show that this visit was part of a carefully choreographed affirmation of the State's position. McDunphy noted in May 1945 that

> after consultation with the government and acting on the authority of the President, I called today on the German minister, Herr Eduard Hempel, at the legation in Northumberland Road, and on behalf of the President expressed condolence on the death of the Fuehrer and Chancellor of the German Reich.[150]

The actual timing of McDunphy's visit to Hempel is also of considerable significance. McDunphy passed on Hyde's condolences with the Government's full knowledge the day after de Valera's sympathy visit to the German Minister and at a time when the adverse international reaction to the Taoiseach's move was making its first waves. As Keogh has noted, 'de Valera had an opportunity to think about his action overnight and had decided not to change his course despite the instantaneous negative reaction in the international press and media'.[151]

[147] ibid.
[148] *Irish Times*, 4 May 1945.
[149] *Irish Press*, 4 May 1945; *Irish Independent,* 4 May 1945.
[150] *Irish Times*, 31 December 2011.
[151] Dermot Keogh, 'Eamon de Valera and Hitler: an analysis of international reaction to the visit to the German Minister, May 1945', *Irish Studies in International Affairs*, vol. 3, no. 1 (1989) 73.

Keogh has also suggested that this 'indicated the government had no second thoughts on this matter'.[152] But, in fact, that is not the full story. The Government had initially viewed de Valera's visit to Hempel, followed by that of the Secretary to the office of President, as a proper manifestation of neutrality and unhesitatingly publicised both events. However, when the initial wave of criticism did not subside, but rather intensified, a shift occurred in Government thinking. International newspapers, particularly in the United States, had been vehement in their criticism of the Irish condolences and the Irish legation in Washington and consulates in other major cities received a huge volume of protest correspondence.[153] This definitely had an effect and it was McDunphy who first perceived and then chronicled a rowing back of the Irish position. McDunphy noted that, following the German surrender, Hempel had called on the Taoiseach on 8 May 1945 to announce the termination of his mission as German Minister.[154] The Government Information Bureau had issued a terse statement arising from this, announcing that Hempel was 'vacating the legation premises' and that the Irish Government would 'take charge' of the properties.[155] On 9 May, the day after Hempel had handed over the keys of the German legation, he contacted McDunphy with a view to paying a farewell visit to the Áras. McDunphy recorded that 'this morning, Dr Hempel asked me for permission to call on me as Secretary to the President, and said that if it were possible he would like also to be received by the President'.[156] Despite Hyde's long-standing amicable relations with Hempel, McDunphy hesitated and kicked to touch. McDunphy was deeply conscious of the furore that his visit and the Taoiseach's visit to Hempel had generated and sought political cover before allowing Hempel to come to the Áras. He wrote:

> In view of the situation I consulted with the Secretary, Department of External Affairs, and he informed me that the view of the Taoiseach, who was also Minister for External Affairs, was that, if the President were willing to receive Dr Hempel it would not in any way conflict with general State policy. He thought however that there was no need to publicise the visit.[157]

[152] Dermot Keogh, *Ireland and Europe 1919–48* (Dublin 1988) 191.
[153] Keogh, 'Eamon de Valera and Hitler', 83–4.
[154] NAI, PRES 1/P519, memo by McDunphy, 9 May 1945.
[155] NAI, PRES 1/P519, press statement issued by Government Information Bureau, 8 May 1945; *Irish Independent*, 9 May 1945
[156] NAI, PRES 1/P519, memo by McDunphy, 9 May 1945.
[157] ibid.

This direction from de Valera constituted a shift in the Government's approach and, though the Government were still happy to treat Hempel with due courtesy, an anxiety now existed about being seen to do anything that would generate further negative international publicity. Hyde willingly agreed to meet Hempel, but this was done under the radar. McDunphy noted 'in the afternoon Dr Hempel called at the Áras and was received by the President.... No notice was issued to the press'.[158]

The covert nature of Hempel's final visit to the Áras showed how badly the Government had been stung by international criticism of the de Valera and McDunphy visits to the German representative. De Valera privately maintained that it was the correct approach not 'to add to his [Hempel's] humiliation in the hour of defeat', but his actions and those of President Hyde's office in expressing 'condolence on the death of the architect of the Holocaust spared Herr Hempel a diplomatic insult, but at the price of insulting the victims of the regime Hempel represented'.[159] The Hitler condolences 'gave the false impression to the world that Ireland had in fact secretly been on the side of the Axis powers' and it allowed David Gray, the US Minister to Ireland, who loathed de Valera and looked on President Hyde with a mixture of condescension and contempt, to unjustly portray de Valera, Hyde and McDunphy to the US State Department as closet Nazi sympathisers.[160] Nevertheless, de Valera's condolence on the death of Hitler did not unduly damage his relationship with Ireland's Jewish community. In 2005, in a letter to *The Irish Times*, Dr Isaac Cohen, who was Chief Rabbi in Ireland from 1956 to 1979, contended that de Valera's 'message of condolence on the death of Hitler was merely an official act which was required by diplomatic protocol and was no judgment on the righteousness of German actions'.[161] Douglas Hyde's condolence on the death of Hitler, expressed via the medium of McDunphy, also, undoubtedly, signified no judgement on the righteousness of German actions, but, with the benefit of hindsight and knowledge of German war-crimes, most Irish people today would surely prefer if our Head of State had not been party to this expression of sympathy to the Nazi regime. Hyde's involvement in this episode was a source of embarrassment to Irish diplomats at this time and for many years to come. On 11 May 1945, John Dulanty, the Irish High Commissioner in London, forwarded on, to the Department of External Affairs, with a sense of distaste, a dubious appreciation letter,

---

[158] ibid.
[159] Gene Kerrigan and Pat Brennan, *This great little nation* (Dublin 1999) 77.
[160] Cathy Molohan, *Germany and Ireland 1945–1955: two nations' friendship* (Dublin 1999) 22; Murphy, *Forgotten patriot*, 222.
[161] *Irish Times*, 29 May 2005.

which he had received from an extreme right-wing organisation, expressing their approval for Hyde's regrets on Hitler's death:

> The British Union of Fascists, which is still in existence, although it had to go underground for the time being, have instructed me to write to your Excellency, and to express their deep appreciation of the news that the secretary to the president of Eire has called on the German minister in Dublin to express condolence on behalf of the president on the death of Adolf Hitler. The British Union of Fascists begs of your Excellency to convey its gratitude to the government of Eire for thus honouring the memory of the greatest German in history.[162]

Against a backdrop of a modern survey where, shockingly and disappointingly, 30% of Irish people surveyed believed that 'Jews still talk too much about what happened to them in the Holocaust', further historical analysis of Irish attitudes to Judaism in this period and beyond is merited.[163] The Holocaust and its horrors should never be forgotten and Ireland's response to this humanitarian nightmare – or lack thereof – is something we should continue to interrogate, even if this means asking uncomfortable questions about the actions or non-actions of a national hero like Douglas Hyde. As our current President, Michael D. Higgins has said, there is a complicity in silence. Our first President, Douglas Hyde, a Protestant head of state of a largely Catholic country, who viewed Jews as 'the most marvelous people in the world' was seen during his tenure in office as a symbol of an inclusive Ireland. By drawing lessons from his life and by being prepared to articulate what this inspirational figure in Irish history may have got wrong – as well as the plenty he got right – we can help ensure that past mistakes are not repeated and we can also work towards building a welcoming, open and tolerant Ireland for the next generation.

BRIAN MURPHY

---

[162] Dermot Keogh, 'De Valera, Hitler & the visit of condolence May 1945', *History Ireland*, issue 3 (Autumn 1997), vol. 5.

[163] Journal.ie, '30% of Irish people "think Jews talk too much about the Holocaust,"' 19 May 2014, available at https://www.thejournal.ie/global-jewish-survey-1472446-May2014/ [accessed 28 October 2020]. This survey was part of a worldwide study on anti-Semitism, published in May 2014, and conducted by the Anti-Defamation League. The survey also found that 28% of Irish people believed 'Jews have too much power in the business world' and that 20% of Irish people admitted to holding anti-Semitic attitudes.